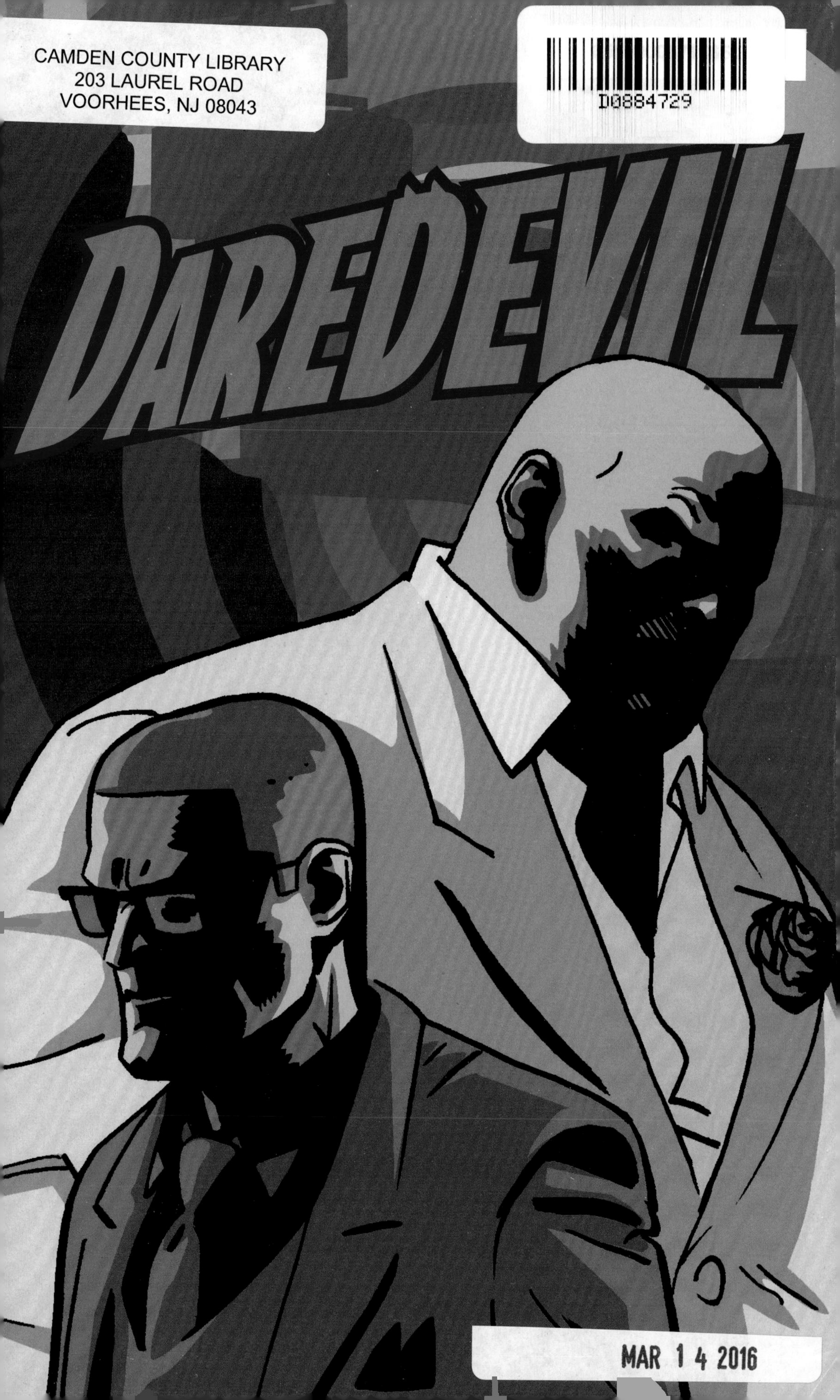
DAREDEVIL

ISSUE #15.1

WRITERS
MARK WAID, MARC GUGGENHEIM & CHRIS SAMNEE

ARTISTS
CHRIS SAMNEE & PETER KRAUSE

COLORIST
MATTHEW WILSON

ISSUES #16-18

STORYTELLERS
MARK WAID & CHRIS SAMNEE

COLORIST
MATTHEW WILSON

LETTERER
VC'S JOE CARAMAGNA

COVER ART
CHRIS SAMNEE & MATTHEW WILSON

ASSISTANT EDITOR
CHARLES BEACHAM

EDITORS
SANA AMANAT & ELLIE PYLE

SENIOR EDITOR
NICK LOWE

COLLECTION EDITOR
JENNIFER GRÜNWALD
ASSISTANT EDITOR
SARAH BRUNSTAD
ASSOCIATE MANAGING EDITOR
ALEX STARBUCK
EDITOR, SPECIAL PROJECTS
MARK D. BEAZLEY
SENIOR EDITOR, SPECIAL PROJECTS
JEFF YOUNGQUIST
SVP PRINT, SALES & MARKETING
DAVID GABRIEL
BOOK DESIGNER
ADAM DEL RE

EDITOR IN CHIEF
AXEL ALONSO
CHIEF CREATIVE OFFICER
JOE QUESADA
PUBLISHER
DAN BUCKLEY
EXECUTIVE PRODUCER
ALAN FINE

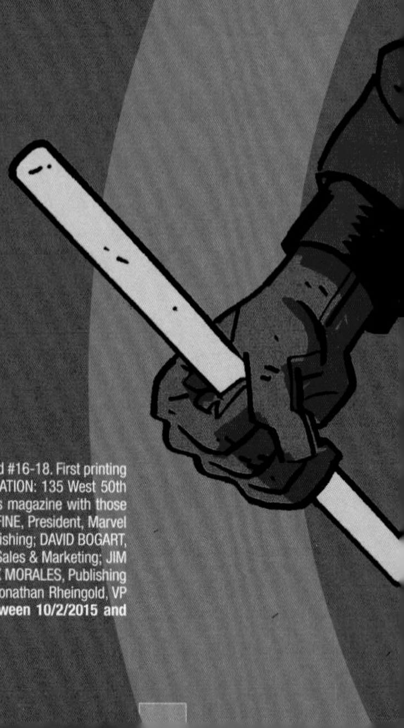

DAREDEVIL VOL. 4: THE AUTOBIOGRAPHY OF MATT MURDOCK. Contains material originally published in magazine form as DAREDEVIL #15.1 and #16-18. First printing 2015. ISBN# 978-0-7851-9802-4. Published by MARVEL WORLDWIDE, INC., a subsidiary of MARVEL ENTERTAINMENT, LLC. OFFICE OF PUBLICATION: 135 West 50th Street, New York, NY 10020. Copyright © 2015 MARVEL No similarity between any of the names, characters, persons, and/or institutions in this magazine with those of any living or dead person or institution is intended, and any such similarity which may exist is purely coincidental. **Printed in Canada.** ALAN FINE, President, Marvel Entertainment; DAN BUCKLEY, President, TV, Publishing and Brand Management; JOE QUESADA, Chief Creative Officer; TOM BREVOORT, SVP of Publishing; DAVID BOGART, SVP of Operations & Procurement, Publishing; C.B. CEBULSKI, VP of International Development & Brand Management; DAVID GABRIEL, SVP Print, Sales & Marketing; JIM O'KEEFE, VP of Operations & Logistics; DAN CARR, Executive Director of Publishing Technology; SUSAN CRESPI, Editorial Operations Manager; ALEX MORALES, Publishing Operations Manager; STAN LEE, Chairman Emeritus. For information regarding advertising in Marvel Comics or on Marvel.com, please contact Jonathan Rheingold, VP of Custom Solutions & Ad Sales, at jrheingold@marvel.com. For Marvel subscription inquiries, please call 800-217-9158. **Manufactured between 10/2/2015 and 11/9/2015** by SOLISCO PRINTERS, SCOTT, QC, CANADA.

10 9 8 7 6 5 4 3 2 1

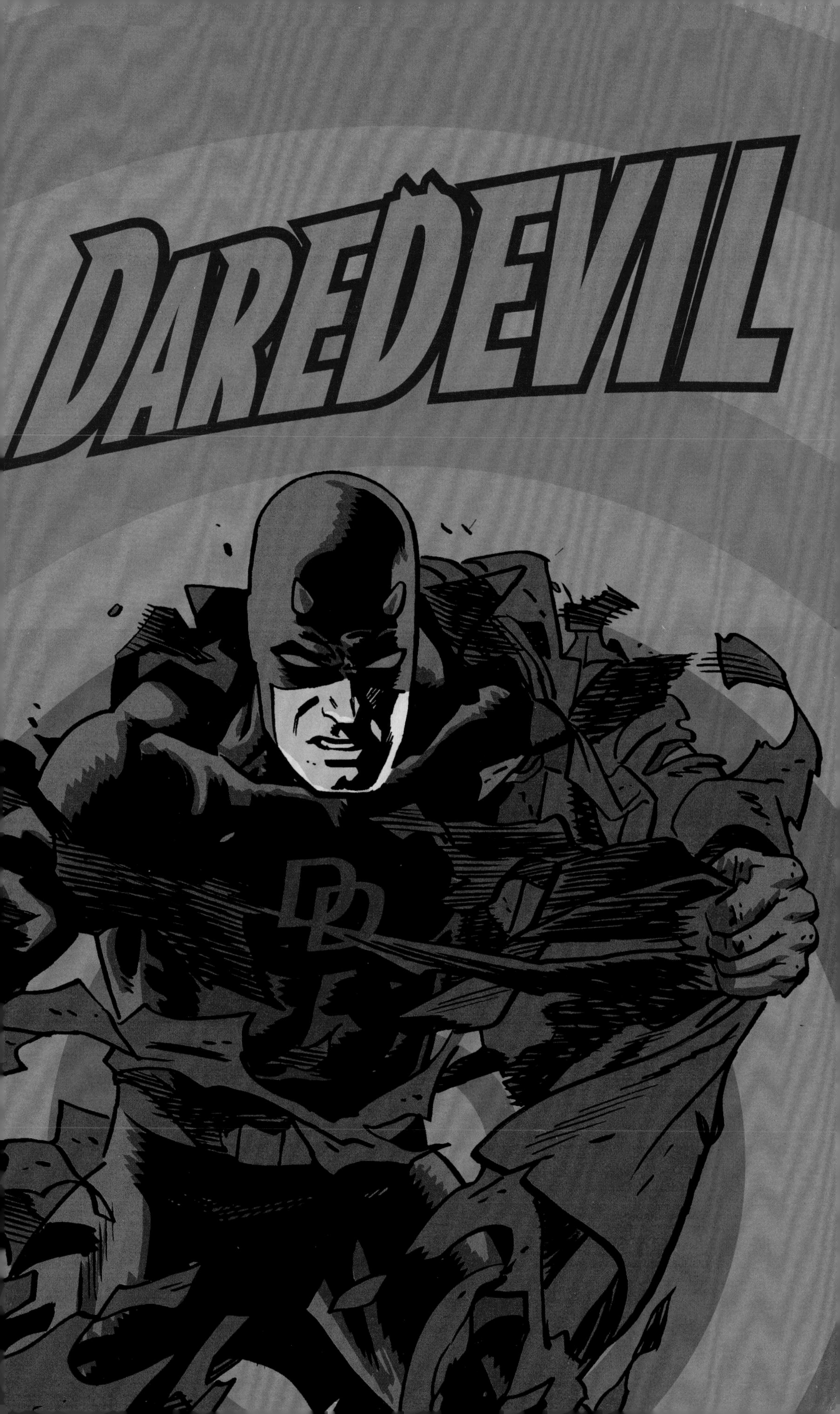
DAREDEVIL
DD

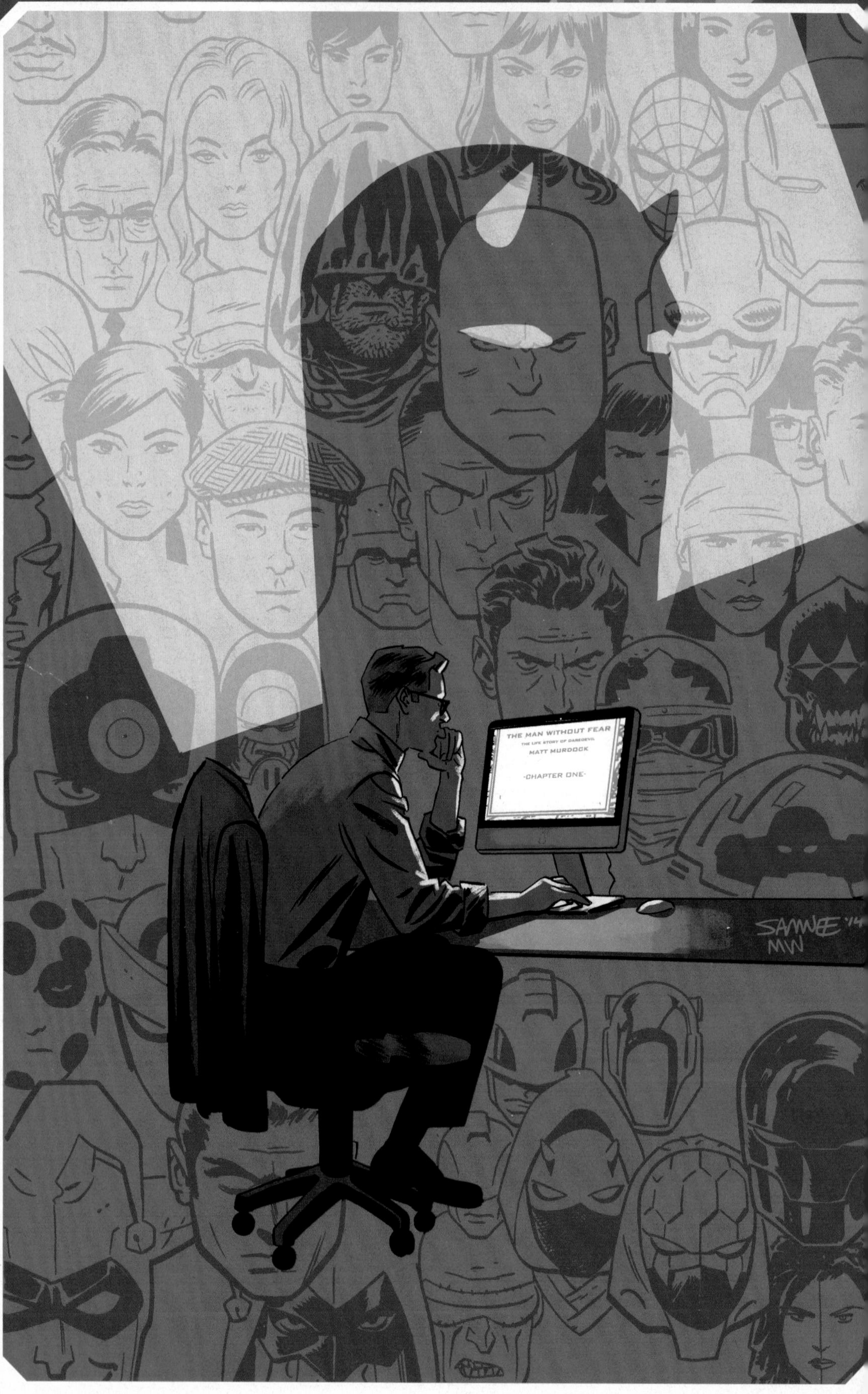
THE MAN WITHOUT FEAR
THE LIFE STORY OF DAREDEVIL
MATT MURDOCK
-CHAPTER ONE-
SAMNEE '14
MW

DAREDEVIL #15.1

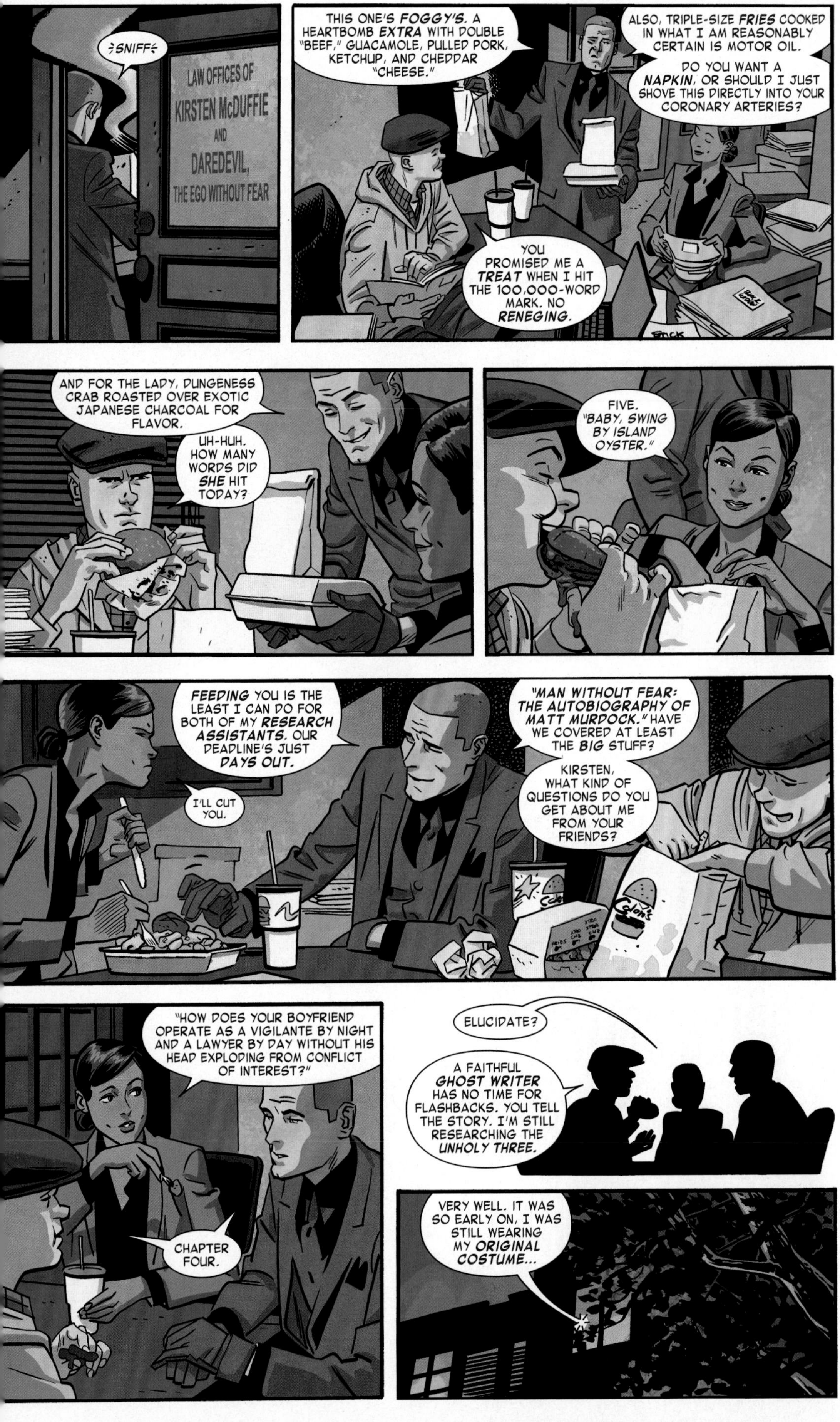

SNIFF
LAW OFFICES OF KIRSTEN McDUFFIE AND DAREDEVIL, THE EGO WITHOUT FEAR
THIS ONE'S FOGGY'S. A HEARTBOMB EXTRA WITH DOUBLE "BEEF," GUACAMOLE, PULLED PORK, KETCHUP, AND CHEDDAR "CHEESE."
ALSO, TRIPLE-SIZE FRIES COOKED IN WHAT I AM REASONABLY CERTAIN IS MOTOR OIL.
DO YOU WANT A NAPKIN, OR SHOULD I JUST SHOVE THIS DIRECTLY INTO YOUR CORONARY ARTERIES?
YOU PROMISED ME A TREAT WHEN I HIT THE 100,000-WORD MARK. NO RENEGING.
AND FOR THE LADY, DUNGENESS CRAB ROASTED OVER EXOTIC JAPANESE CHARCOAL FOR FLAVOR.
UH-HUH. HOW MANY WORDS DID SHE HIT TODAY?
FIVE. "BABY, SWING BY ISLAND OYSTER."
FEEDING YOU IS THE LEAST I CAN DO FOR BOTH OF MY RESEARCH ASSISTANTS. OUR DEADLINE'S JUST DAYS OUT.
I'LL CUT YOU.
"MAN WITHOUT FEAR: THE AUTOBIOGRAPHY OF MATT MURDOCK." HAVE WE COVERED AT LEAST THE BIG STUFF?
KIRSTEN, WHAT KIND OF QUESTIONS DO YOU GET ABOUT ME FROM YOUR FRIENDS?
"HOW DOES YOUR BOYFRIEND OPERATE AS A VIGILANTE BY NIGHT AND A LAWYER BY DAY WITHOUT HIS HEAD EXPLODING FROM CONFLICT OF INTEREST?"
CHAPTER FOUR.
ELUCIDATE?
A FAITHFUL GHOST WRITER HAS NO TIME FOR FLASHBACKS. YOU TELL THE STORY. I'M STILL RESEARCHING THE UNHOLY THREE.
VERY WELL. IT WAS SO EARLY ON, I WAS STILL WEARING MY ORIGINAL COSTUME...

PREVIOUSLY:

Since outing himself as Daredevil in a court of law, blind lawyer Matt Murdock has faked the death of his best friend, Foggy Nelson, moved out west to start a new practice with his girlfriend, Kirsten McDuffie, and had more than a few run-ins with old foes looking to get even.

Recently, Matt cast off his cowl and completely embraced his role as The Man Without Fear–he's even writing a biography about his vigilante adventures. As his Daredevil duties have a tendency to take his attention away from authoring, Matt enlisted Foggy to help as his ghost writer.

With a deadline looming, Team Daredevil has hunkered down for a late night of storytelling...

*The following takes place before Daredevil #15.

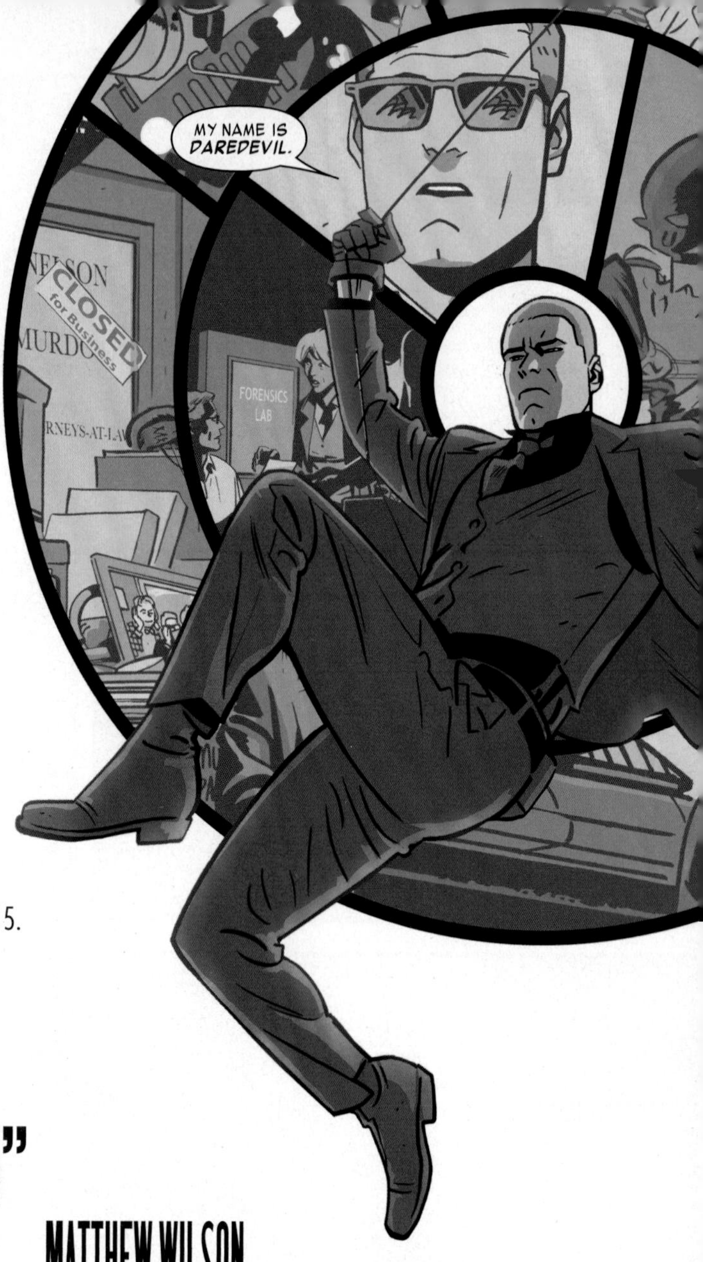
MY NAME IS DAREDEVIL.
CLOSED for Business
FORENSICS LAB

"RETROSPECTION"

MARK WAID & CHRIS SAMNEE — STORYTELLERS
MATTHEW WILSON — COLORIST

"WORLDS COLLIDE"

MARC GUGGENHEIM — WRITER
PETER KRAUSE — ARTIST
MATTHEW WILSON — COLORIST

"CHASING THE DEVIL"

CHRIS SAMNEE — WRITER/ARTIST
MATTHEW WILSON — COLORIST

VC'S JOE CARAMAGNA — LETTERER
SAMNEE & WILSON — COVER
RYAN STEGMA MARTE GRAC — COVER

CHARLES BEACHAM — ASSISTANT EDITOR
SANA AMANAT — EDITOR
NICK LOWE — SENIOR EDITOR
AXEL ALONSO — EDITOR IN CHIEF
JOE QUESADA — CHIEF CREATIVE OFFICER
DAN BUCKLEY — PUBLISHER
ALAN FI — EXEC. PRODUC

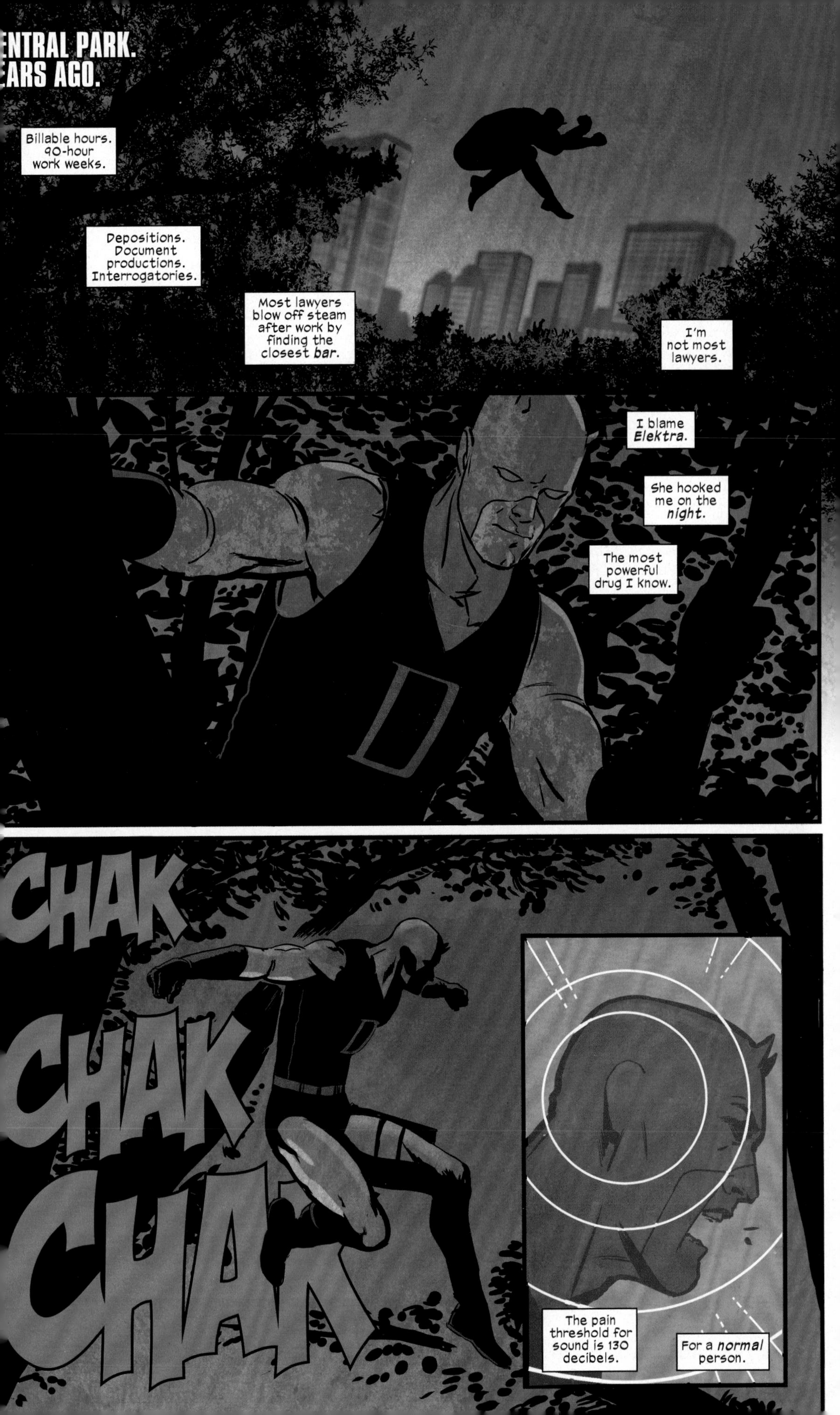

ENTRAL PARK.
EARS AGO.
Billable hours. 90-hour work weeks.
Depositions. Document productions. Interrogatories.
Most lawyers blow off steam after work by finding the closest *bar*.
I'm not most lawyers.
I blame *Elektra*.
She hooked me on the *night*.
The most powerful drug I know.
CHAK
CHAK
CHAK
The pain threshold for sound is 130 decibels.
For a *normal* person.

Those were 170-decibel *gunshots.*

Feels like repeatedly slamming my head against the express train.

Shake it off.

Follow the echoes. The shots were .38 caliber from the sound of them.

And they seem to have done their work.

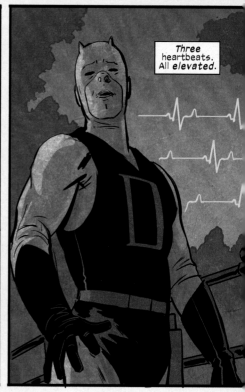

Three heartbeats. All *elevated.*

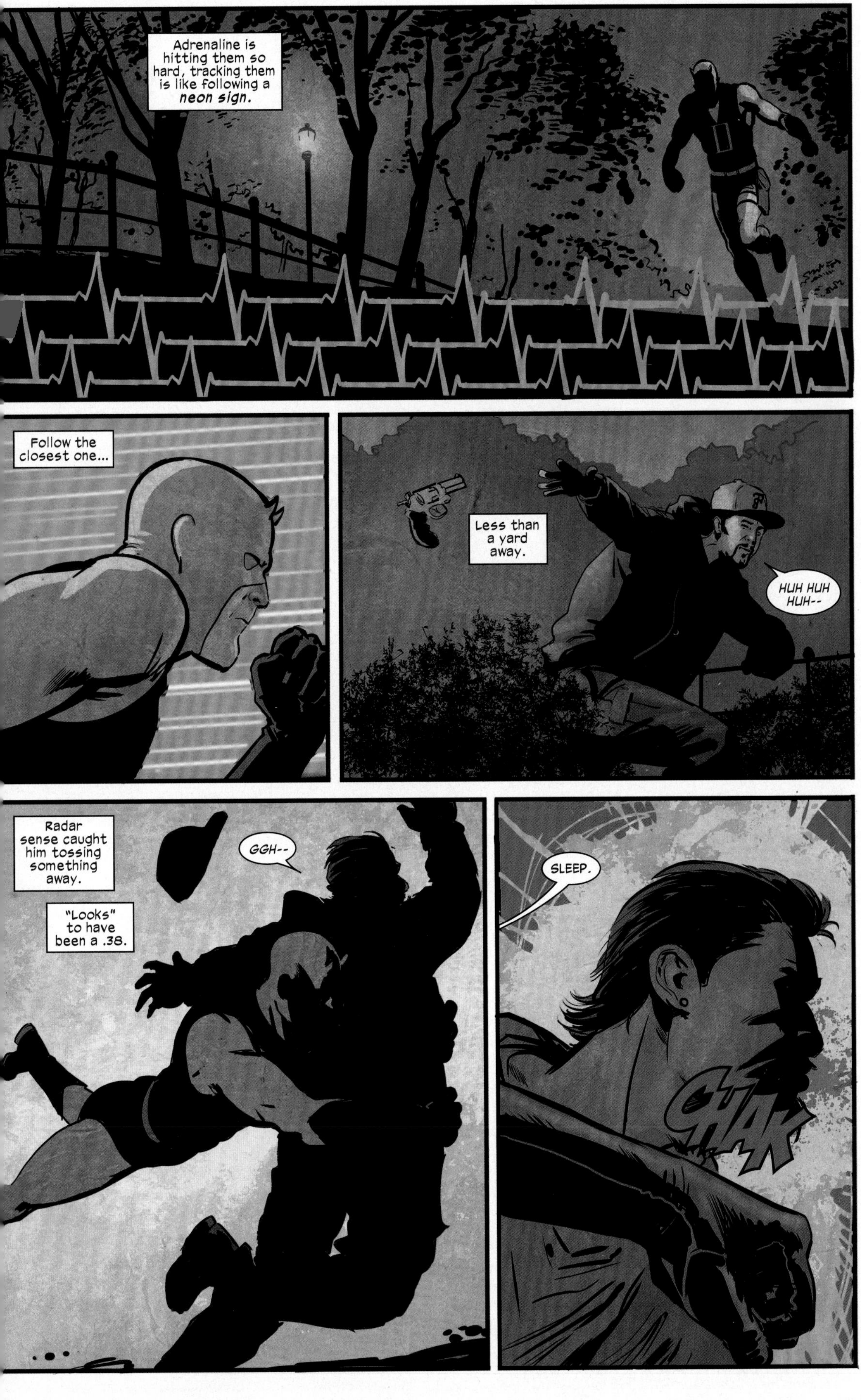
Adrenaline is hitting them so hard, tracking them is like following a *neon sign.*
Follow the closest one...
Less than a yard away.
HUH HUH HUH--
Radar sense caught him tossing something away.
GGH--
"Looks" to have been a .38.
SLEEP.
CHAK

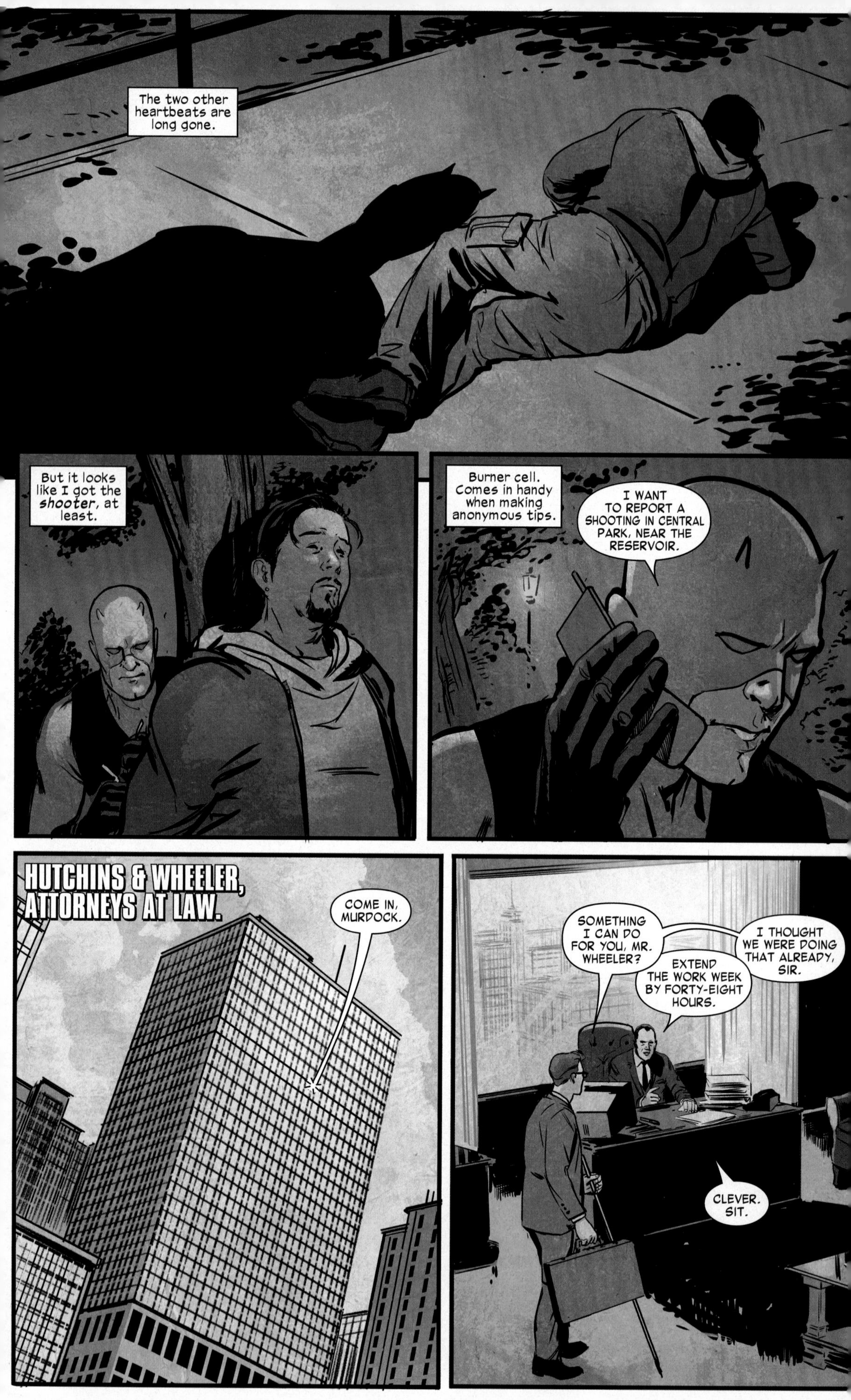
The two other heartbeats are long gone.
But it looks like I got the *shooter*, at least.
Burner cell. Comes in handy when making anonymous tips.
I WANT TO REPORT A SHOOTING IN CENTRAL PARK, NEAR THE RESERVOIR.
HUTCHINS & WHEELER, ATTORNEYS AT LAW.
COME IN, MURDOCK.
SOMETHING I CAN DO FOR YOU, MR. WHEELER?
EXTEND THE WORK WEEK BY FORTY-EIGHT HOURS.
I THOUGHT WE WERE DOING THAT ALREADY, SIR.
CLEVER. SIT.

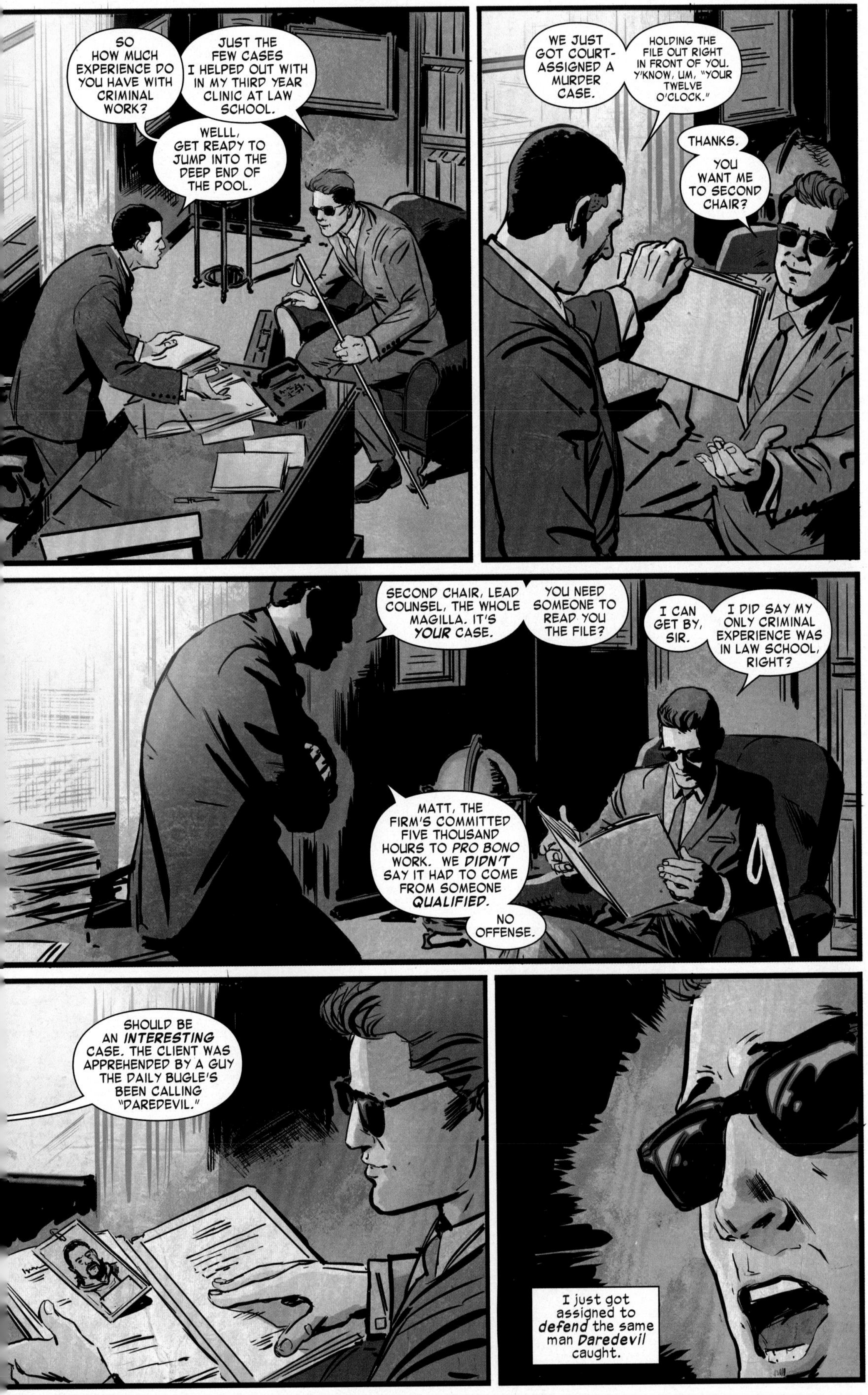

SO HOW MUCH EXPERIENCE DO YOU HAVE WITH CRIMINAL WORK?
JUST THE FEW CASES I HELPED OUT WITH IN MY THIRD YEAR CLINIC AT LAW SCHOOL.
WELLL, GET READY TO JUMP INTO THE DEEP END OF THE POOL.
WE JUST GOT COURT-ASSIGNED A MURDER CASE.
HOLDING THE FILE OUT RIGHT IN FRONT OF YOU. Y'KNOW, UM, "YOUR TWELVE O'CLOCK."
THANKS.
YOU WANT ME TO SECOND CHAIR?
SECOND CHAIR, LEAD COUNSEL, THE WHOLE MAGILLA. IT'S YOUR CASE.
YOU NEED SOMEONE TO READ YOU THE FILE?
I CAN GET BY, SIR.
I DID SAY MY ONLY CRIMINAL EXPERIENCE WAS IN LAW SCHOOL, RIGHT?
MATT, THE FIRM'S COMMITTED FIVE THOUSAND HOURS TO PRO BONO WORK. WE DIDN'T SAY IT HAD TO COME FROM SOMEONE QUALIFIED.
NO OFFENSE.
SHOULD BE AN INTERESTING CASE. THE CLIENT WAS APPREHENDED BY A GUY THE DAILY BUGLE'S BEEN CALLING "DAREDEVIL."
I just got assigned to defend the same man Daredevil caught.

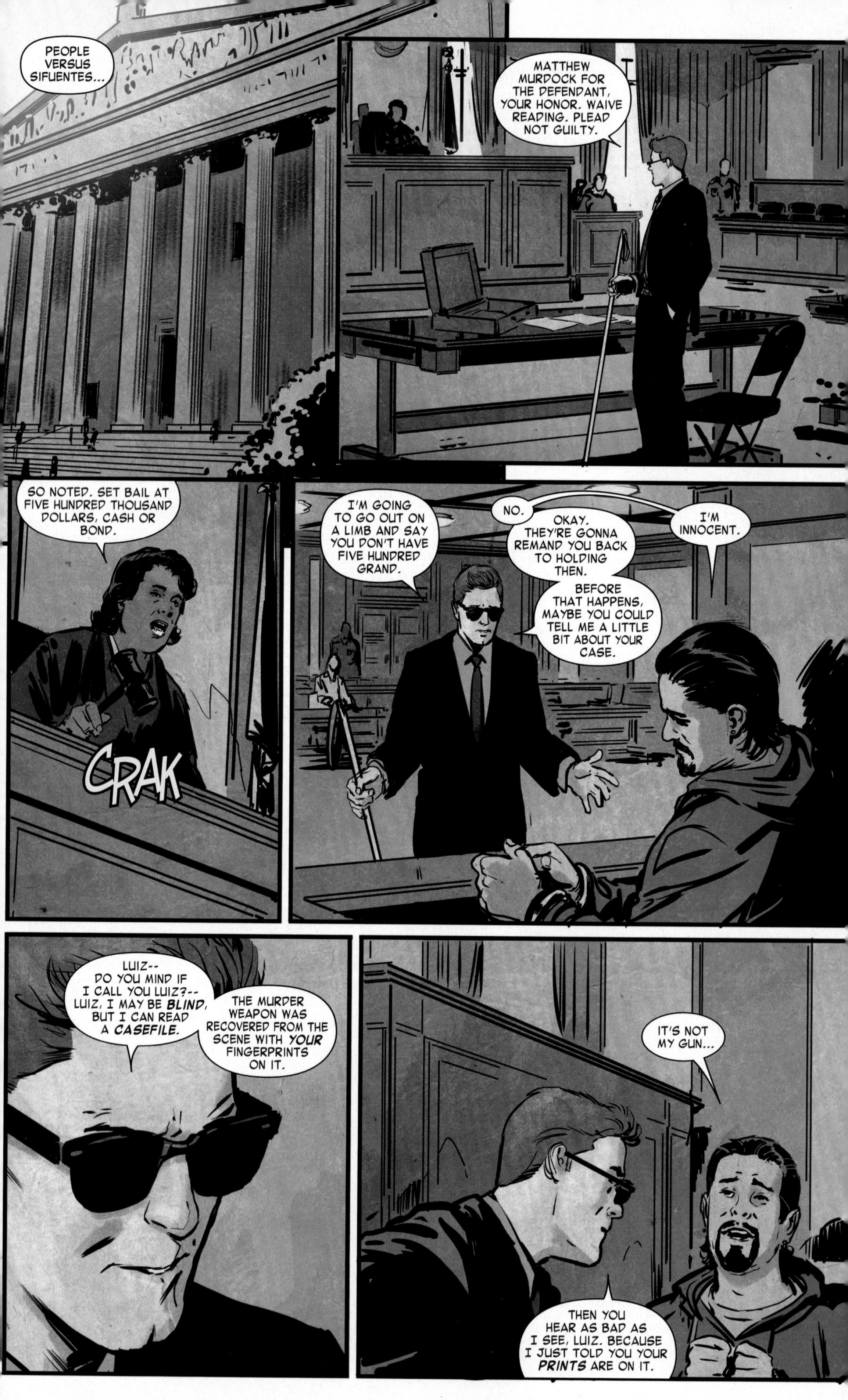
PEOPLE VERSUS SIFUENTES...
MATTHEW MURDOCK FOR THE DEFENDANT, YOUR HONOR. WAIVE READING. PLEAD NOT GUILTY.
SO NOTED. SET BAIL AT FIVE HUNDRED THOUSAND DOLLARS, CASH OR BOND.
CRAK
I'M GOING TO GO OUT ON A LIMB AND SAY YOU DON'T HAVE FIVE HUNDRED GRAND.
NO.
I'M INNOCENT.
OKAY. THEY'RE GONNA REMAND YOU BACK TO HOLDING THEN.
BEFORE THAT HAPPENS, MAYBE YOU COULD TELL ME A LITTLE BIT ABOUT YOUR CASE.
LUIZ-- DO YOU MIND IF I CALL YOU LUIZ?-- LUIZ, I MAY BE ***BLIND***, BUT I CAN READ A ***CASEFILE***.
THE MURDER WEAPON WAS RECOVERED FROM THE SCENE WITH ***YOUR*** FINGERPRINTS ON IT.
IT'S NOT MY GUN...
THEN YOU HEAR AS BAD AS I SEE, LUIZ. BECAUSE I JUST TOLD YOU YOUR ***PRINTS*** ARE ON IT.

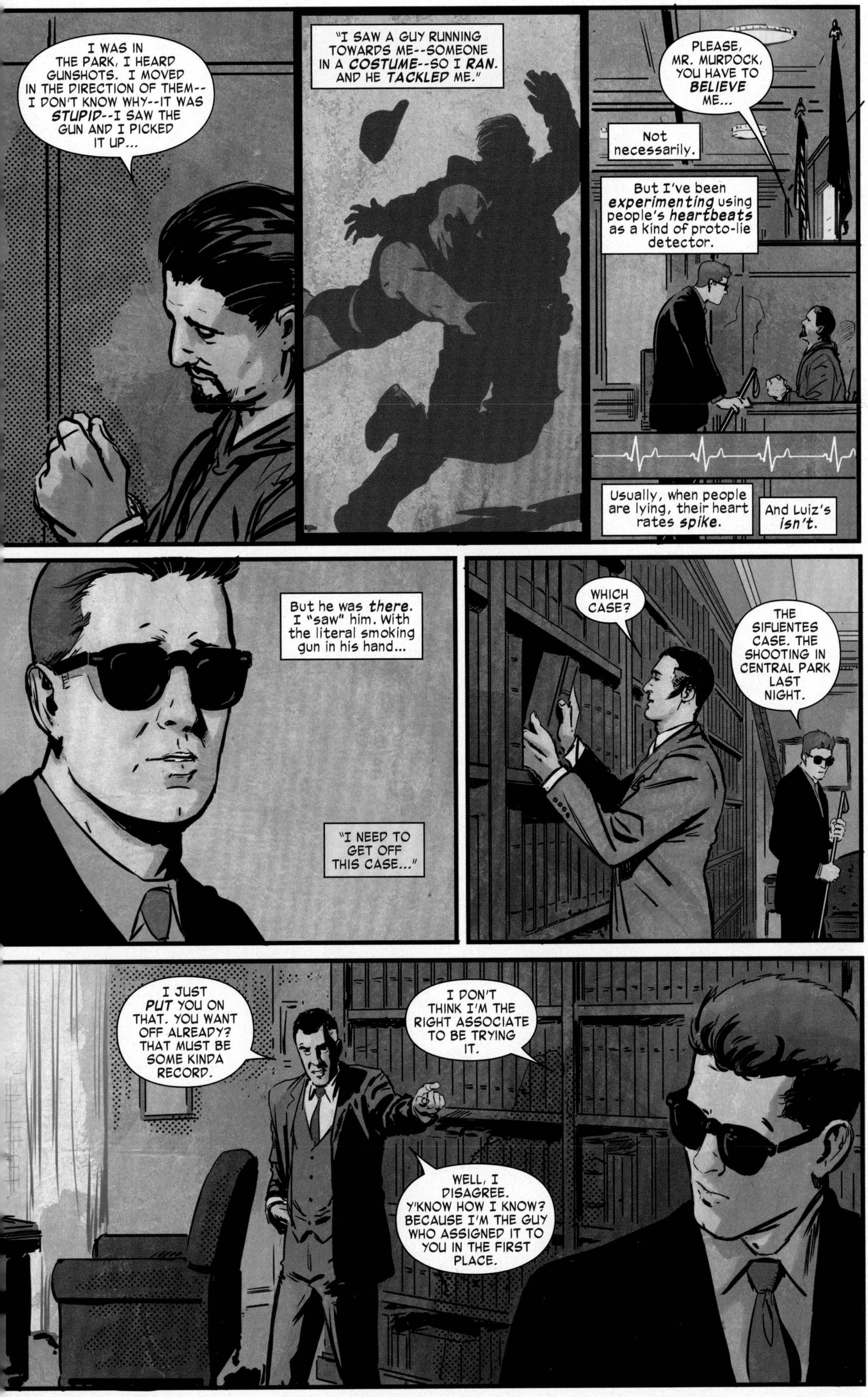

I WAS IN THE PARK, I HEARD GUNSHOTS. I MOVED IN THE DIRECTION OF THEM--I DON'T KNOW WHY--IT WAS *STUPID*--I SAW THE GUN AND I PICKED IT UP...
"I SAW A GUY RUNNING TOWARDS ME--SOMEONE IN A *COSTUME*--SO I *RAN*. AND HE *TACKLED* ME."
PLEASE, MR. MURDOCK, YOU HAVE TO *BELIEVE* ME...
Not necessarily.
But I've been *experimenting* using people's *heartbeats* as a kind of proto-lie detector.
Usually, when people are lying, their heart rates *spike*.
And Luiz's *isn't*.
But he was *there*. I "saw" him. With the literal smoking gun in his hand...
"I NEED TO GET OFF THIS CASE..."
WHICH CASE?
THE SIFUENTES CASE. THE SHOOTING IN CENTRAL PARK LAST NIGHT.
I JUST *PUT* YOU ON THAT. YOU WANT OFF ALREADY? THAT MUST BE SOME KINDA RECORD.
I DON'T THINK I'M THE RIGHT ASSOCIATE TO BE TRYING IT.
WELL, I DISAGREE. Y'KNOW HOW I KNOW? BECAUSE I'M THE GUY WHO ASSIGNED IT TO YOU IN THE FIRST PLACE.

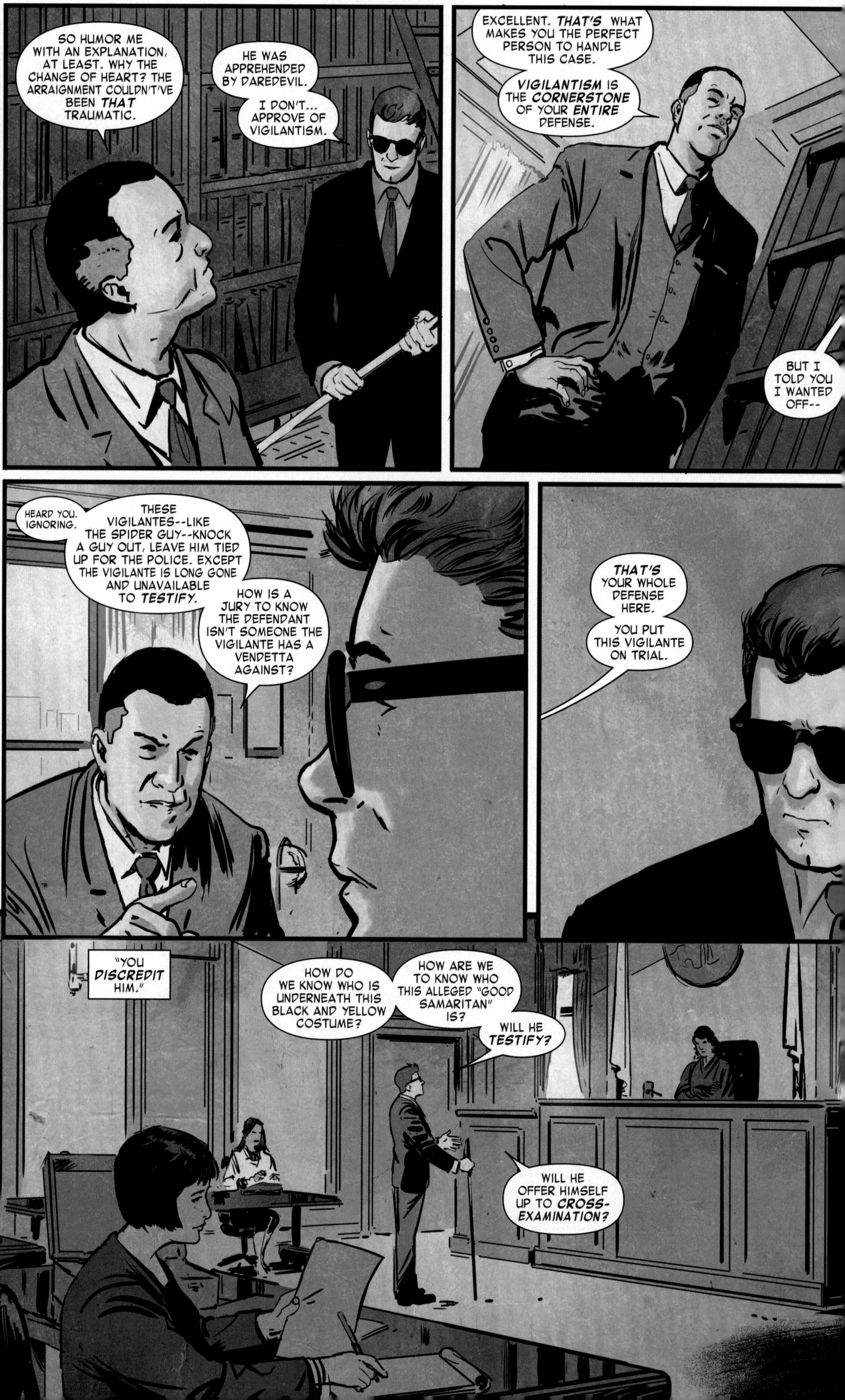
SO HUMOR ME WITH AN EXPLANATION, AT LEAST. WHY THE CHANGE OF HEART? THE ARRAIGNMENT COULDN'T'VE BEEN THAT TRAUMATIC.
HE WAS APPREHENDED BY DAREDEVIL.
I DON'T... APPROVE OF VIGILANTISM.
EXCELLENT. THAT'S WHAT MAKES YOU THE PERFECT PERSON TO HANDLE THIS CASE.
VIGILANTISM IS THE CORNERSTONE OF YOUR ENTIRE DEFENSE.
BUT I TOLD YOU I WANTED OFF--
HEARD YOU. IGNORING.
THESE VIGILANTES--LIKE THE SPIDER GUY--KNOCK A GUY OUT, LEAVE HIM TIED UP FOR THE POLICE. EXCEPT THE VIGILANTE IS LONG GONE AND UNAVAILABLE TO TESTIFY.
HOW IS A JURY TO KNOW THE DEFENDANT ISN'T SOMEONE THE VIGILANTE HAS A VENDETTA AGAINST?
THAT'S YOUR WHOLE DEFENSE HERE.
YOU PUT THIS VIGILANTE ON TRIAL.
"YOU DISCREDIT HIM."
HOW DO WE KNOW WHO IS UNDERNEATH THIS BLACK AND YELLOW COSTUME?
HOW ARE WE TO KNOW WHO THIS ALLEGED "GOOD SAMARITAN" IS?
WILL HE TESTIFY?
WILL HE OFFER HIMSELF UP TO CROSS-EXAMINATION?

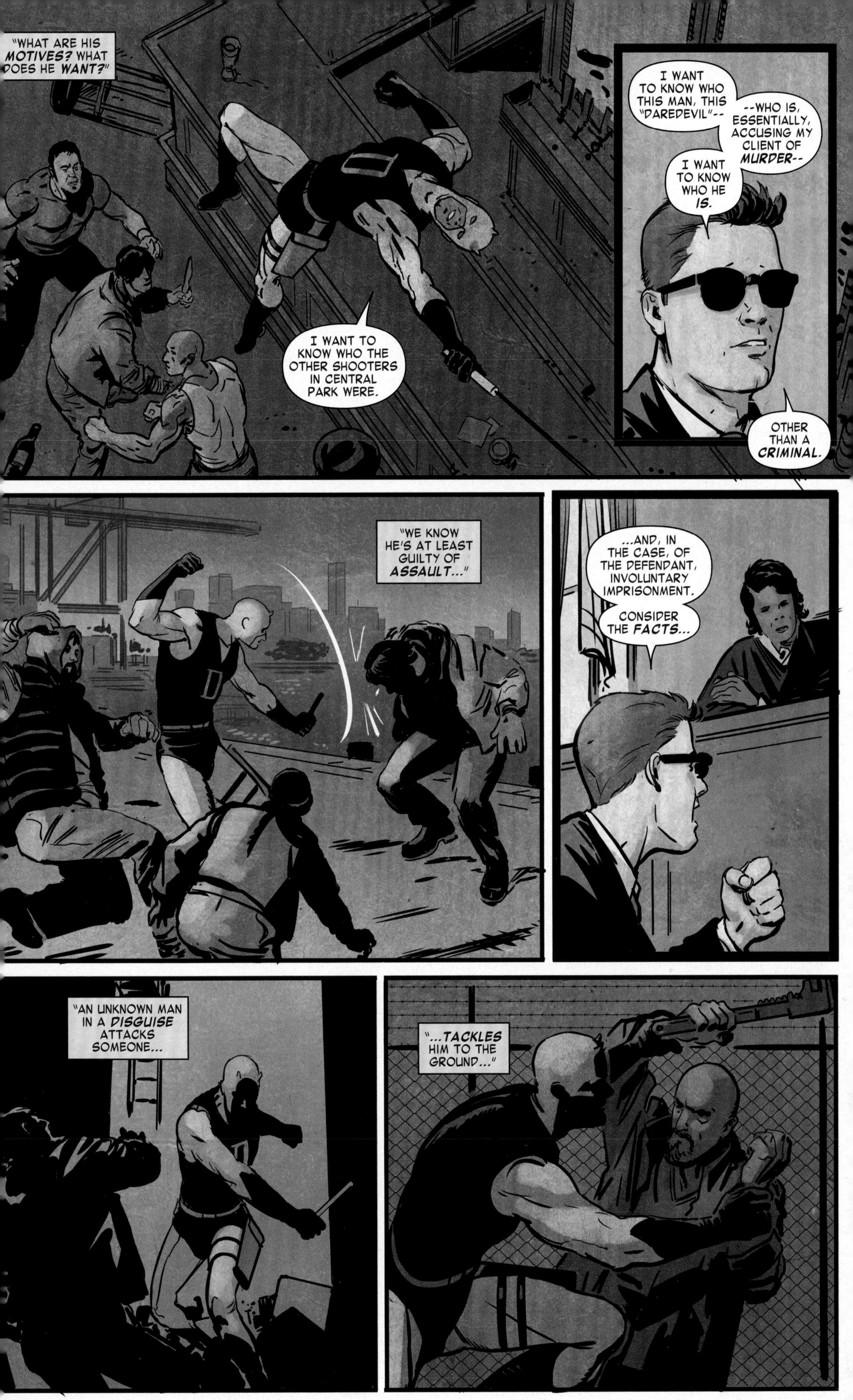
"WHAT ARE HIS MOTIVES? WHAT DOES HE WANT?"
I WANT TO KNOW WHO THE OTHER SHOOTERS IN CENTRAL PARK WERE.
I WANT TO KNOW WHO THIS MAN, THIS "DAREDEVIL"--
--WHO IS, ESSENTIALLY, ACCUSING MY CLIENT OF MURDER--
I WANT TO KNOW WHO HE IS.
OTHER THAN A CRIMINAL.
"WE KNOW HE'S AT LEAST GUILTY OF ASSAULT..."
...AND, IN THE CASE, OF THE DEFENDANT, INVOLUNTARY IMPRISONMENT.
CONSIDER THE FACTS...
"AN UNKNOWN MAN IN A DISGUISE ATTACKS SOMEONE...
"...TACKLES HIM TO THE GROUND..."

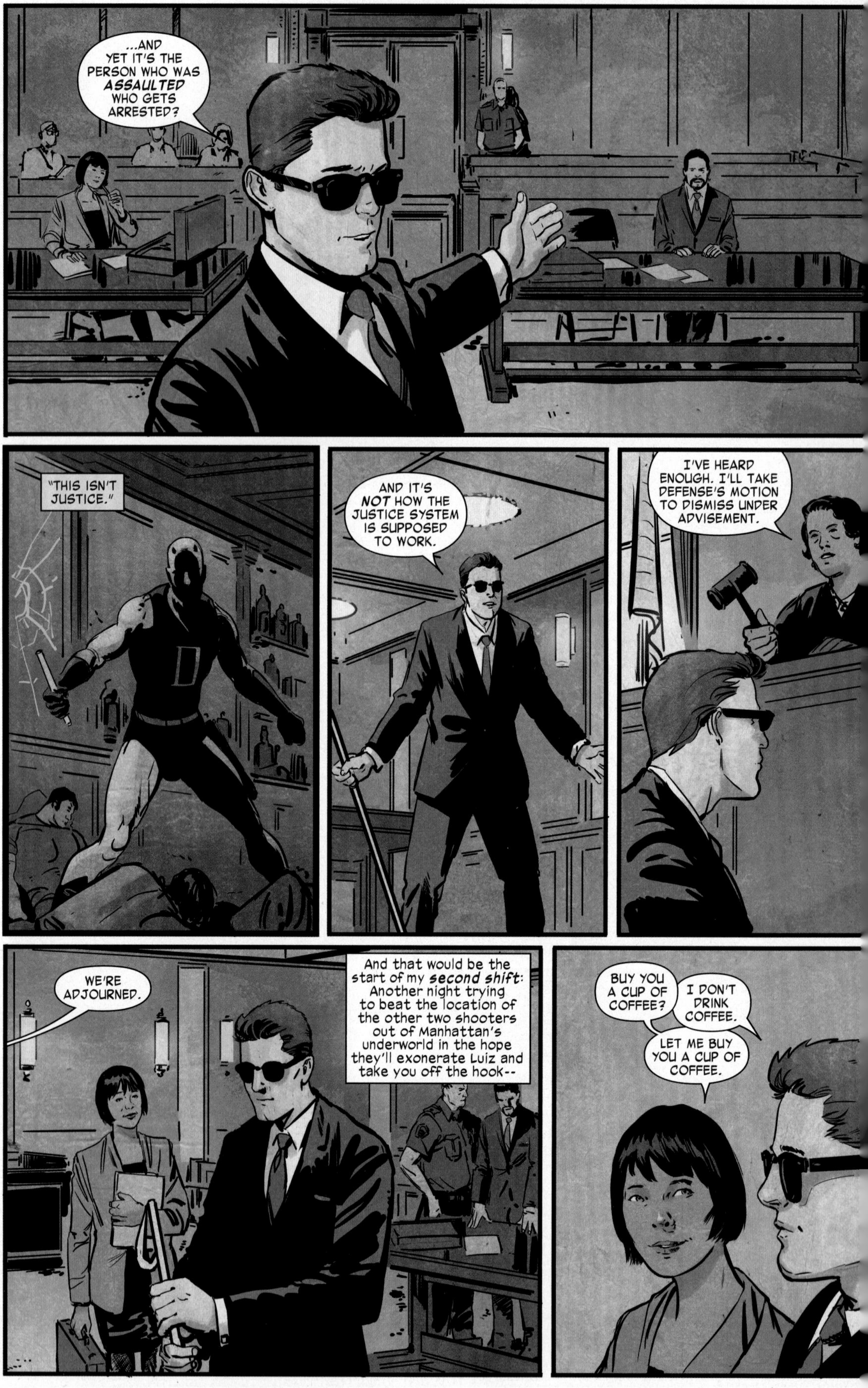
...AND YET IT'S THE PERSON WHO WAS ASSAULTED WHO GETS ARRESTED?
"THIS ISN'T JUSTICE."
AND IT'S NOT HOW THE JUSTICE SYSTEM IS SUPPOSED TO WORK.
I'VE HEARD ENOUGH. I'LL TAKE DEFENSE'S MOTION TO DISMISS UNDER ADVISEMENT.
WE'RE ADJOURNED.
And that would be the start of my second shift: Another night trying to beat the location of the other two shooters out of Manhattan's underworld in the hope they'll exonerate Luiz and take you off the hook--
BUY YOU A CUP OF COFFEE?
I DON'T DRINK COFFEE.
LET ME BUY YOU A CUP OF COFFEE.

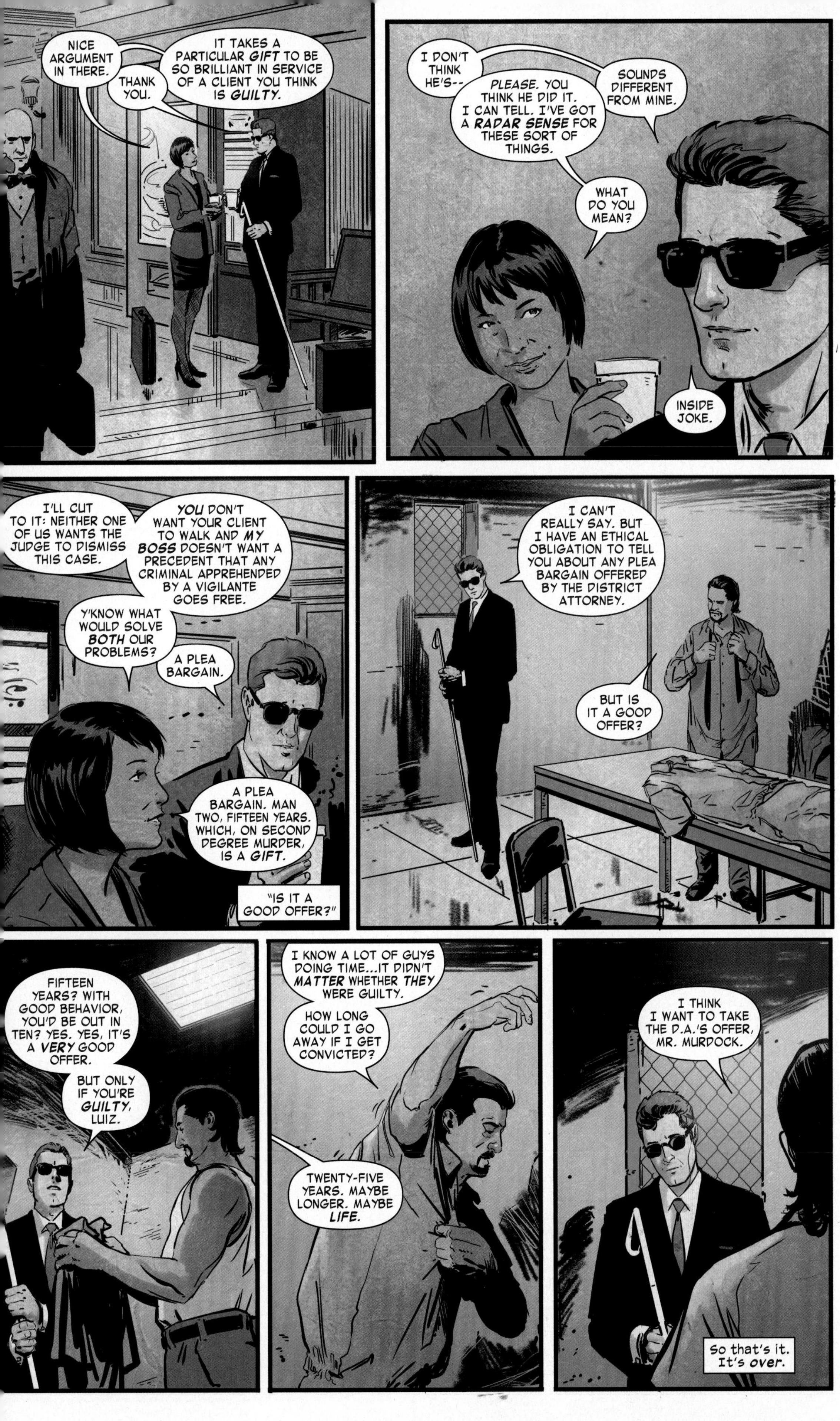
NICE ARGUMENT IN THERE.
THANK YOU.
IT TAKES A PARTICULAR GIFT TO BE SO BRILLIANT IN SERVICE OF A CLIENT YOU THINK IS GUILTY.
I DON'T THINK HE'S--
PLEASE. YOU THINK HE DID IT. I CAN TELL. I'VE GOT A RADAR SENSE FOR THESE SORT OF THINGS.
SOUNDS DIFFERENT FROM MINE.
WHAT DO YOU MEAN?
INSIDE JOKE.
I'LL CUT TO IT: NEITHER ONE OF US WANTS THE JUDGE TO DISMISS THIS CASE.
YOU DON'T WANT YOUR CLIENT TO WALK AND MY BOSS DOESN'T WANT A PRECEDENT THAT ANY CRIMINAL APPREHENDED BY A VIGILANTE GOES FREE.
Y'KNOW WHAT WOULD SOLVE BOTH OUR PROBLEMS?
A PLEA BARGAIN.
A PLEA BARGAIN. MAN TWO, FIFTEEN YEARS. WHICH, ON SECOND DEGREE MURDER, IS A GIFT.
"IS IT A GOOD OFFER?"
I CAN'T REALLY SAY. BUT I HAVE AN ETHICAL OBLIGATION TO TELL YOU ABOUT ANY PLEA BARGAIN OFFERED BY THE DISTRICT ATTORNEY.
BUT IS IT A GOOD OFFER?
FIFTEEN YEARS? WITH GOOD BEHAVIOR, YOU'D BE OUT IN TEN? YES. YES, IT'S A VERY GOOD OFFER.
BUT ONLY IF YOU'RE GUILTY, LUIZ.
I KNOW A LOT OF GUYS DOING TIME...IT DIDN'T MATTER WHETHER THEY WERE GUILTY.
HOW LONG COULD I GO AWAY IF I GET CONVICTED?
TWENTY-FIVE YEARS. MAYBE LONGER. MAYBE LIFE.
I THINK I WANT TO TAKE THE D.A.'S OFFER, MR. MURDOCK.
So that's it. It's over.

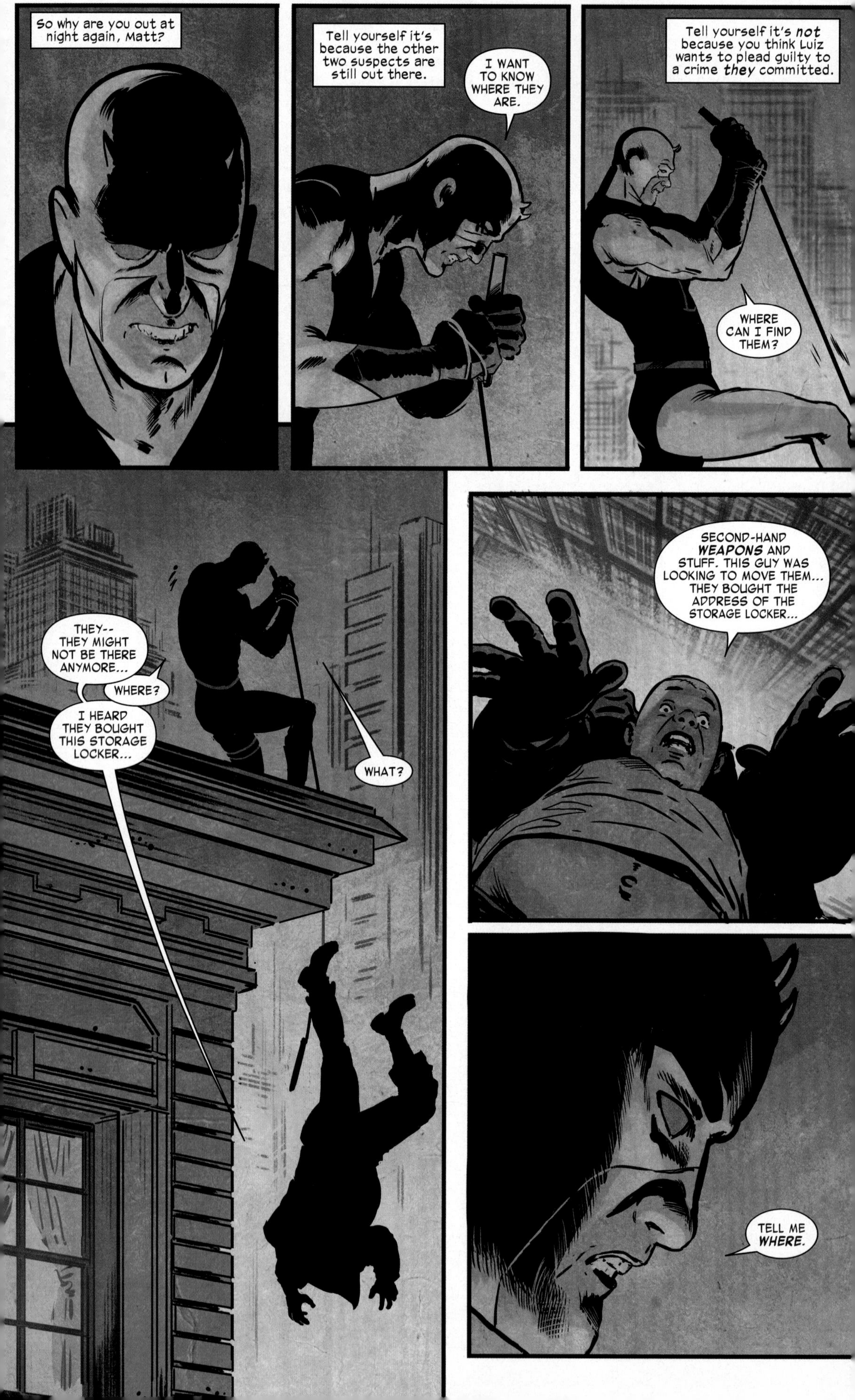
So why are you out at night again, Matt?
Tell yourself it's because the other two suspects are still out there.
I WANT TO KNOW WHERE THEY ARE.
Tell yourself it's not because you think Luiz wants to plead guilty to a crime they committed.
WHERE CAN I FIND THEM?
THEY-- THEY MIGHT NOT BE THERE ANYMORE...
WHERE?
I HEARD THEY BOUGHT THIS STORAGE LOCKER...
WHAT?
SECOND-HAND WEAPONS AND STUFF. THIS GUY WAS LOOKING TO MOVE THEM... THEY BOUGHT THE ADDRESS OF THE STORAGE LOCKER...
TELL ME WHERE.

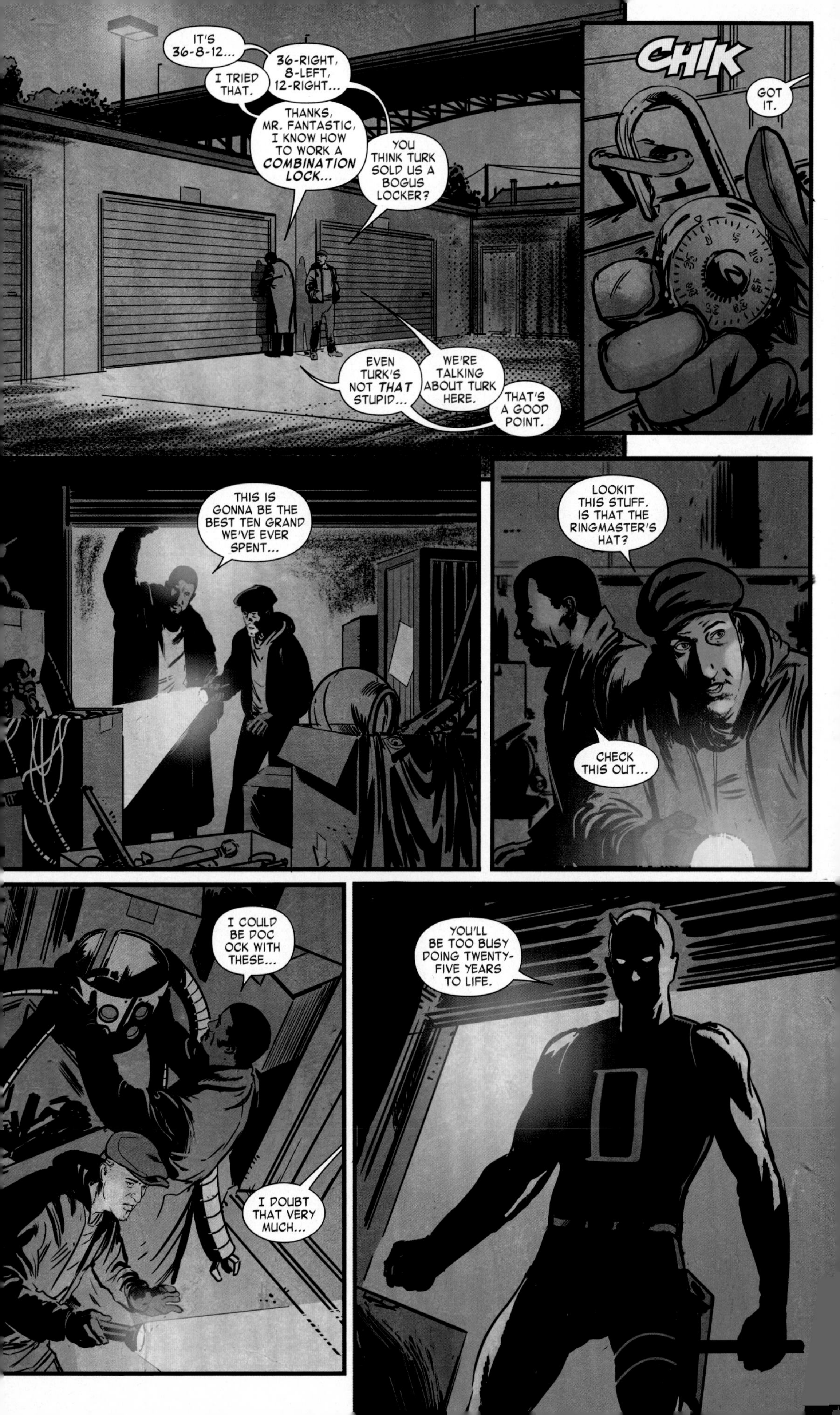
IT'S 36-8-12...
I TRIED THAT.
36-RIGHT, 8-LEFT, 12-RIGHT...
THANKS, MR. FANTASTIC, I KNOW HOW TO WORK A COMBINATION LOCK...
YOU THINK TURK SOLD US A BOGUS LOCKER?
EVEN TURK'S NOT THAT STUPID...
WE'RE TALKING ABOUT TURK HERE.
THAT'S A GOOD POINT.
CHIK
GOT IT.
THIS IS GONNA BE THE BEST TEN GRAND WE'VE EVER SPENT...
LOOKIT THIS STUFF. IS THAT THE RINGMASTER'S HAT?
CHECK THIS OUT...
I COULD BE DOC OCK WITH THESE...
I DOUBT THAT VERY MUCH...
YOU'LL BE TOO BUSY DOING TWENTY-FIVE YEARS TO LIFE.

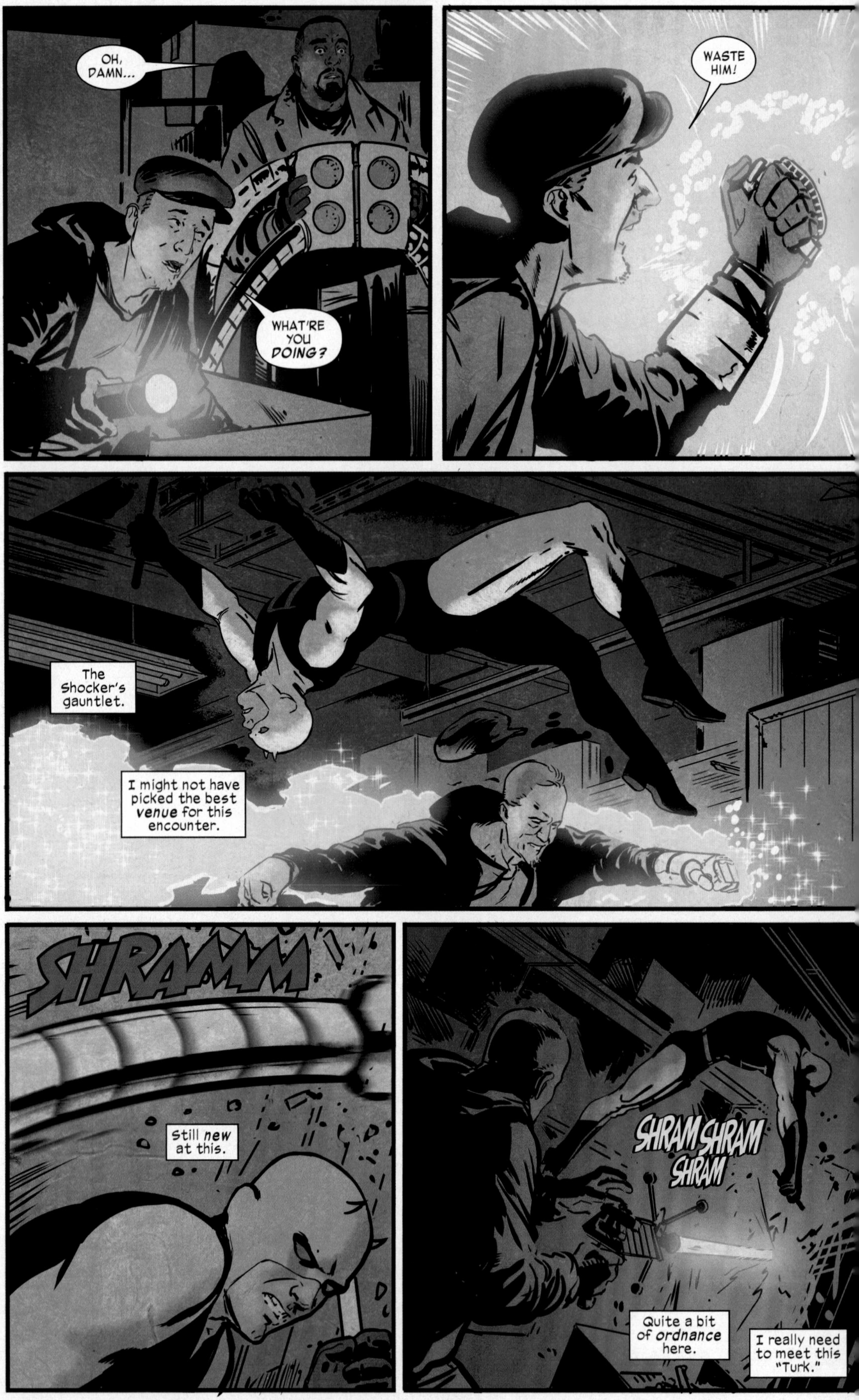

OH, DAMN...
WHAT'RE YOU *DOING?*
WASTE HIM!
The Shocker's gauntlet.
I might not have picked the best *venue* for this encounter.
SHRAMM
Still *new* at this.
SHRAM SHRAM SHRAM
Quite a bit of *ordnance* here.
I really need to meet this "Turk."

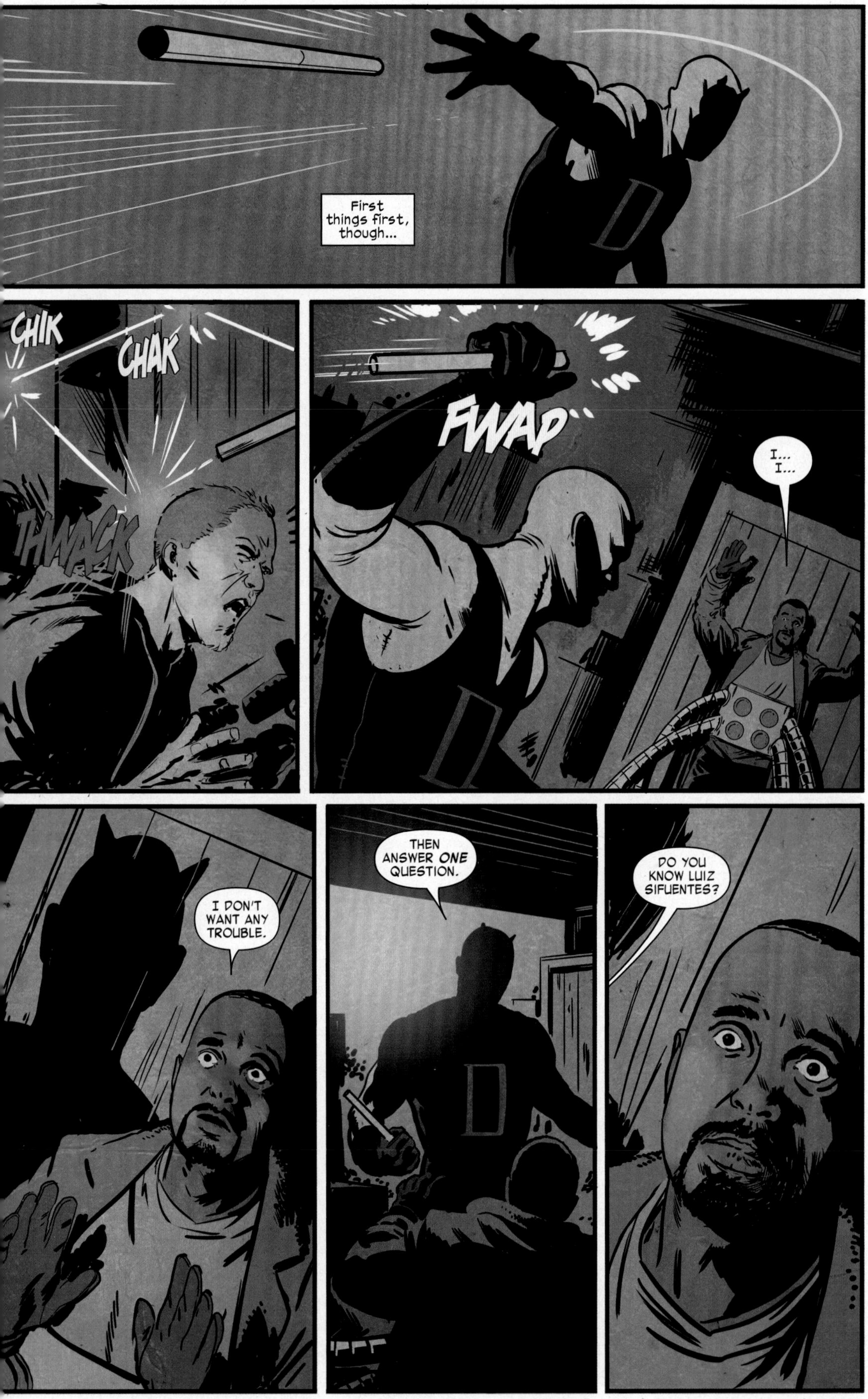
First things first, though...
CHIK
CHAK
THWACK
FWAP
I... I...
I DON'T WANT ANY TROUBLE.
THEN ANSWER *ONE* QUESTION.
DO YOU KNOW LUIZ SIFUENTES?

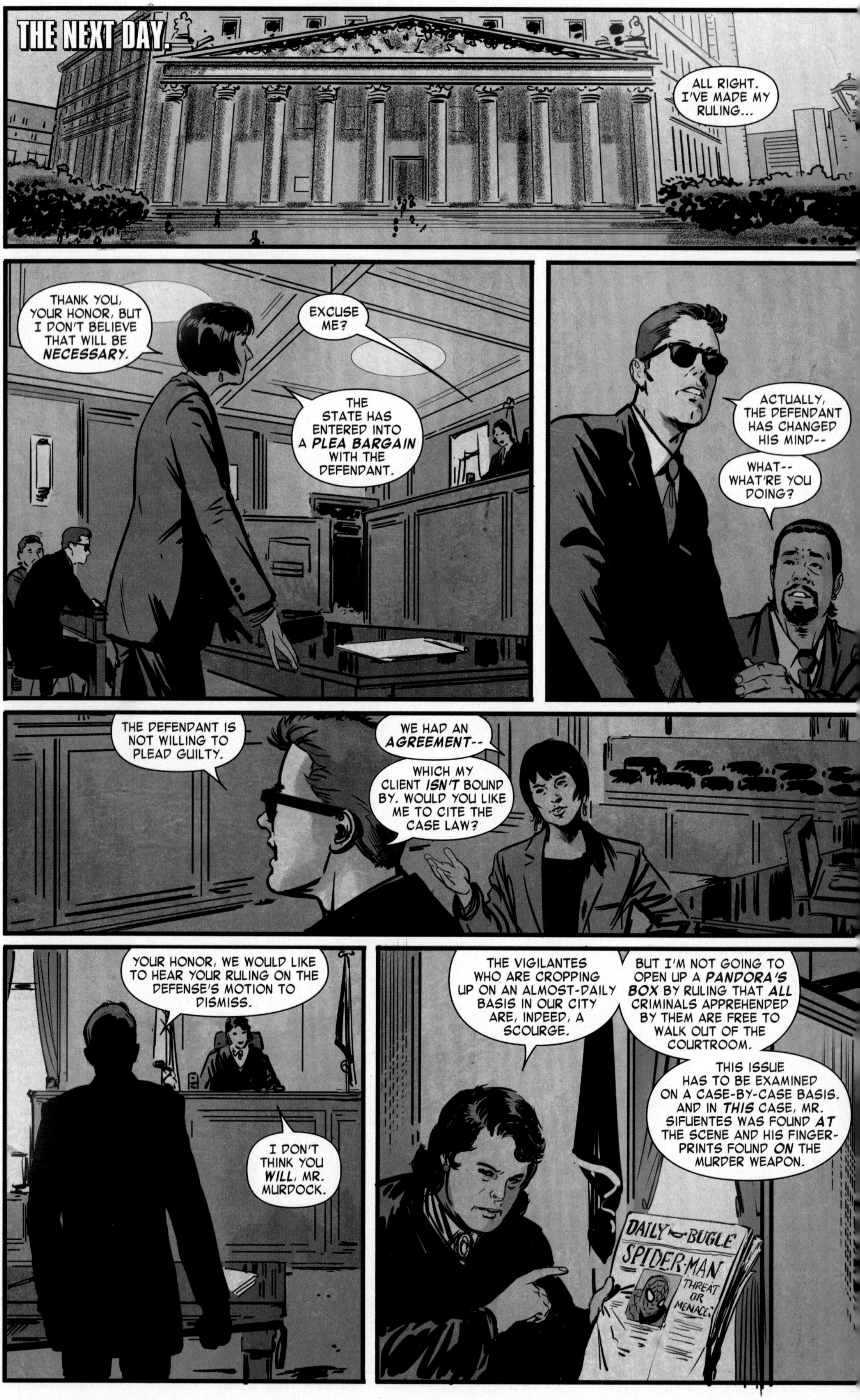
THE NEXT DAY.
ALL RIGHT. I'VE MADE MY RULING...
THANK YOU, YOUR HONOR, BUT I DON'T BELIEVE THAT WILL BE NECESSARY.
EXCUSE ME?
THE STATE HAS ENTERED INTO A PLEA BARGAIN WITH THE DEFENDANT.
ACTUALLY, THE DEFENDANT HAS CHANGED HIS MIND--
WHAT-- WHAT'RE YOU DOING?
THE DEFENDANT IS NOT WILLING TO PLEAD GUILTY.
WE HAD AN AGREEMENT--
WHICH MY CLIENT ISN'T BOUND BY. WOULD YOU LIKE ME TO CITE THE CASE LAW?
YOUR HONOR, WE WOULD LIKE TO HEAR YOUR RULING ON THE DEFENSE'S MOTION TO DISMISS.
I DON'T THINK YOU WILL, MR. MURDOCK.
THE VIGILANTES WHO ARE CROPPING UP ON AN ALMOST-DAILY BASIS IN OUR CITY ARE, INDEED, A SCOURGE.
BUT I'M NOT GOING TO OPEN UP A PANDORA'S BOX BY RULING THAT ALL CRIMINALS APPREHENDED BY THEM ARE FREE TO WALK OUT OF THE COURTROOM.
THIS ISSUE HAS TO BE EXAMINED ON A CASE-BY-CASE BASIS. AND IN THIS CASE, MR. SIFUENTES WAS FOUND AT THE SCENE AND HIS FINGER-PRINTS FOUND ON THE MURDER WEAPON.
DAILY BUGLE
SPIDER-MAN
THREAT OR MENACE?

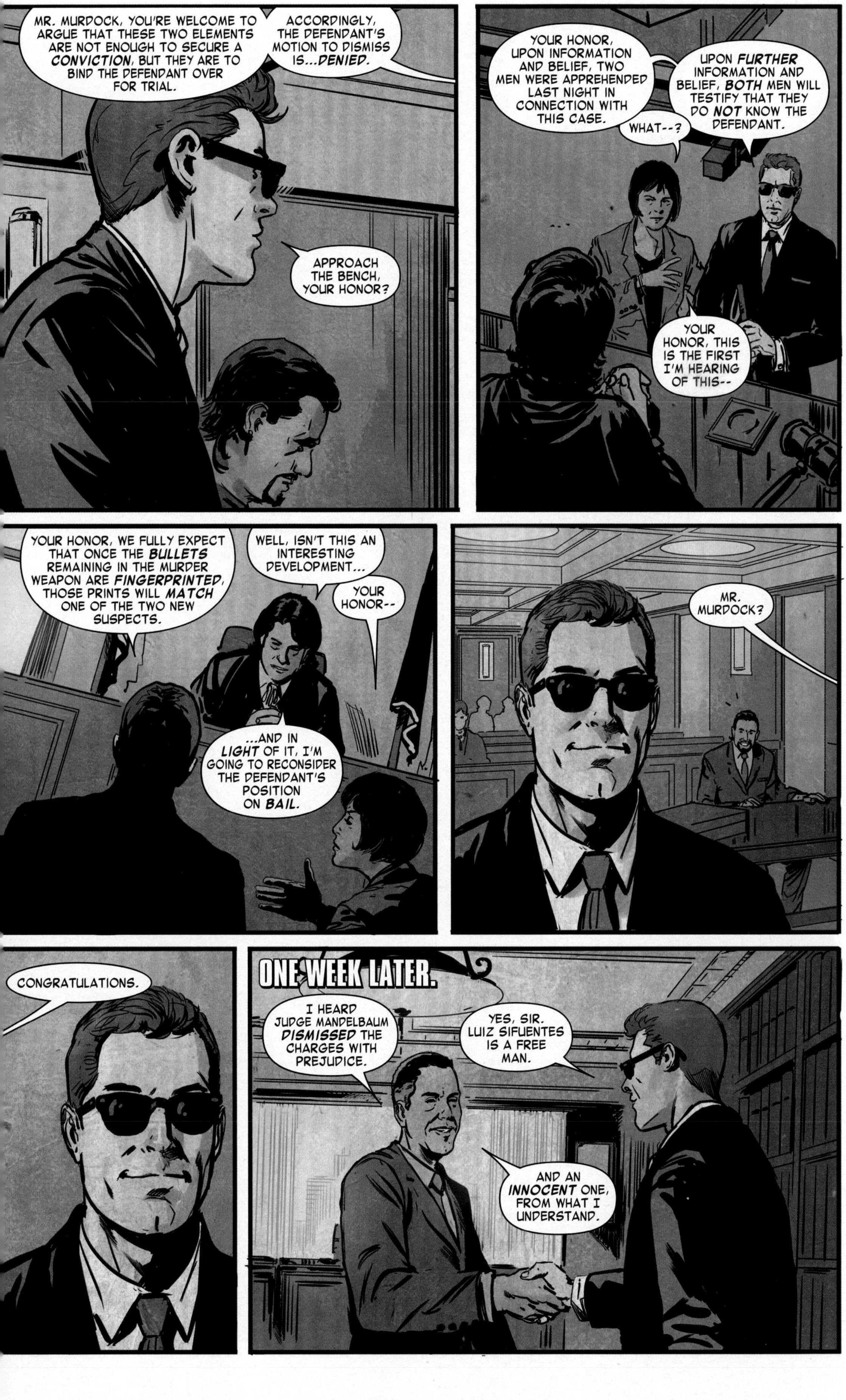

MR. MURDOCK, YOU'RE WELCOME TO ARGUE THAT THESE TWO ELEMENTS ARE NOT ENOUGH TO SECURE A *CONVICTION*, BUT THEY ARE TO BIND THE DEFENDANT OVER FOR TRIAL.
ACCORDINGLY, THE DEFENDANT'S MOTION TO DISMISS IS...*DENIED.*
APPROACH THE BENCH, YOUR HONOR?
YOUR HONOR, UPON INFORMATION AND BELIEF, TWO MEN WERE APPREHENDED LAST NIGHT IN CONNECTION WITH THIS CASE.
WHAT--?
UPON *FURTHER* INFORMATION AND BELIEF, *BOTH* MEN WILL TESTIFY THAT THEY DO *NOT* KNOW THE DEFENDANT.
YOUR HONOR, THIS IS THE FIRST I'M HEARING OF THIS--
YOUR HONOR, WE FULLY EXPECT THAT ONCE THE *BULLETS* REMAINING IN THE MURDER WEAPON ARE *FINGERPRINTED*, THOSE PRINTS WILL *MATCH* ONE OF THE TWO NEW SUSPECTS.
WELL, ISN'T THIS AN INTERESTING DEVELOPMENT...
YOUR HONOR--
...AND IN *LIGHT* OF IT, I'M GOING TO RECONSIDER THE DEFENDANT'S POSITION ON *BAIL*.
MR. MURDOCK?
CONGRATULATIONS.
ONE WEEK LATER.
I HEARD JUDGE MANDELBAUM *DISMISSED* THE CHARGES WITH PREJUDICE.
YES, SIR. LUIZ SIFUENTES IS A FREE MAN.
AND AN *INNOCENT* ONE, FROM WHAT I UNDERSTAND.

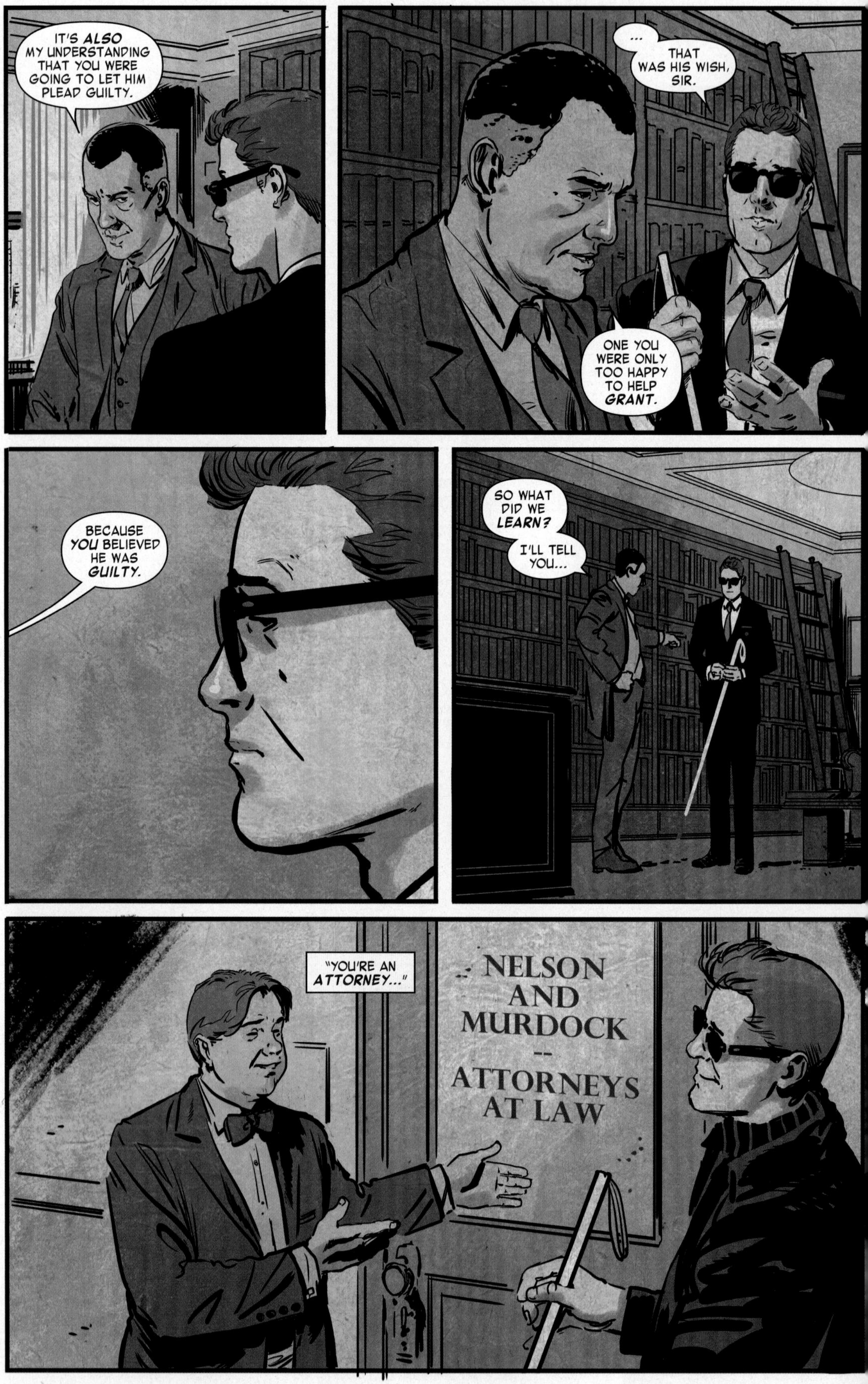
IT'S ALSO MY UNDERSTANDING THAT YOU WERE GOING TO LET HIM PLEAD GUILTY.
...
THAT WAS HIS WISH, SIR.
ONE YOU WERE ONLY TOO HAPPY TO HELP GRANT.
BECAUSE YOU BELIEVED HE WAS GUILTY.
SO WHAT DID WE LEARN?
I'LL TELL YOU...
"YOU'RE AN ATTORNEY..."
NELSON AND MURDOCK -- ATTORNEYS AT LAW

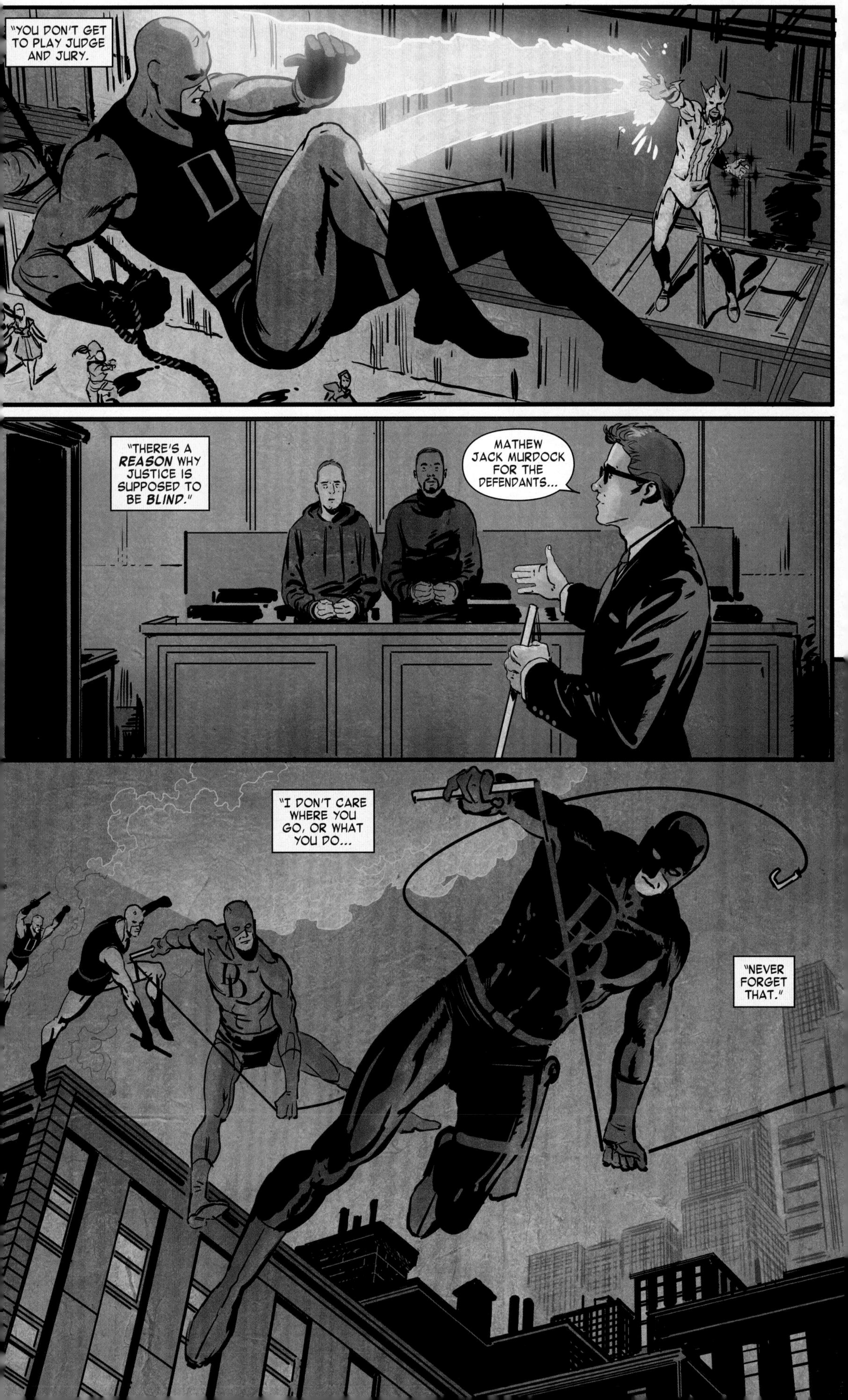
"YOU DON'T GET TO PLAY JUDGE AND JURY.
"THERE'S A REASON WHY JUSTICE IS SUPPOSED TO BE BLIND."
MATHEW JACK MURDOCK FOR THE DEFENDANTS...
"I DON'T CARE WHERE YOU GO, OR WHAT YOU DO...
"NEVER FORGET THAT."

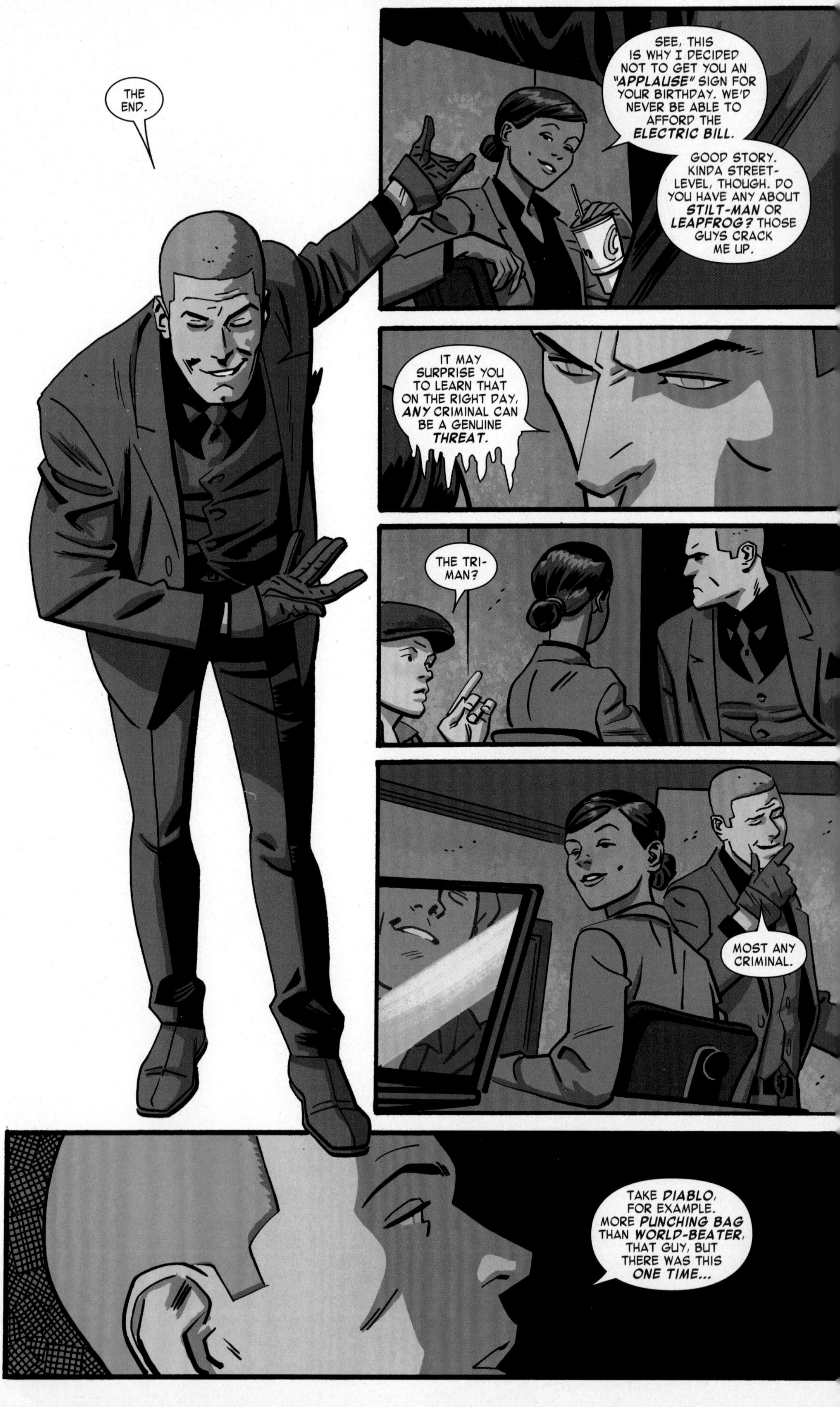
THE END.
SEE, THIS IS WHY I DECIDED NOT TO GET YOU AN "APPLAUSE" SIGN FOR YOUR BIRTHDAY. WE'D NEVER BE ABLE TO AFFORD THE ELECTRIC BILL.
GOOD STORY. KINDA STREET-LEVEL, THOUGH. DO YOU HAVE ANY ABOUT STILT-MAN OR LEAPFROG? THOSE GUYS CRACK ME UP.
IT MAY SURPRISE YOU TO LEARN THAT ON THE RIGHT DAY, ANY CRIMINAL CAN BE A GENUINE THREAT.
THE TRI-MAN?
MOST ANY CRIMINAL.
TAKE DIABLO, FOR EXAMPLE. MORE PUNCHING BAG THAN WORLD-BEATER, THAT GUY, BUT THERE WAS THIS ONE TIME...

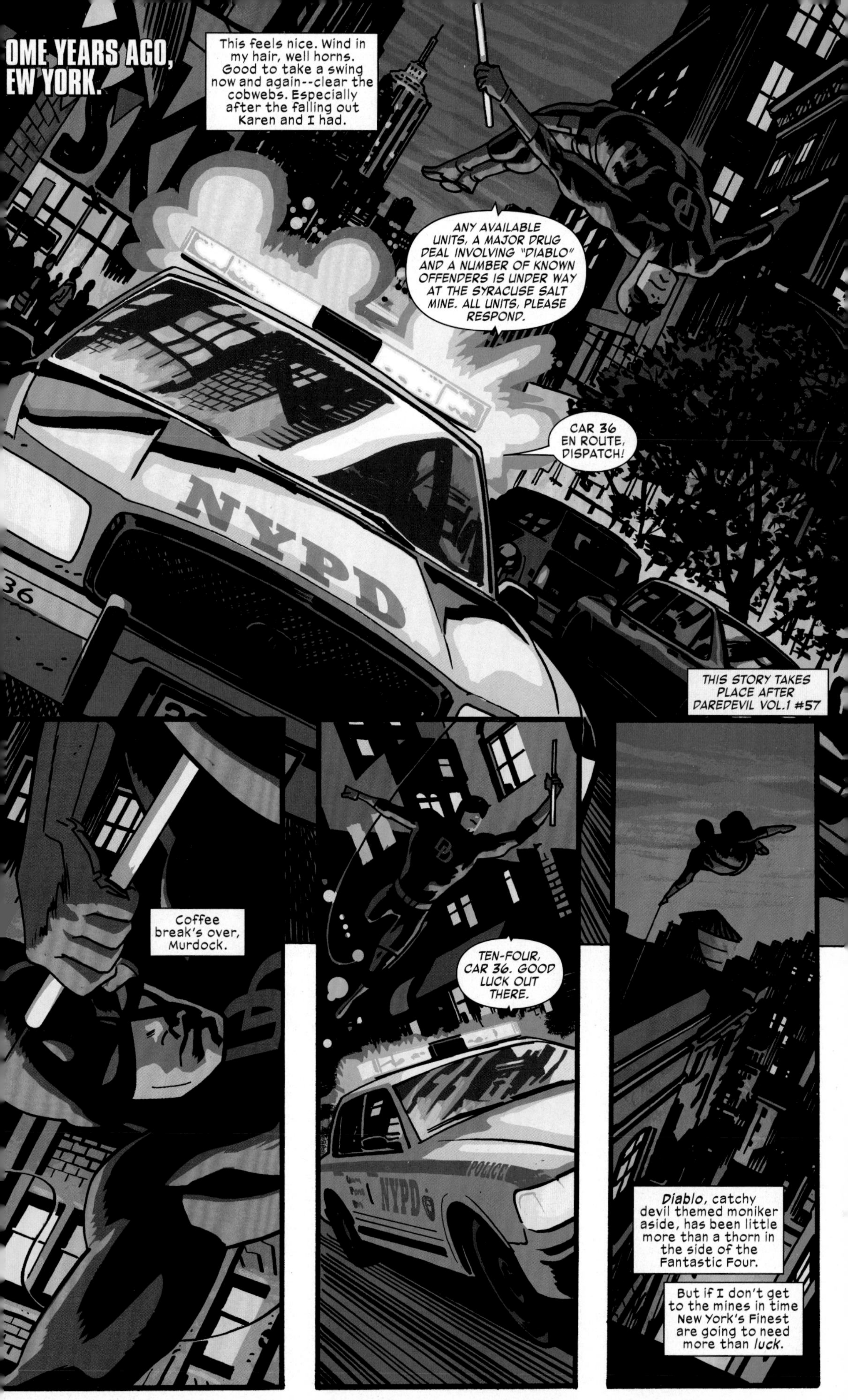
OME YEARS AGO,
EW YORK.
This feels nice. Wind in my hair, well horns. Good to take a swing now and again--clear the cobwebs. Especially after the falling out Karen and I had.
ANY AVAILABLE UNITS, A MAJOR DRUG DEAL INVOLVING "DIABLO" AND A NUMBER OF KNOWN OFFENDERS IS UNDER WAY AT THE SYRACUSE SALT MINE. ALL UNITS, PLEASE RESPOND.
CAR 36 EN ROUTE, DISPATCH!
NYPD
36
THIS STORY TAKES PLACE AFTER DAREDEVIL VOL.1 #57
Coffee break's over, Murdock.
TEN-FOUR, CAR 36. GOOD LUCK OUT THERE.
POLICE
NYPD
Diablo, catchy devil themed moniker aside, has been little more than a thorn in the side of the Fantastic Four.
But if I don't get to the mines in time New York's Finest are going to need more than *luck*.

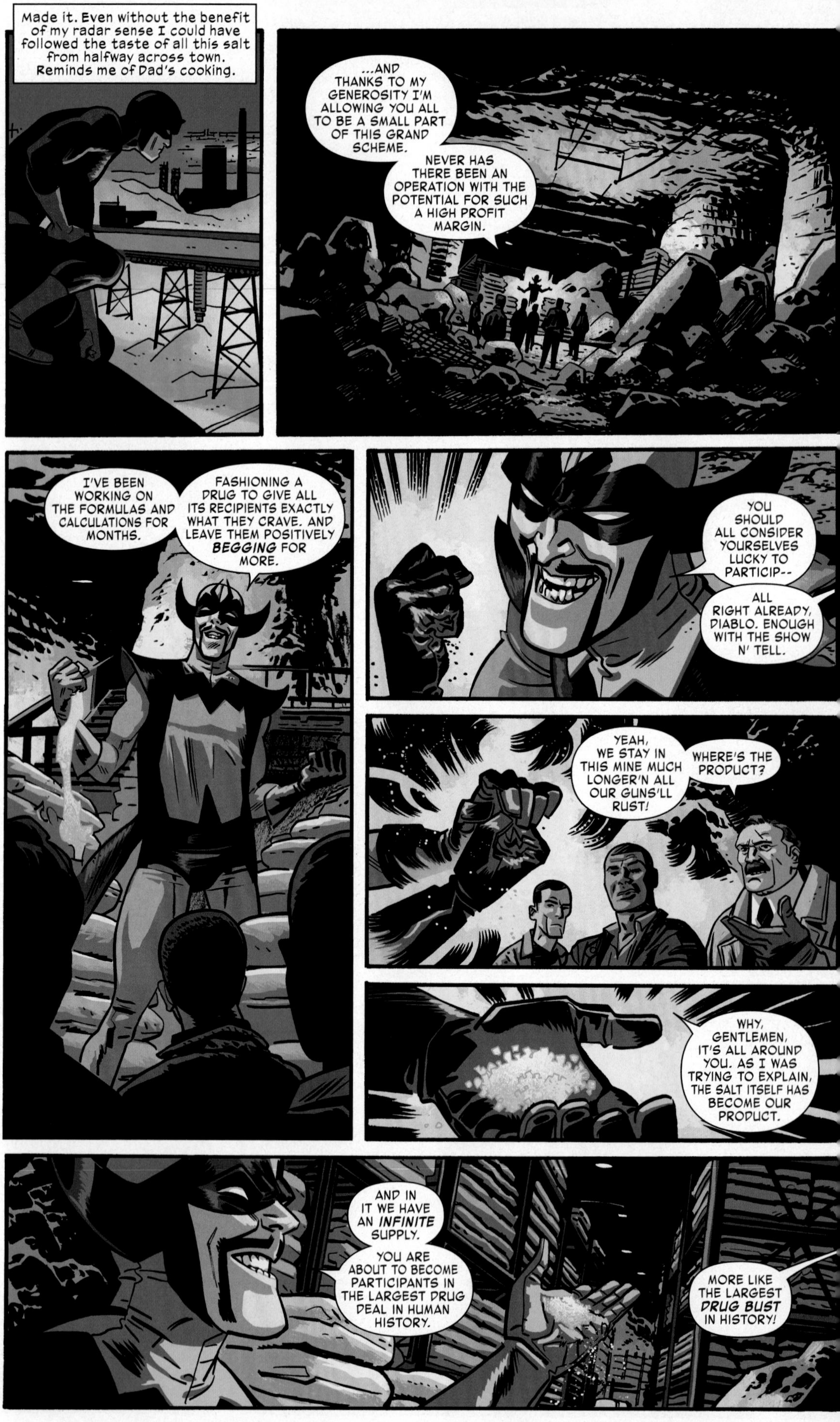

Made it. Even without the benefit of my radar sense I could have followed the taste of all this salt from halfway across town. Reminds me of Dad's cooking.
...AND THANKS TO MY GENEROSITY I'M ALLOWING YOU ALL TO BE A SMALL PART OF THIS GRAND SCHEME.
NEVER HAS THERE BEEN AN OPERATION WITH THE POTENTIAL FOR SUCH A HIGH PROFIT MARGIN.
I'VE BEEN WORKING ON THE FORMULAS AND CALCULATIONS FOR MONTHS.
FASHIONING A DRUG TO GIVE ALL ITS RECIPIENTS EXACTLY WHAT THEY CRAVE. AND LEAVE THEM POSITIVELY *BEGGING* FOR MORE.
YOU SHOULD ALL CONSIDER YOURSELVES LUCKY TO PARTICIP--
ALL RIGHT ALREADY, DIABLO. ENOUGH WITH THE SHOW N' TELL.
YEAH, WE STAY IN THIS MINE MUCH LONGER'N ALL OUR GUNS'LL RUST!
WHERE'S THE PRODUCT?
WHY, GENTLEMEN, IT'S ALL AROUND YOU. AS I WAS TRYING TO EXPLAIN, THE SALT ITSELF HAS BECOME OUR PRODUCT.
AND IN IT WE HAVE AN *INFINITE* SUPPLY.
YOU ARE ABOUT TO BECOME PARTICIPANTS IN THE LARGEST DRUG DEAL IN HUMAN HISTORY.
MORE LIKE THE LARGEST ***DRUG BUST*** IN HISTORY!

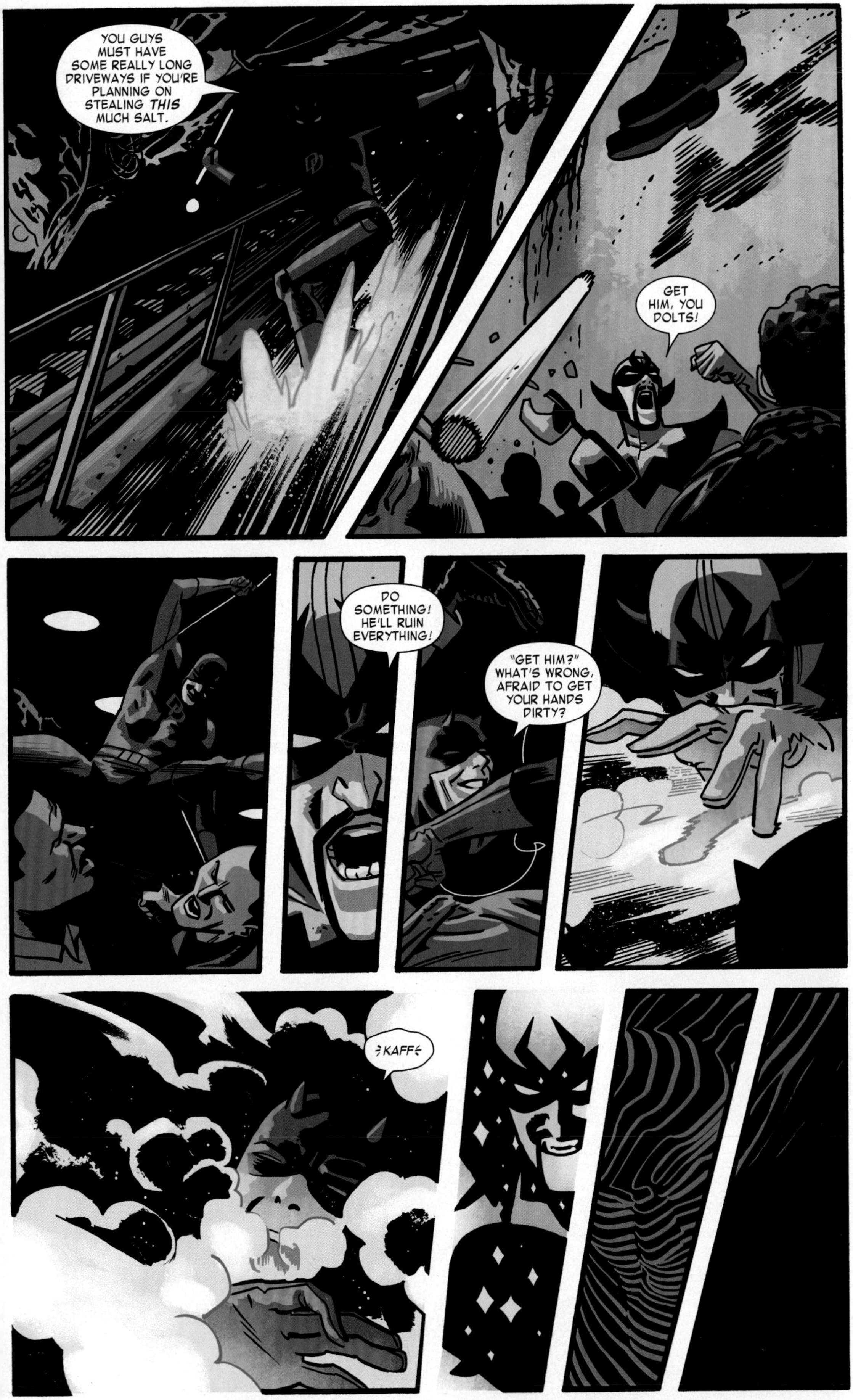
YOU GUYS MUST HAVE SOME REALLY LONG DRIVEWAYS IF YOU'RE PLANNING ON STEALING *THIS* MUCH SALT.
GET HIM, YOU DOLTS!
DO SOMETHING! HE'LL RUIN EVERYTHING!
"GET HIM?" WHAT'S WRONG, AFRAID TO GET YOUR HANDS DIRTY?
KAFF

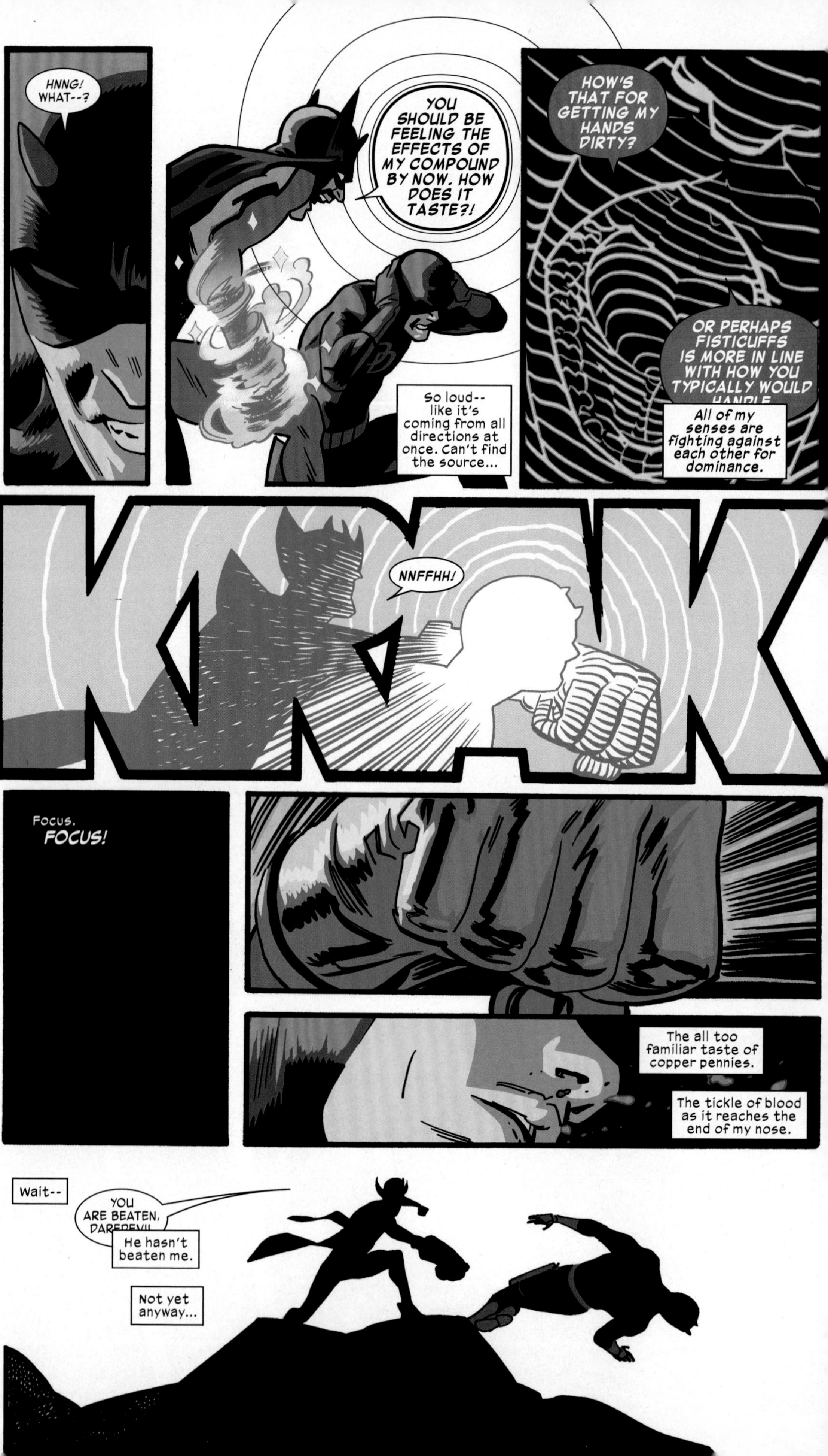

HNNG! WHAT--?
YOU SHOULD BE FEELING THE EFFECTS OF MY COMPOUND BY NOW. HOW DOES IT TASTE?!
So loud--like it's coming from all directions at once. Can't find the source...
HOW'S THAT FOR GETTING MY HANDS DIRTY?
OR PERHAPS FISTICUFFS IS MORE IN LINE WITH HOW YOU TYPICALLY WOULD
All of my senses are fighting against each other for dominance.
KRAK
NNFFHH!
Focus. FOCUS!
The all too familiar taste of copper pennies.
The tickle of blood as it reaches the end of my nose.
Wait--
YOU ARE BEATEN,
He hasn't beaten me.
Not yet anyway...

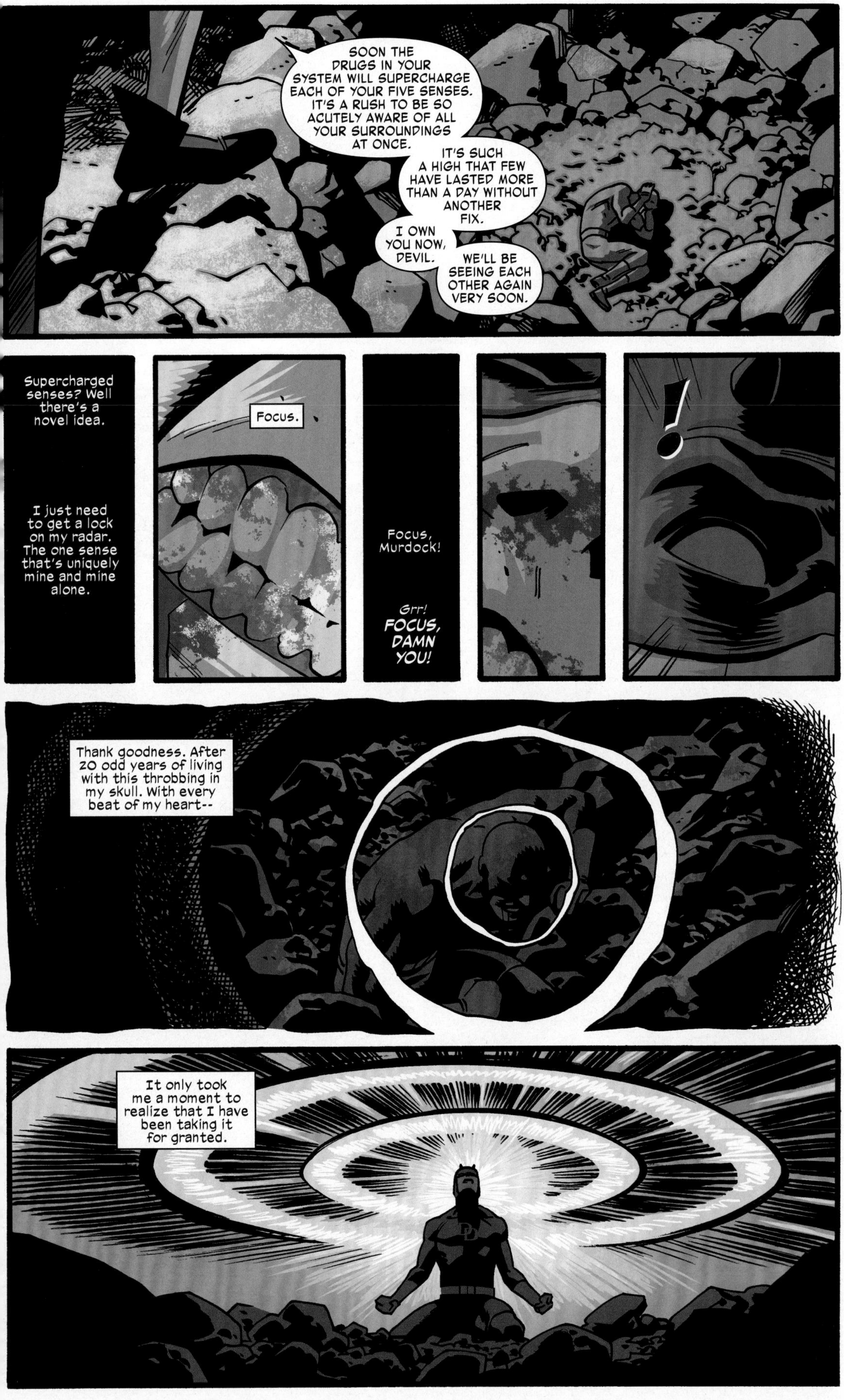
SOON THE DRUGS IN YOUR SYSTEM WILL SUPERCHARGE EACH OF YOUR FIVE SENSES. IT'S A RUSH TO BE SO ACUTELY AWARE OF ALL YOUR SURROUNDINGS AT ONCE.
IT'S SUCH A HIGH THAT FEW HAVE LASTED MORE THAN A DAY WITHOUT ANOTHER FIX.
I OWN YOU NOW, DEVIL.
WE'LL BE SEEING EACH OTHER AGAIN VERY SOON.
Supercharged senses? Well there's a novel idea.
I just need to get a lock on my radar. The one sense that's uniquely mine and mine alone.
Focus.
Focus, Murdock!
Grr! FOCUS, DAMN YOU!
!
Thank goodness. After 20 odd years of living with this throbbing in my skull. With every beat of my heart--
It only took me a moment to realize that I have been taking it for granted.

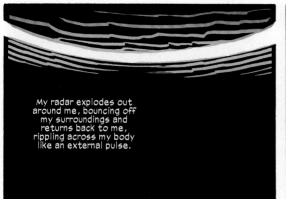

My radar explodes out around me, bouncing off my surroundings and returns back to me, rippling across my body like an external pulse.

Not so fast...

HKKKT!

YOU CAN'T ESCAPE JUSTICE, DIABLO!

LET ME GO, YOU BIG RED BUFFOON!

GYAAAAHHHH!

WEE-OOO WEE-OOO

All of my senses are completely raw.

I've got to get a handle on this--

Who says the police are never around when you need them?

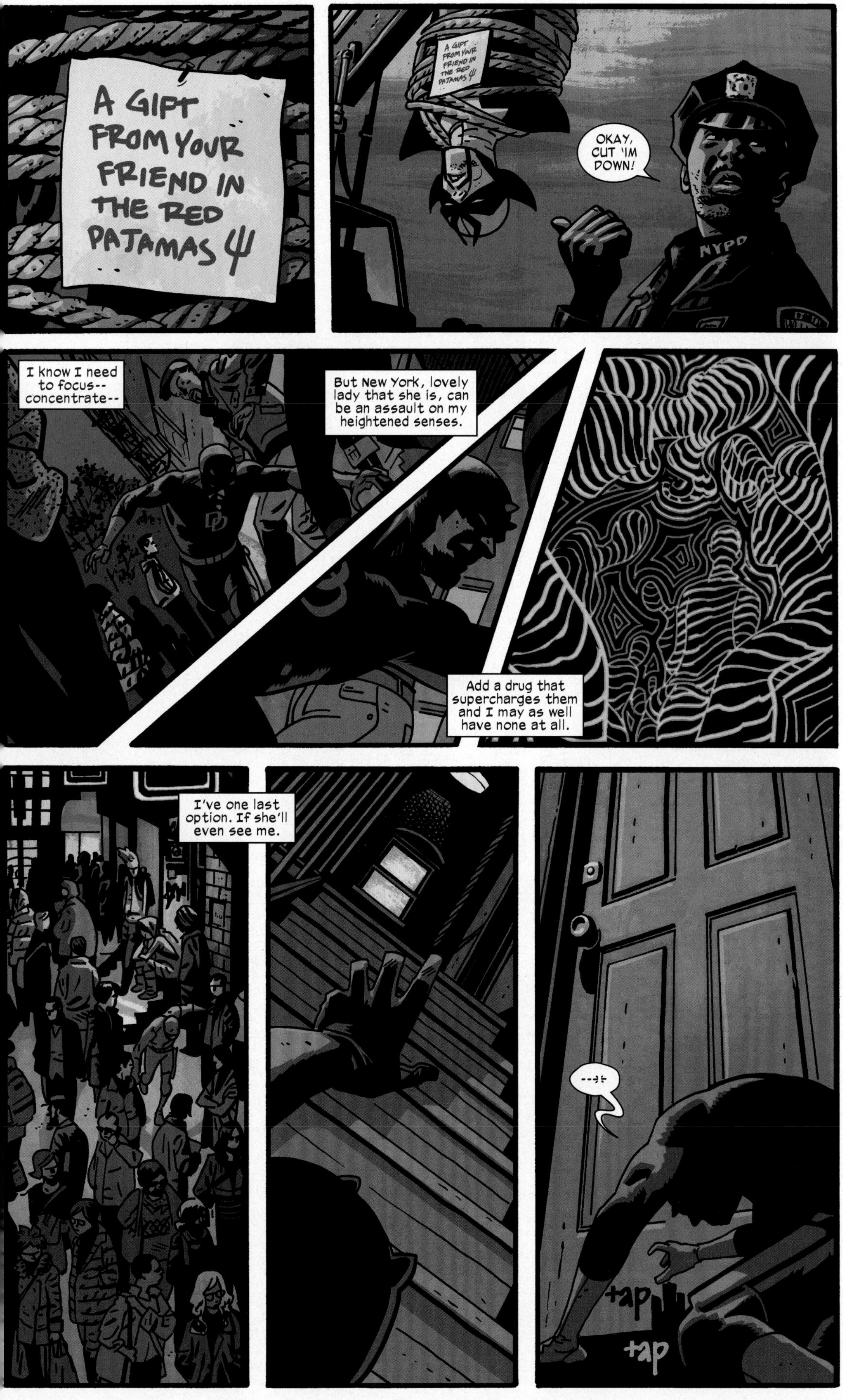
A GIFT FROM YOUR FRIEND IN THE RED PAJAMAS
A GIFT FROM YOUR FRIEND IN THE RED PAJAMAS
OKAY, CUT 'IM DOWN!
NYPD
I know I need to focus--concentrate--
But New York, lovely lady that she is, can be an assault on my heightened senses.
Add a drug that supercharges them and I may as well have none at all.
I've one last option. If she'll even see me.
tap
tap

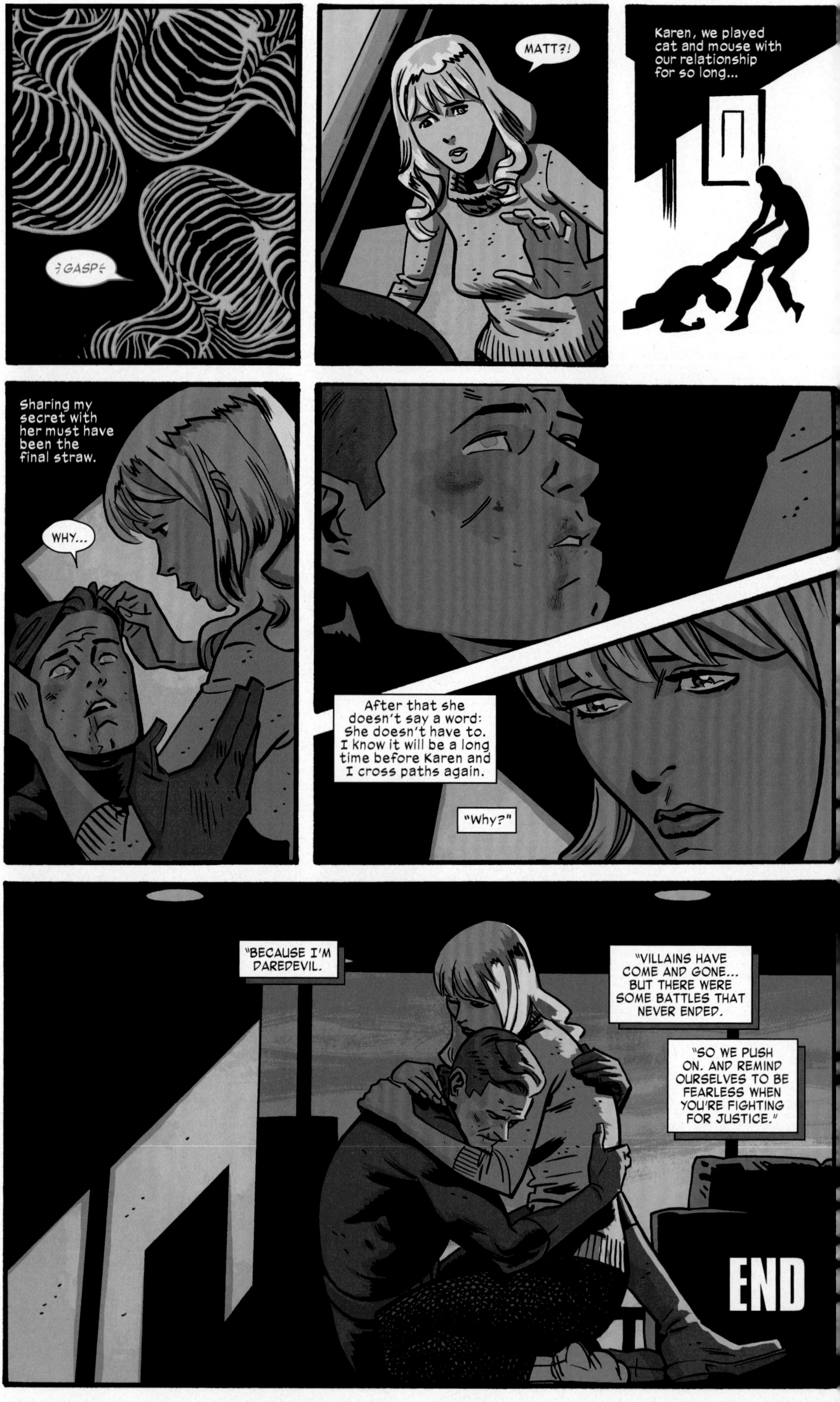

GASP
MATT?!
Karen, we played cat and mouse with our relationship for so long...
Sharing my secret with her must have been the final straw.
WHY...
After that she doesn't say a word: She doesn't have to. I know it will be a long time before Karen and I cross paths again.
"Why?"
"BECAUSE I'M DAREDEVIL.
"VILLAINS HAVE COME AND GONE... BUT THERE WERE SOME BATTLES THAT NEVER ENDED.
"SO WE PUSH ON. AND REMIND OURSELVES TO BE FEARLESS WHEN YOU'RE FIGHTING FOR JUSTICE."
END

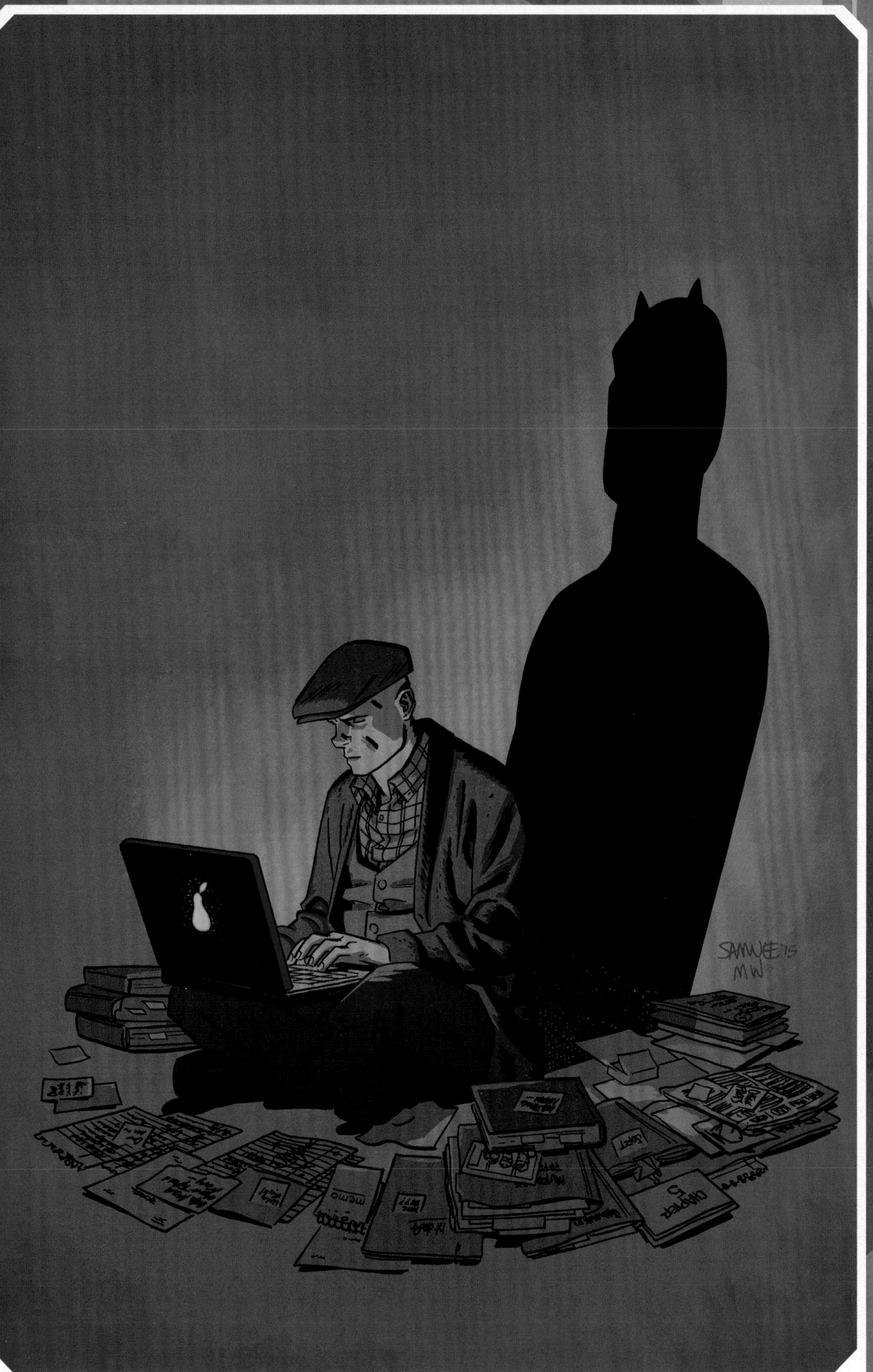
memo

DAREDEVIL #16

PREVIOUSLY:

After years of maintaining a secret identity, Matt Murdock has come clean to the world: He is Daredevil. His heightened senses, including 360-degree radar sense, are now a matter of public record.

In order to protect his best friend Foggy Nelson from Daredevil's enemies, Matt very publically faked Foggy's death. They then moved to San Francisco, where Matt opened a new law practice with his girlfriend, Kirsten McDuffie.

With his identity out in the open, Matt Murdock recently cast off his cowl, fully embracing his role as The Man Without Fear. While chasing a rumor of The Owl's escape, Matt wound up working with his foe's daughter, Jubula Pride, who has abilities like her father. A strong lead sent them to Alcatraz Island where they found The Owl inextricably connected to a surveillance super computer by his captor...The Shroud!

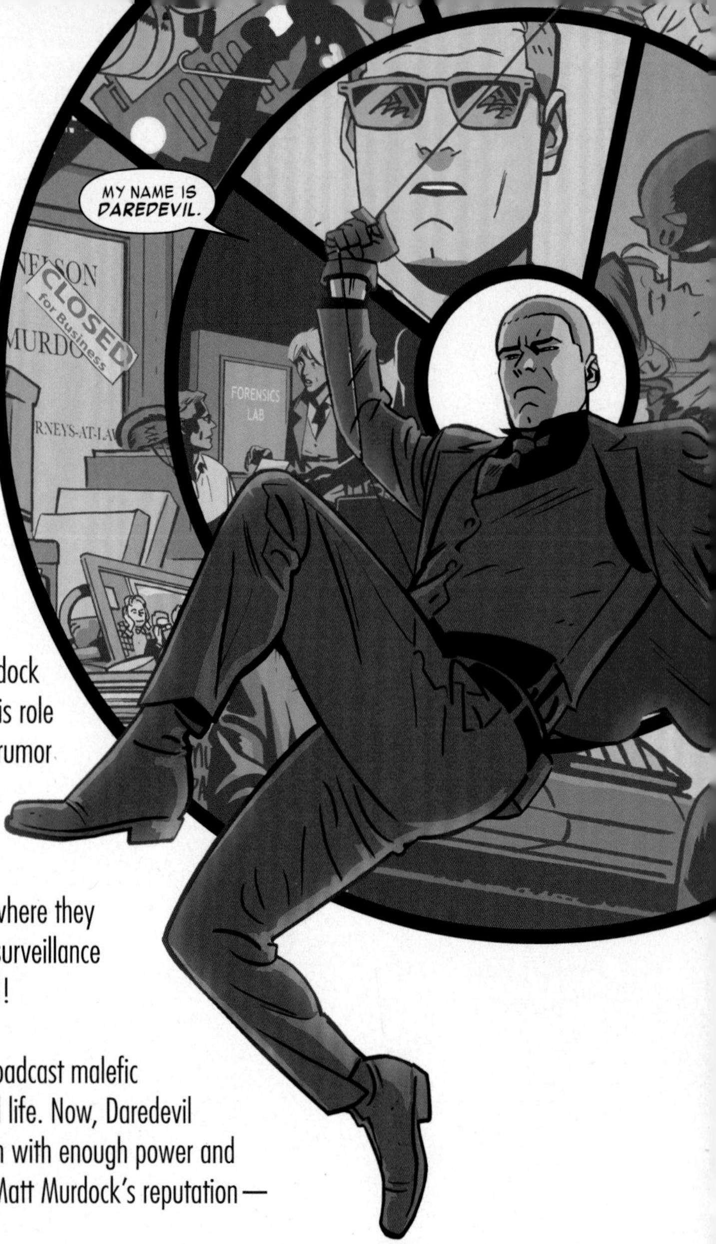
MY NAME IS DAREDEVIL.
CLOSED
for Business
FORENSICS LAB

The pair fled, but not before The Shroud broadcast malefic footage of Matt's personal and professional life. Now, Daredevil has no choice but to turn to the only person with enough power and influence to repair the shattered pieces of Matt Murdock's reputation—Wilson Fisk a.k.a. The Kingpin!

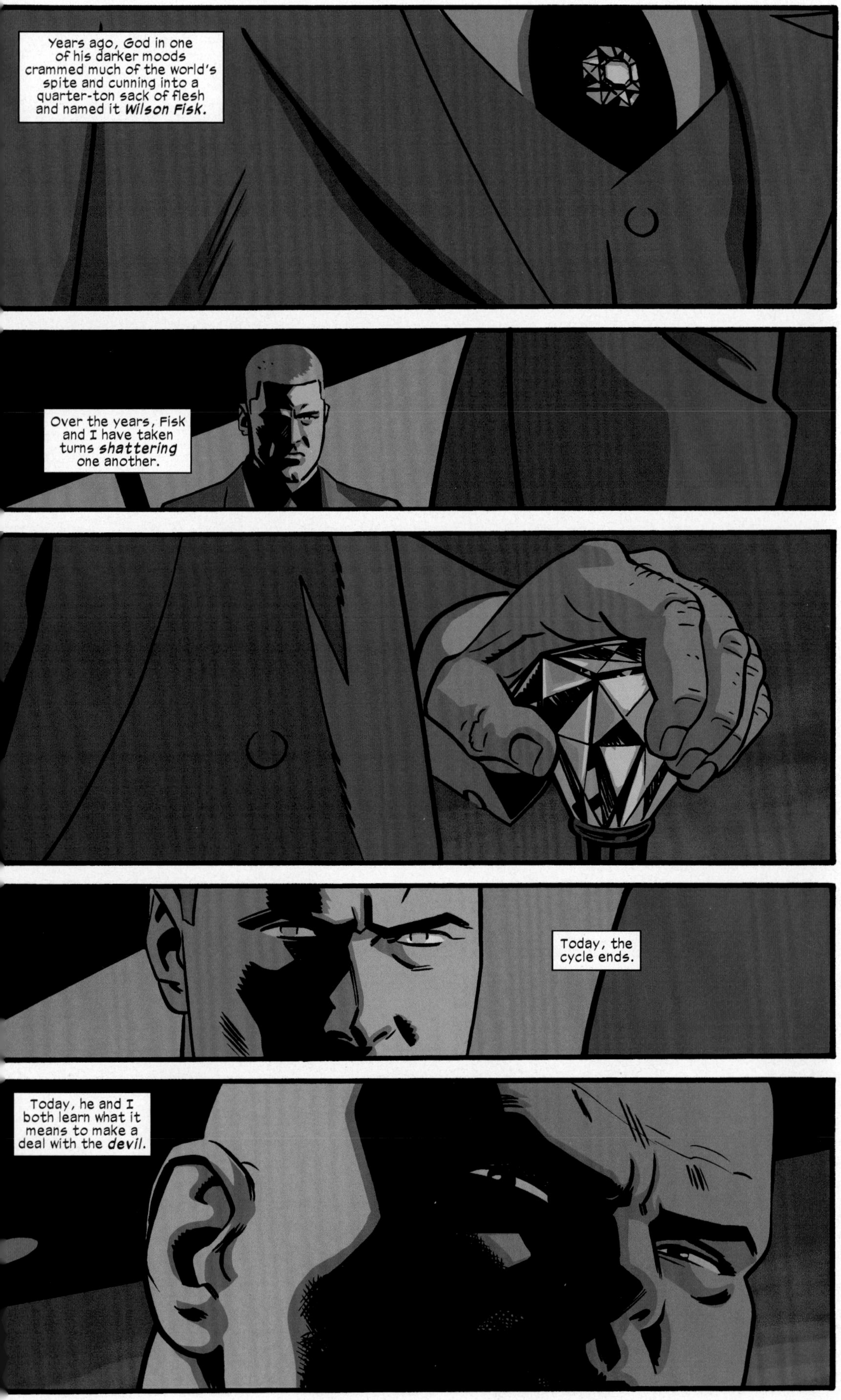
Years ago, God in one of his darker moods crammed much of the world's spite and cunning into a quarter-ton sack of flesh and named it *Wilson Fisk*.
Over the years, Fisk and I have taken turns *shattering* one another.
Today, the cycle ends.
Today, he and I both learn what it means to make a deal with the *devil*.

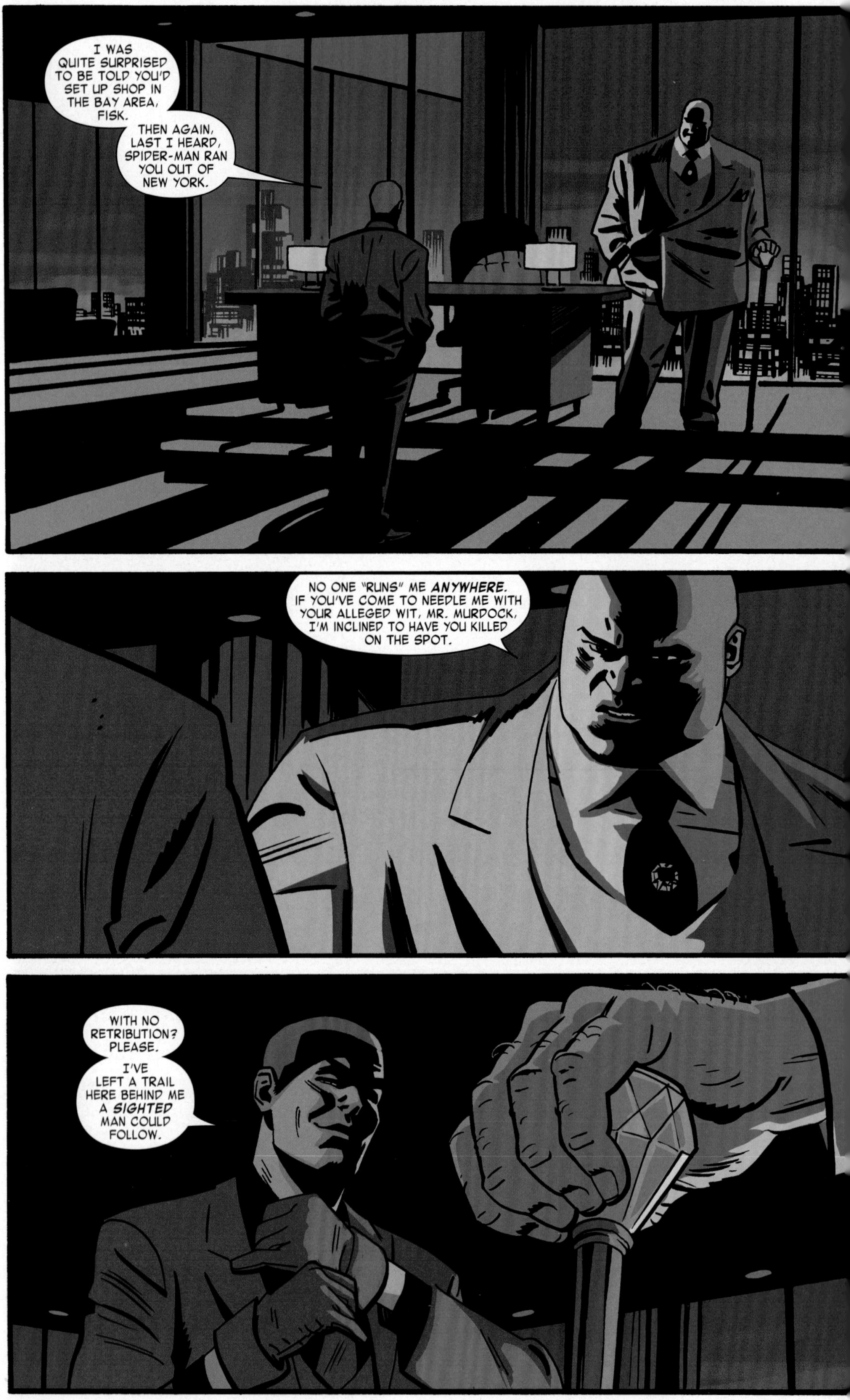
I WAS QUITE SURPRISED TO BE TOLD YOU'D SET UP SHOP IN THE BAY AREA, FISK.
THEN AGAIN, LAST I HEARD, SPIDER-MAN RAN YOU OUT OF NEW YORK.
NO ONE "RUNS" ME ***ANYWHERE.*** IF YOU'VE COME TO NEEDLE ME WITH YOUR ALLEGED WIT, MR. MURDOCK, I'M INCLINED TO HAVE YOU KILLED ON THE SPOT.
WITH NO RETRIBUTION? PLEASE.
I'VE LEFT A TRAIL HERE BEHIND ME A ***SIGHTED*** MAN COULD FOLLOW.

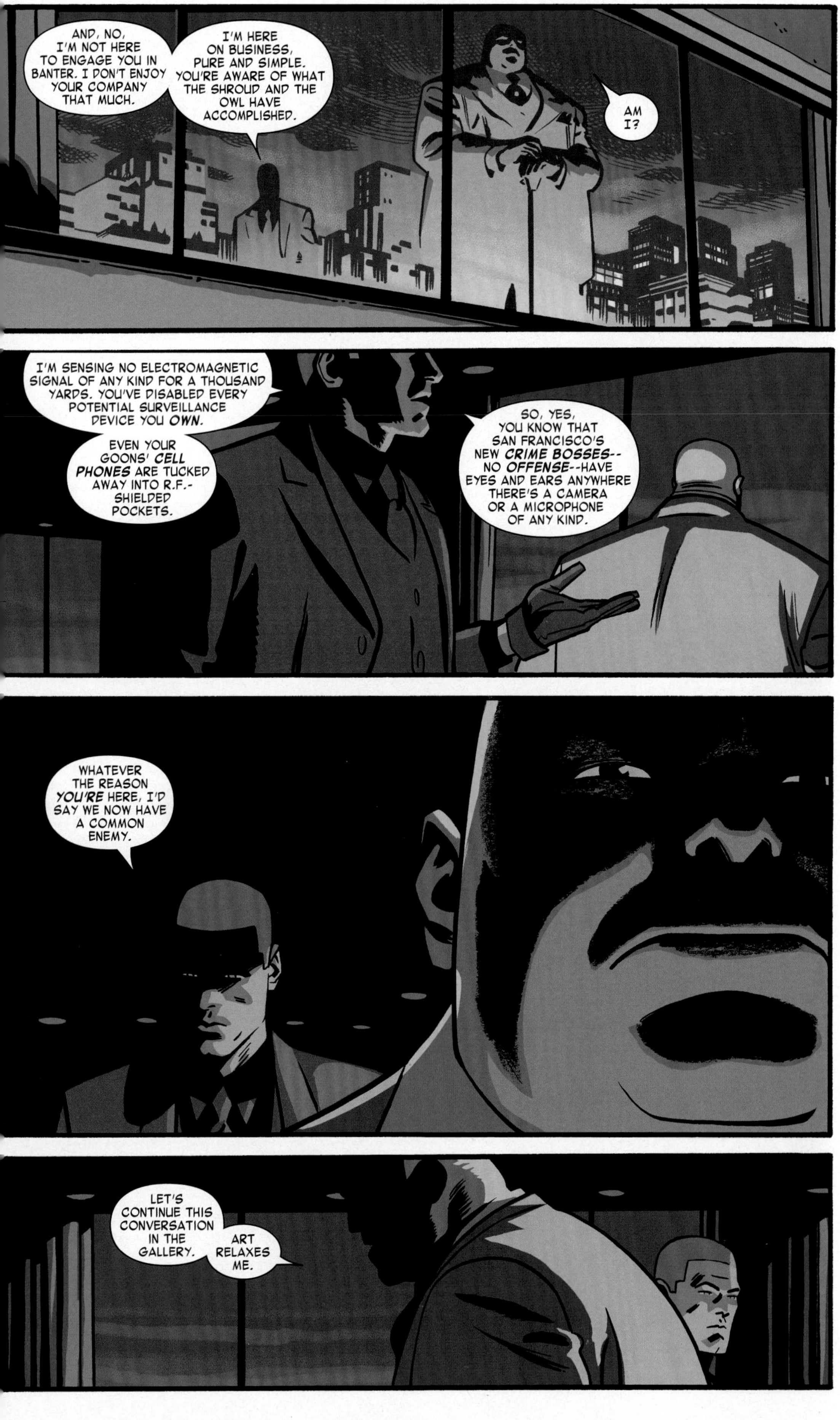
AND, NO, I'M NOT HERE TO ENGAGE YOU IN BANTER. I DON'T ENJOY YOUR COMPANY THAT MUCH.
I'M HERE ON BUSINESS, PURE AND SIMPLE. YOU'RE AWARE OF WHAT THE SHROUD AND THE OWL HAVE ACCOMPLISHED.
AM I?
I'M SENSING NO ELECTROMAGNETIC SIGNAL OF ANY KIND FOR A THOUSAND YARDS. YOU'VE DISABLED EVERY POTENTIAL SURVEILLANCE DEVICE YOU OWN.
EVEN YOUR GOONS' CELL PHONES ARE TUCKED AWAY INTO R.F.-SHIELDED POCKETS.
SO, YES, YOU KNOW THAT SAN FRANCISCO'S NEW CRIME BOSSES--NO OFFENSE--HAVE EYES AND EARS ANYWHERE THERE'S A CAMERA OR A MICROPHONE OF ANY KIND.
WHATEVER THE REASON YOU'RE HERE, I'D SAY WE NOW HAVE A COMMON ENEMY.
LET'S CONTINUE THIS CONVERSATION IN THE GALLERY.
ART RELAXES ME.

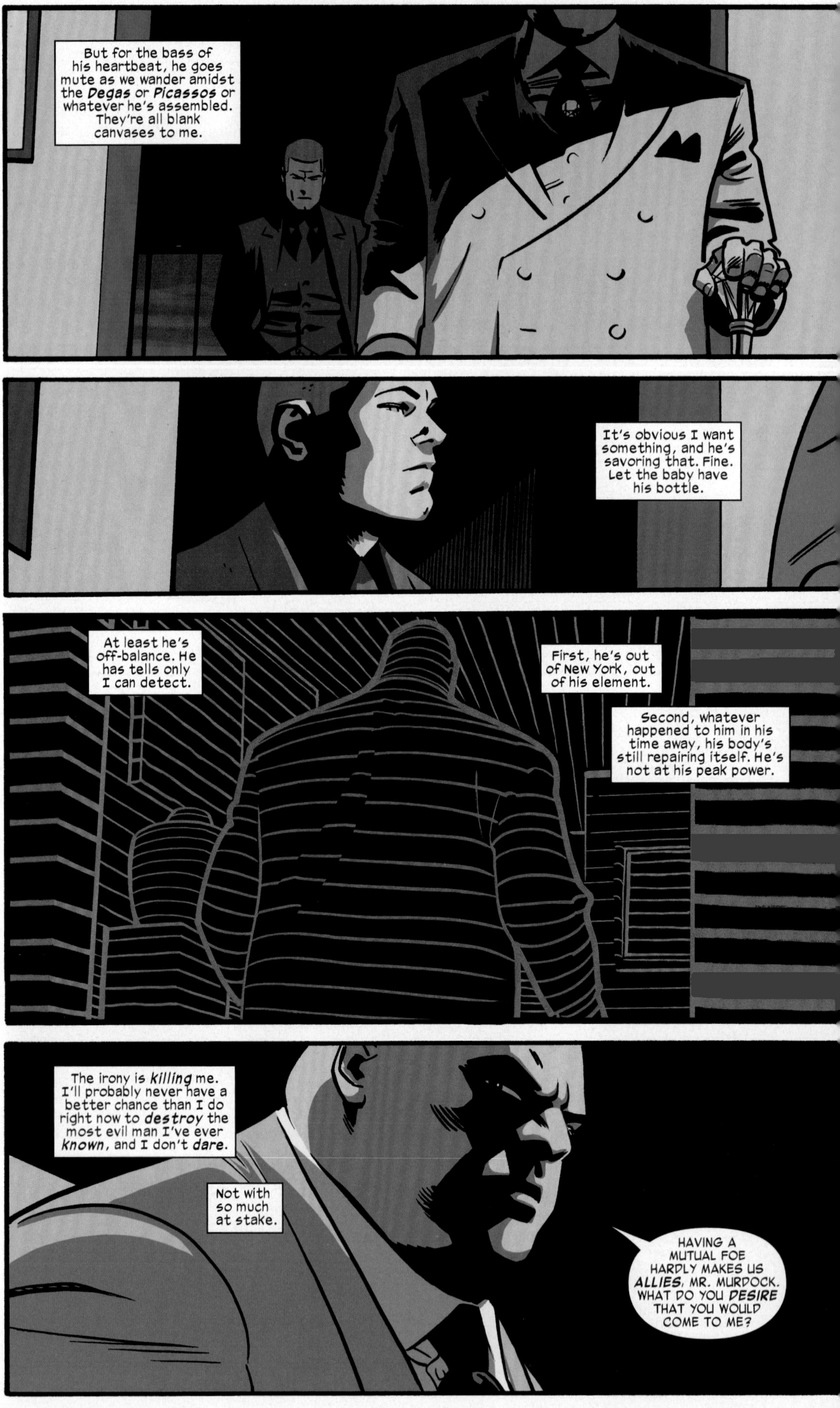

But for the bass of his heartbeat, he goes mute as we wander amidst the *Degas* or *Picassos* or whatever he's assembled. They're all blank canvases to me.
It's obvious I want something, and he's savoring that. Fine. Let the baby have his bottle.
At least he's off-balance. He has tells only I can detect.
First, he's out of New York, out of his element.
Second, whatever happened to him in his time away, his body's still repairing itself. He's not at his peak power.
The irony is *killing* me. I'll probably never have a better chance than I do right now to *destroy* the most evil man I've ever *known*, and I don't *dare*.
Not with so much at stake.
HAVING A MUTUAL FOE HARDLY MAKES US *ALLIES*, MR. MURDOCK. WHAT DO YOU *DESIRE* THAT YOU WOULD COME TO ME?

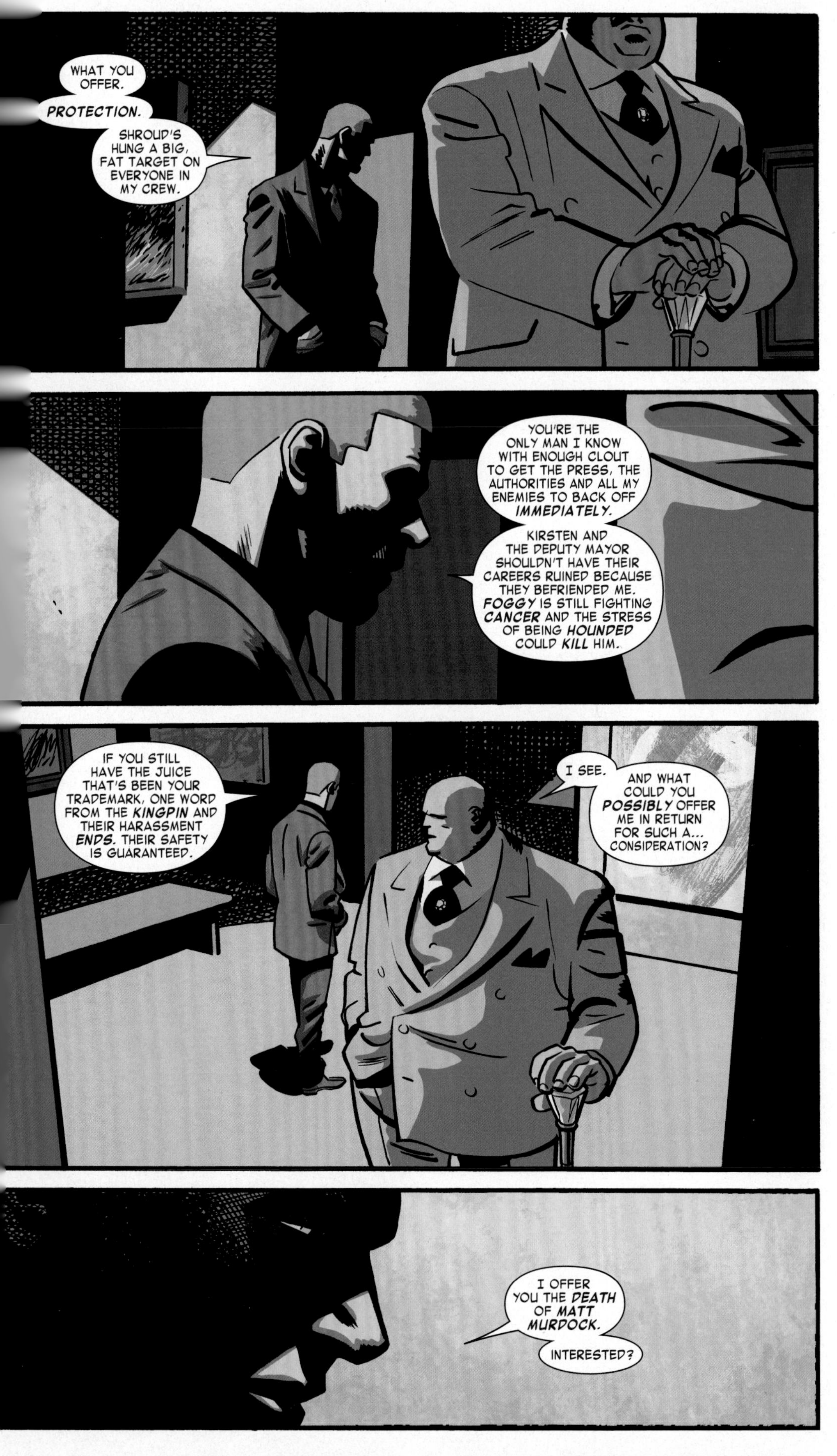
WHAT YOU OFFER.
PROTECTION.
SHROUD'S HUNG A BIG, FAT TARGET ON EVERYONE IN MY CREW.
YOU'RE THE ONLY MAN I KNOW WITH ENOUGH CLOUT TO GET THE PRESS, THE AUTHORITIES AND ALL MY ENEMIES TO BACK OFF IMMEDIATELY.
KIRSTEN AND THE DEPUTY MAYOR SHOULDN'T HAVE THEIR CAREERS RUINED BECAUSE THEY BEFRIENDED ME. FOGGY IS STILL FIGHTING CANCER AND THE STRESS OF BEING HOUNDED COULD KILL HIM.
IF YOU STILL HAVE THE JUICE THAT'S BEEN YOUR TRADEMARK, ONE WORD FROM THE KINGPIN AND THEIR HARASSMENT ENDS. THEIR SAFETY IS GUARANTEED.
I SEE.
AND WHAT COULD YOU POSSIBLY OFFER ME IN RETURN FOR SUCH A... CONSIDERATION?
I OFFER YOU THE DEATH OF MATT MURDOCK.
INTERESTED?

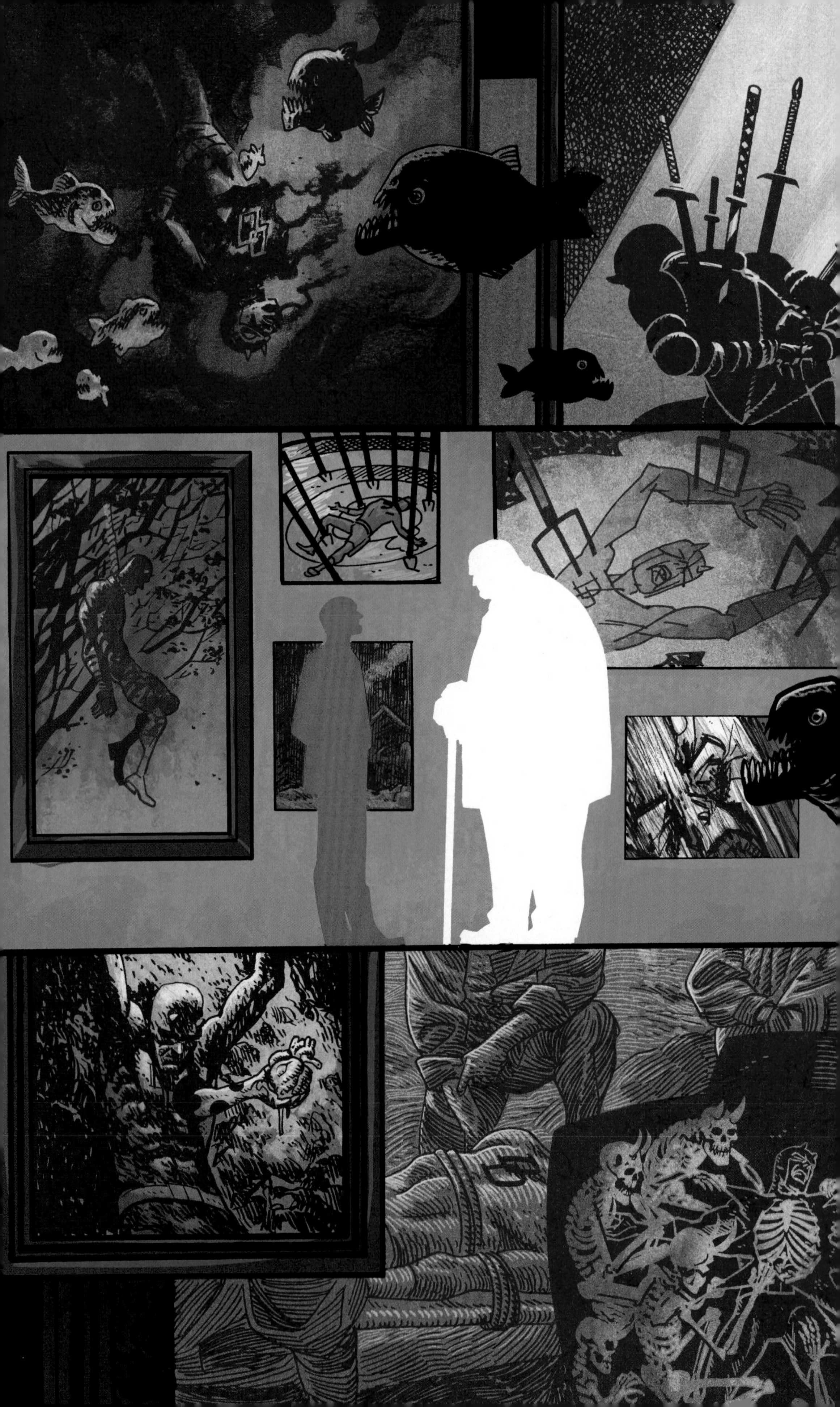

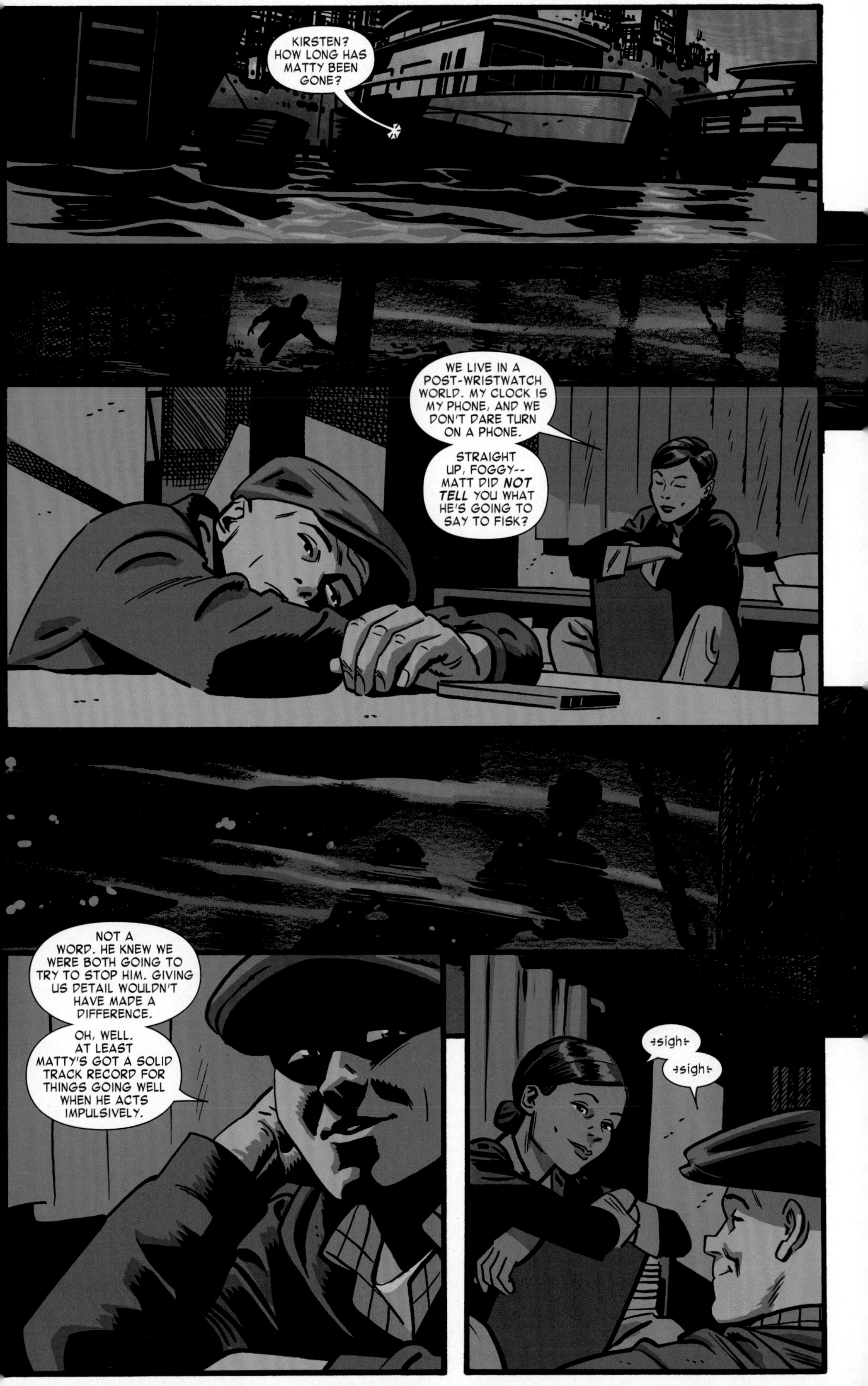
KIRSTEN? HOW LONG HAS MATTY BEEN GONE?
WE LIVE IN A POST-WRISTWATCH WORLD. MY CLOCK IS MY PHONE, AND WE DON'T DARE TURN ON A PHONE.
STRAIGHT UP, FOGGY-- MATT DID **NOT TELL** YOU WHAT HE'S GOING TO SAY TO FISK?
NOT A WORD. HE KNEW WE WERE BOTH GOING TO TRY TO STOP HIM. GIVING US DETAIL WOULDN'T HAVE MADE A DIFFERENCE.
OH, WELL. AT LEAST MATTY'S GOT A SOLID TRACK RECORD FOR THINGS GOING WELL WHEN HE ACTS IMPULSIVELY.
sigh
sigh

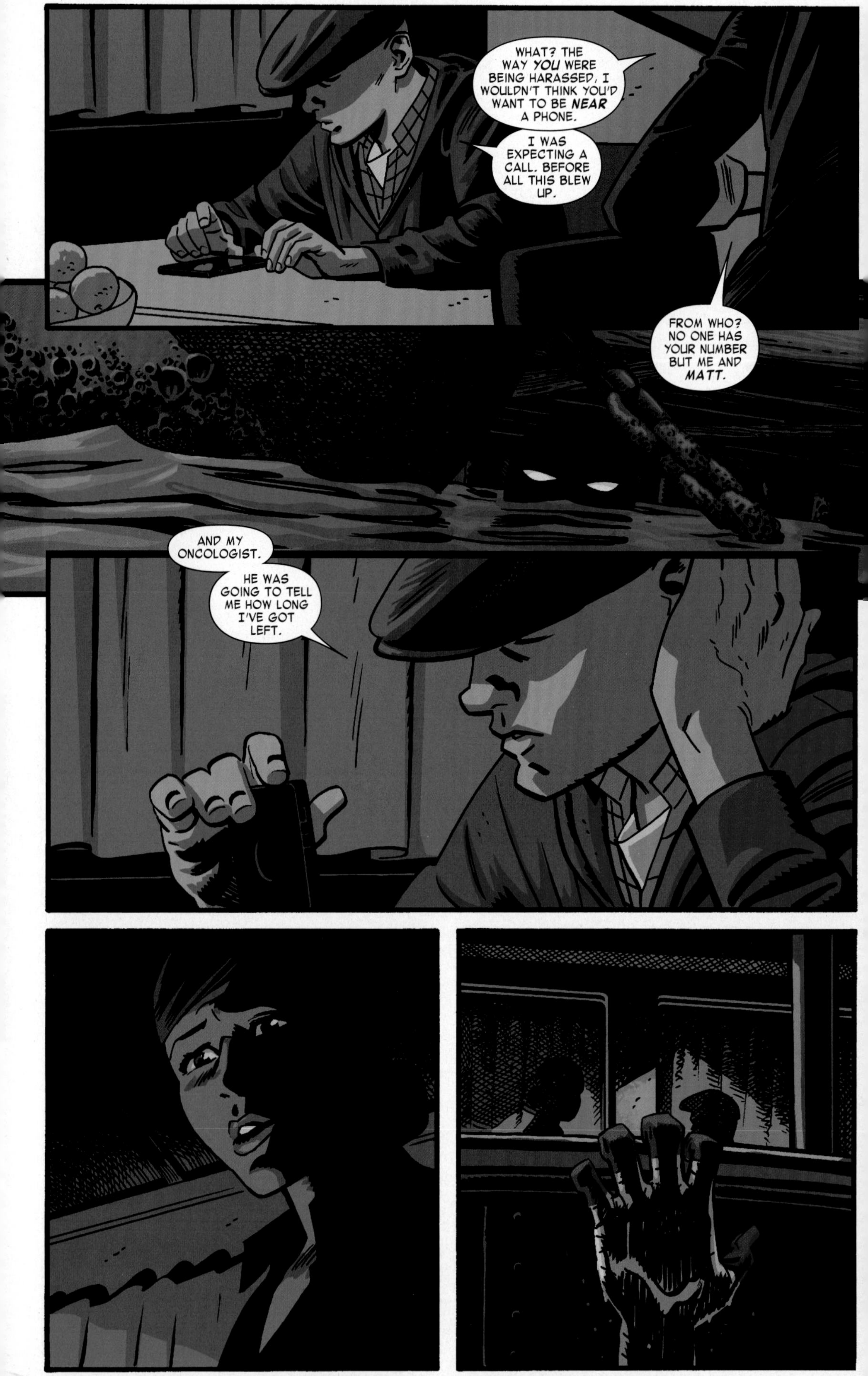
WHAT? THE WAY YOU WERE BEING HARASSED, I WOULDN'T THINK YOU'D WANT TO BE NEAR A PHONE.
I WAS EXPECTING A CALL. BEFORE ALL THIS BLEW UP.
FROM WHO? NO ONE HAS YOUR NUMBER BUT ME AND MATT.
AND MY ONCOLOGIST.
HE WAS GOING TO TELL ME HOW LONG I'VE GOT LEFT.

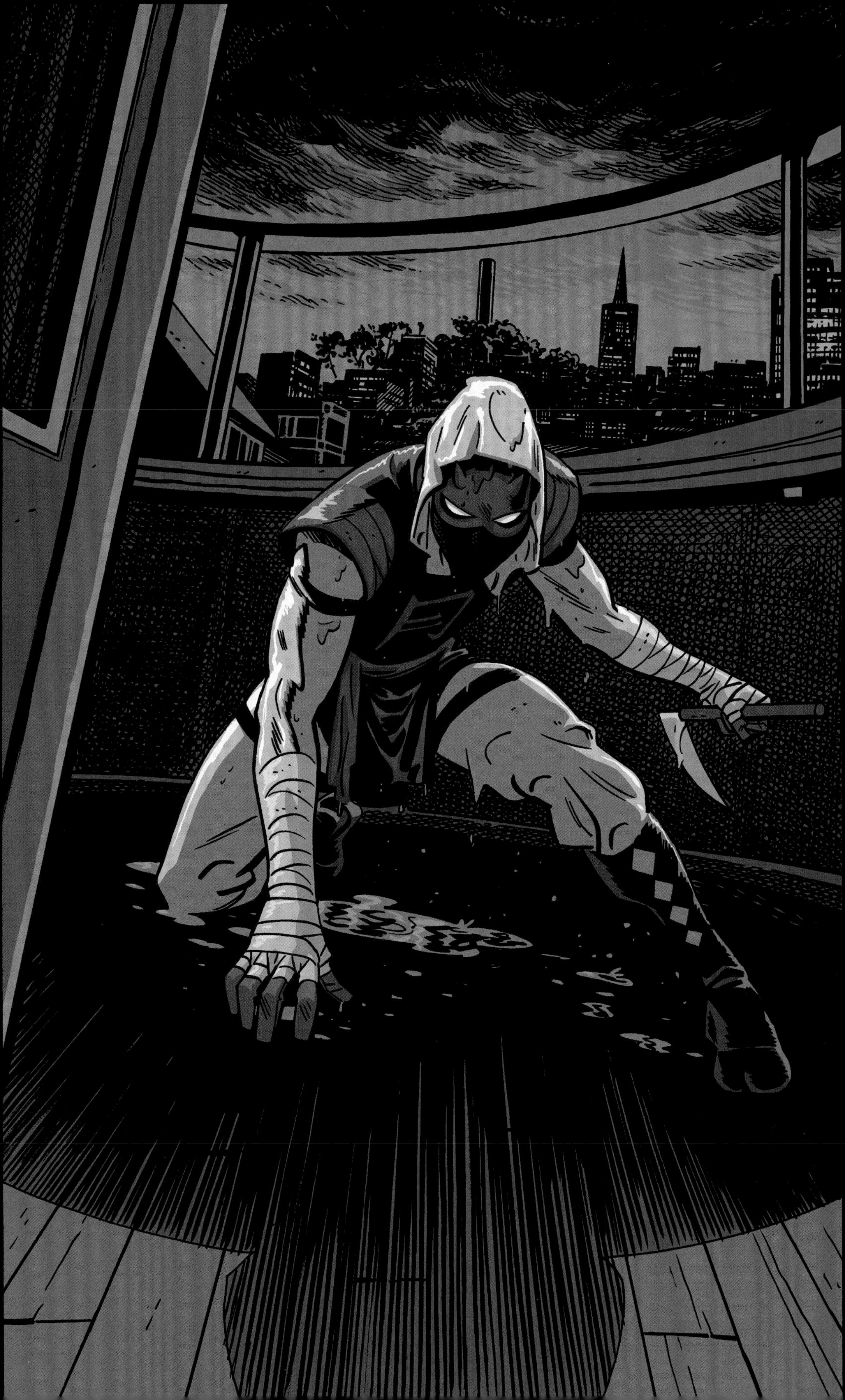

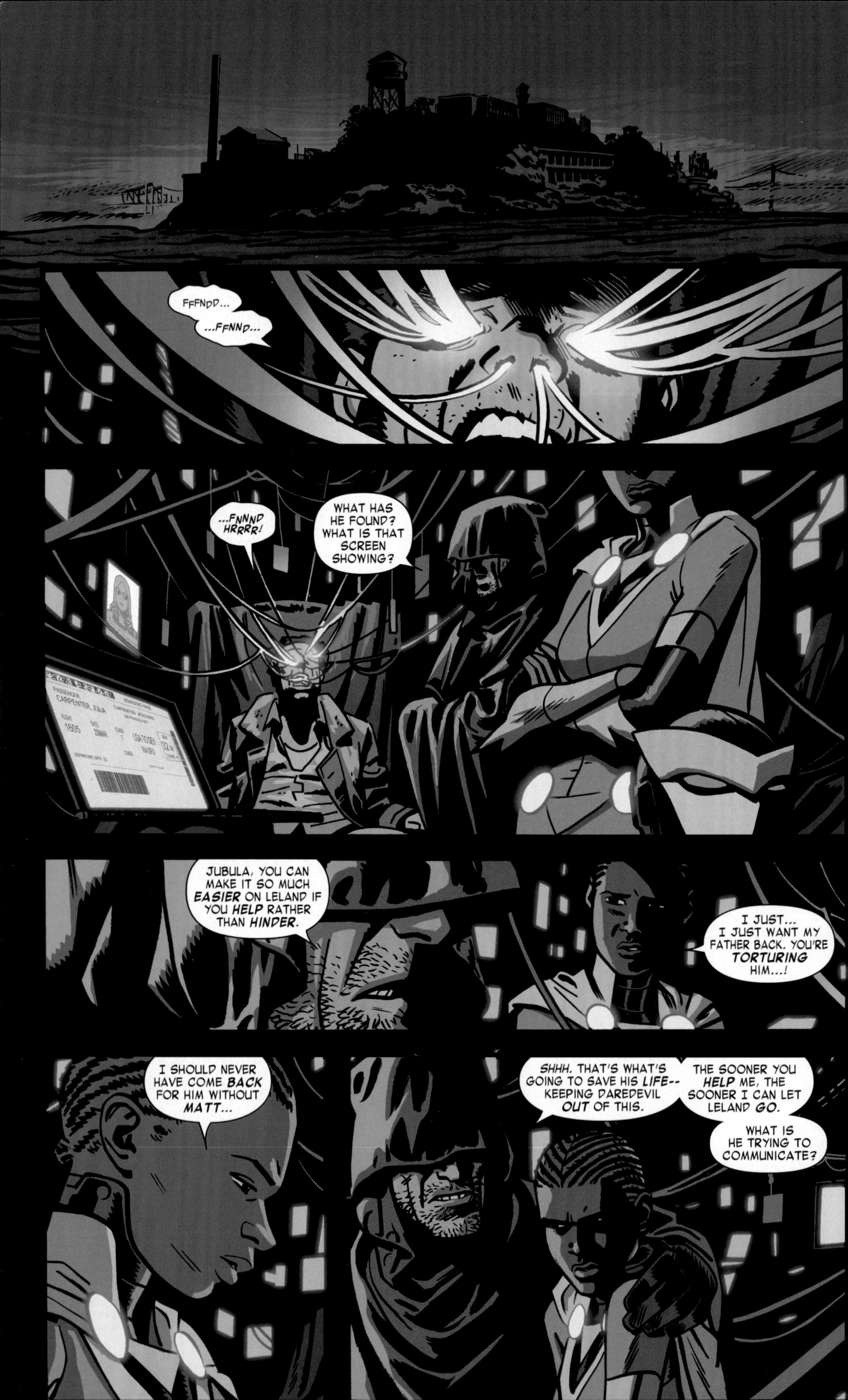
FFFNDD...
...FFNND...
...FNNND HRRRR!
WHAT HAS HE FOUND? WHAT IS THAT SCREEN SHOWING?
CARPENTER, JULIA
1605
JUBULA, YOU CAN MAKE IT SO MUCH EASIER ON LELAND IF YOU HELP RATHER THAN HINDER.
I JUST... I JUST WANT MY FATHER BACK. YOU'RE TORTURING HIM...!
I SHOULD NEVER HAVE COME BACK FOR HIM WITHOUT MATT...
SHHH. THAT'S WHAT'S GOING TO SAVE HIS LIFE-- KEEPING DAREDEVIL OUT OF THIS.
THE SOONER YOU HELP ME, THE SOONER I CAN LET LELAND GO.
WHAT IS HE TRYING TO COMMUNICATE?

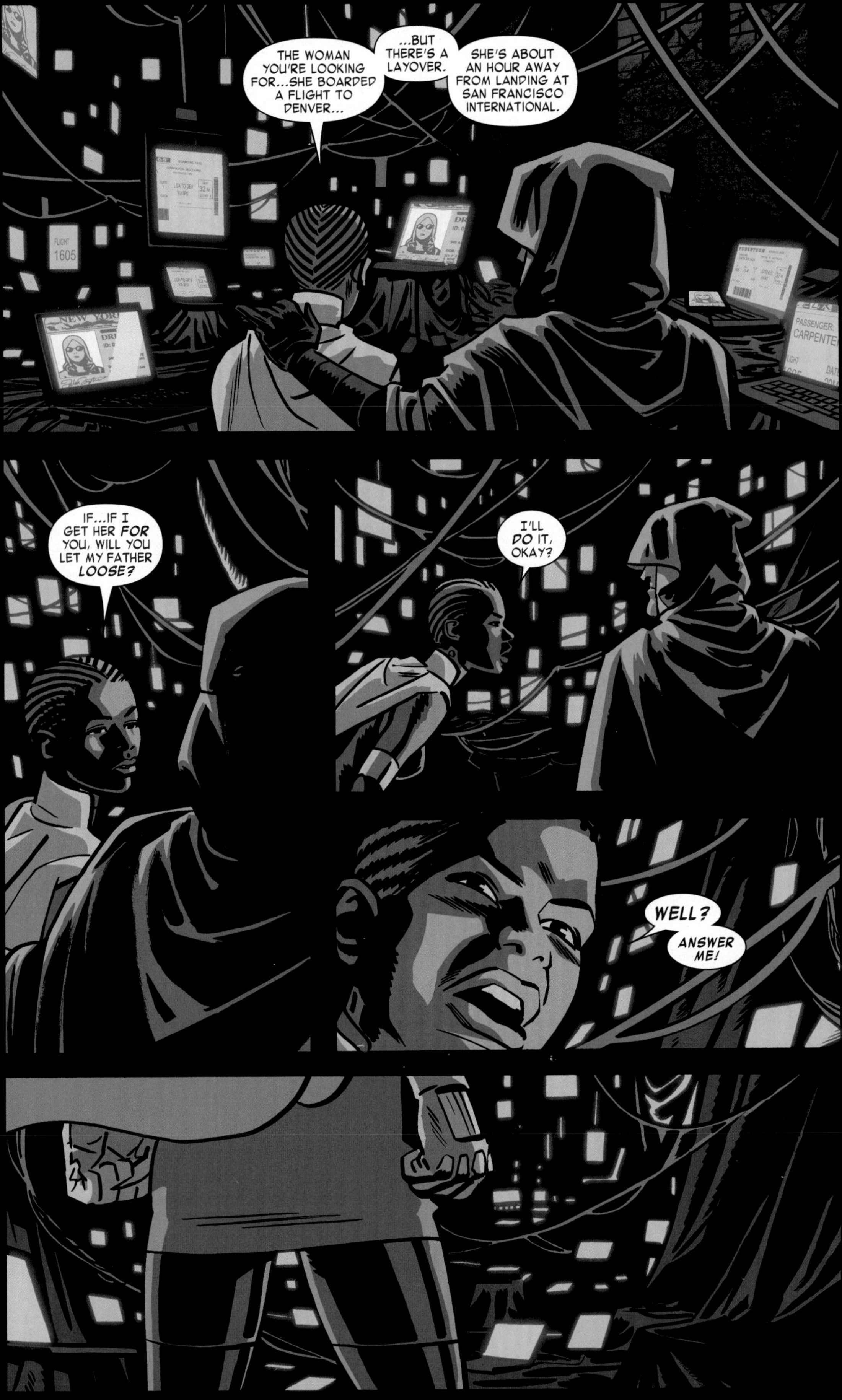
THE WOMAN YOU'RE LOOKING FOR...SHE BOARDED A FLIGHT TO DENVER...
...BUT THERE'S A LAYOVER.
SHE'S ABOUT AN HOUR AWAY FROM LANDING AT SAN FRANCISCO INTERNATIONAL.
FLIGHT 1605
NEW YORK
PASSENGER: CARPENTER
IF...IF I GET HER FOR YOU, WILL YOU LET MY FATHER LOOSE?
I'LL DO IT, OKAY?
WELL?
ANSWER ME!

 AREN'T YOU A DEVOTED *CATHOLIC,* MR. MURDOCK? DOESN'T THE CHURCH CONSIDER SUICIDE A *MORTAL SIN?*

YOU *HAVE* CHANGED. THE NOTION OF DAREDEVIL'S *DEATH* AT HIS *OWN* HANDS--

YOU MISUNDERSTAND. DAREDEVIL *LIVES.*

IT'S *MATT MURDOCK* WHO GOES AWAY.

"ONCE UPON A TIME, DAREDEVIL'S IDENTITY WAS A *SECRET.*"

"AND YOU *DIDN'T* LIKE THAT. AT ALL.

"SO YOU HAD YOUR MEN *DIG* AND *TORTURE* AND *STRONG-ARM* THEIR WAY THROUGH MY LIFE UNTIL YOU GOT MY NAME.

"YOU MADE ME VULNERABLE, THEN YOU EXPLOITED THAT SECRET TO ANNIHILATE ME...MANIPULATE ME...HURT *OTHERS.*

"I CAN ONLY IMAGINE THE MONEY AND THE TIME YOU INVESTED IN FINDING THAT ONE PIECE OF LEVERAGE OVER ME. THE ONE THAT ONLY YOU HAD."

BUT I *CAN* GUESS HOW *LIVID* IT MADE YOU WHEN I *TORE* IT FROM YOU BY UNMASKING BEFORE THE *WHOLE* WORLD.

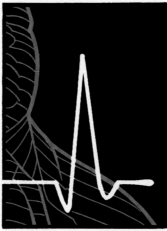

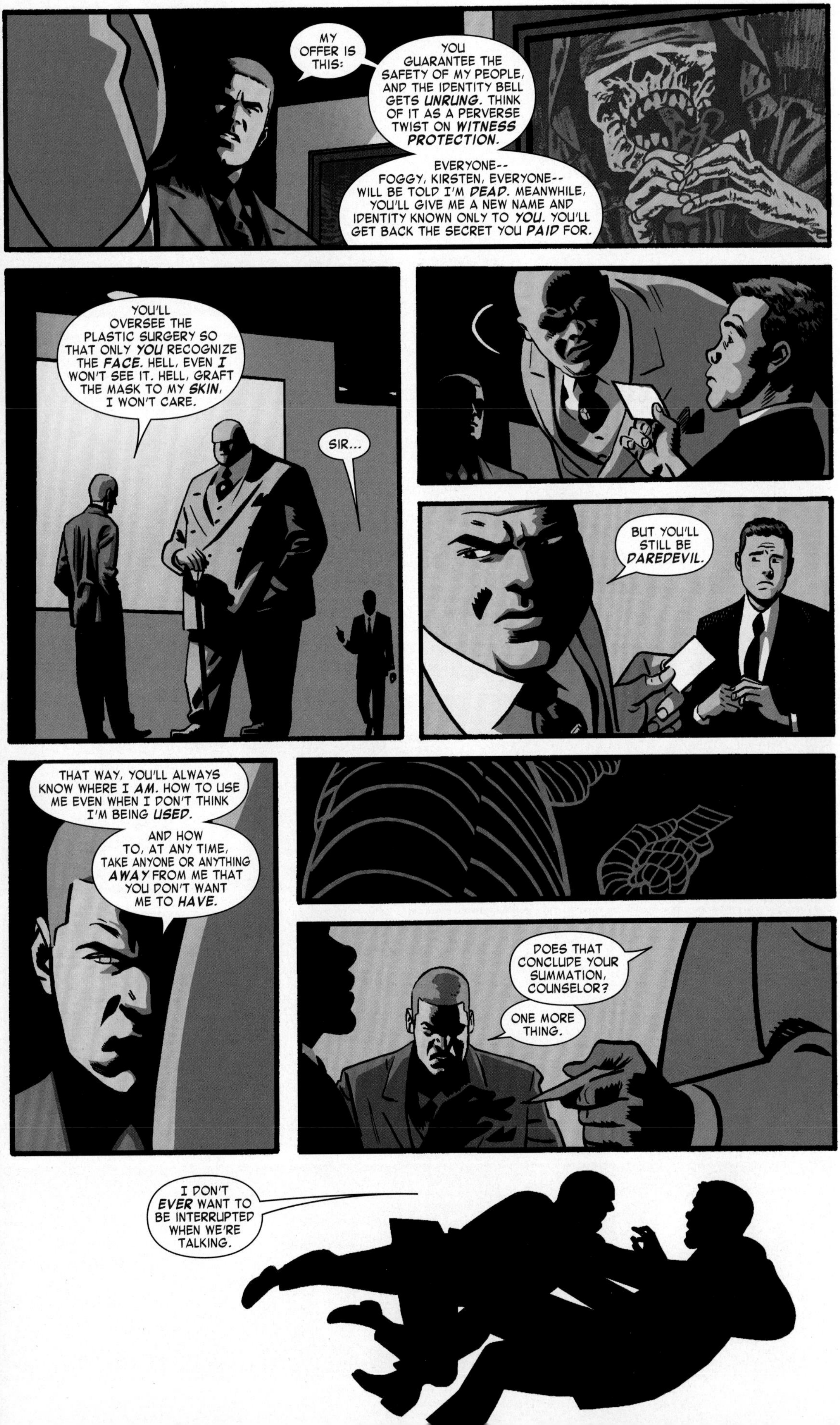
MY OFFER IS THIS:
YOU GUARANTEE THE SAFETY OF MY PEOPLE, AND THE IDENTITY BELL GETS UNRUNG. THINK OF IT AS A PERVERSE TWIST ON WITNESS PROTECTION.
EVERYONE-- FOGGY, KIRSTEN, EVERYONE-- WILL BE TOLD I'M DEAD. MEANWHILE, YOU'LL GIVE ME A NEW NAME AND IDENTITY KNOWN ONLY TO YOU. YOU'LL GET BACK THE SECRET YOU PAID FOR.
YOU'LL OVERSEE THE PLASTIC SURGERY SO THAT ONLY YOU RECOGNIZE THE FACE. HELL, EVEN I WON'T SEE IT. HELL, GRAFT THE MASK TO MY SKIN, I WON'T CARE.
SIR...
BUT YOU'LL STILL BE DAREDEVIL.
THAT WAY, YOU'LL ALWAYS KNOW WHERE I AM. HOW TO USE ME EVEN WHEN I DON'T THINK I'M BEING USED.
AND HOW TO, AT ANY TIME, TAKE ANYONE OR ANYTHING AWAY FROM ME THAT YOU DON'T WANT ME TO HAVE.
DOES THAT CONCLUDE YOUR SUMMATION, COUNSELOR?
ONE MORE THING.
I DON'T EVER WANT TO BE INTERRUPTED WHEN WE'RE TALKING.

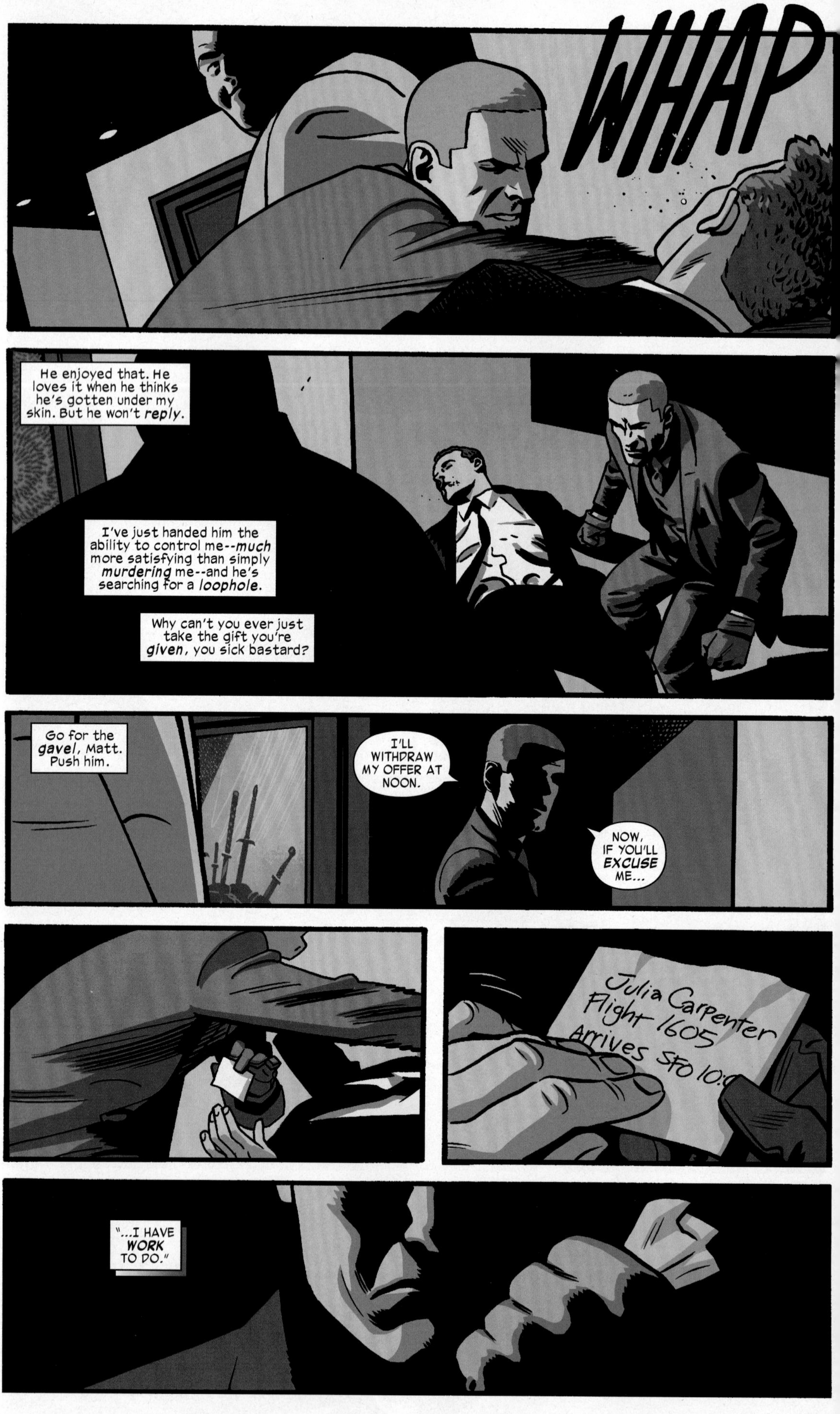
WHAP
He enjoyed that. He loves it when he thinks he's gotten under my skin. But he won't *reply*.
I've just handed him the ability to control me--*much* more satisfying than simply *murdering* me--and he's searching for a *loophole*.
Why can't you ever just take the gift you're *given*, you sick bastard?
Go for the *gavel*, Matt. Push him.
I'LL WITHDRAW MY OFFER AT NOON.
NOW, IF YOU'LL **EXCUSE** ME...
Julia Carpenter
Flight 1605
Arrives SFO 10:
"...I HAVE **WORK** TO DO."

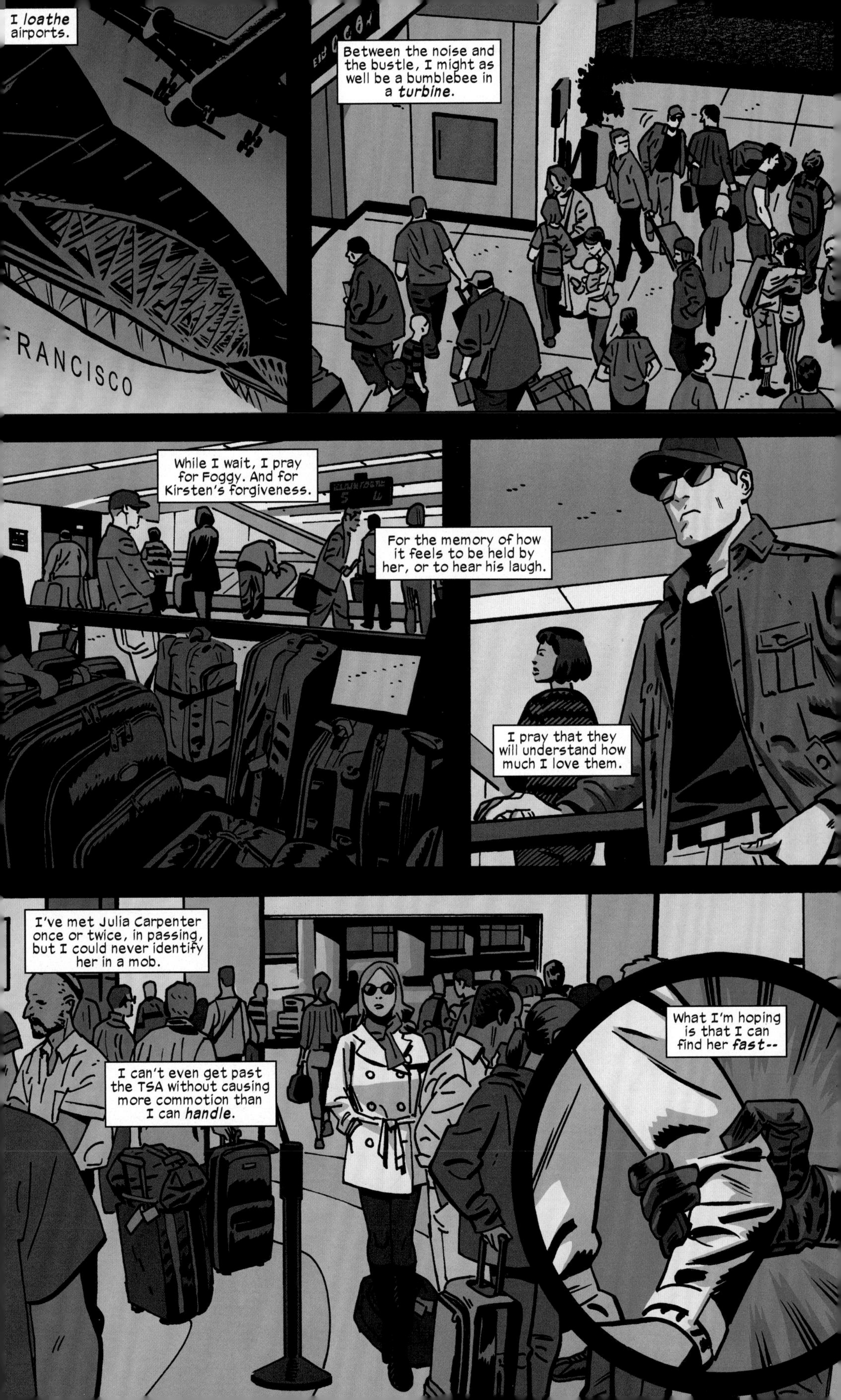

I *loathe* airports.
FRANCISCO
Between the noise and the bustle, I might as well be a bumblebee in a *turbine*.
While I wait, I pray for Foggy. And for Kirsten's forgiveness.
For the memory of how it feels to be held by her, or to hear his laugh.
I pray that they will understand how much I love them.
I've met Julia Carpenter once or twice, in passing, but I could never identify her in a mob.
I can't even get past the TSA without causing more commotion than I can *handle*.
What I'm hoping is that I can find her *fast*--

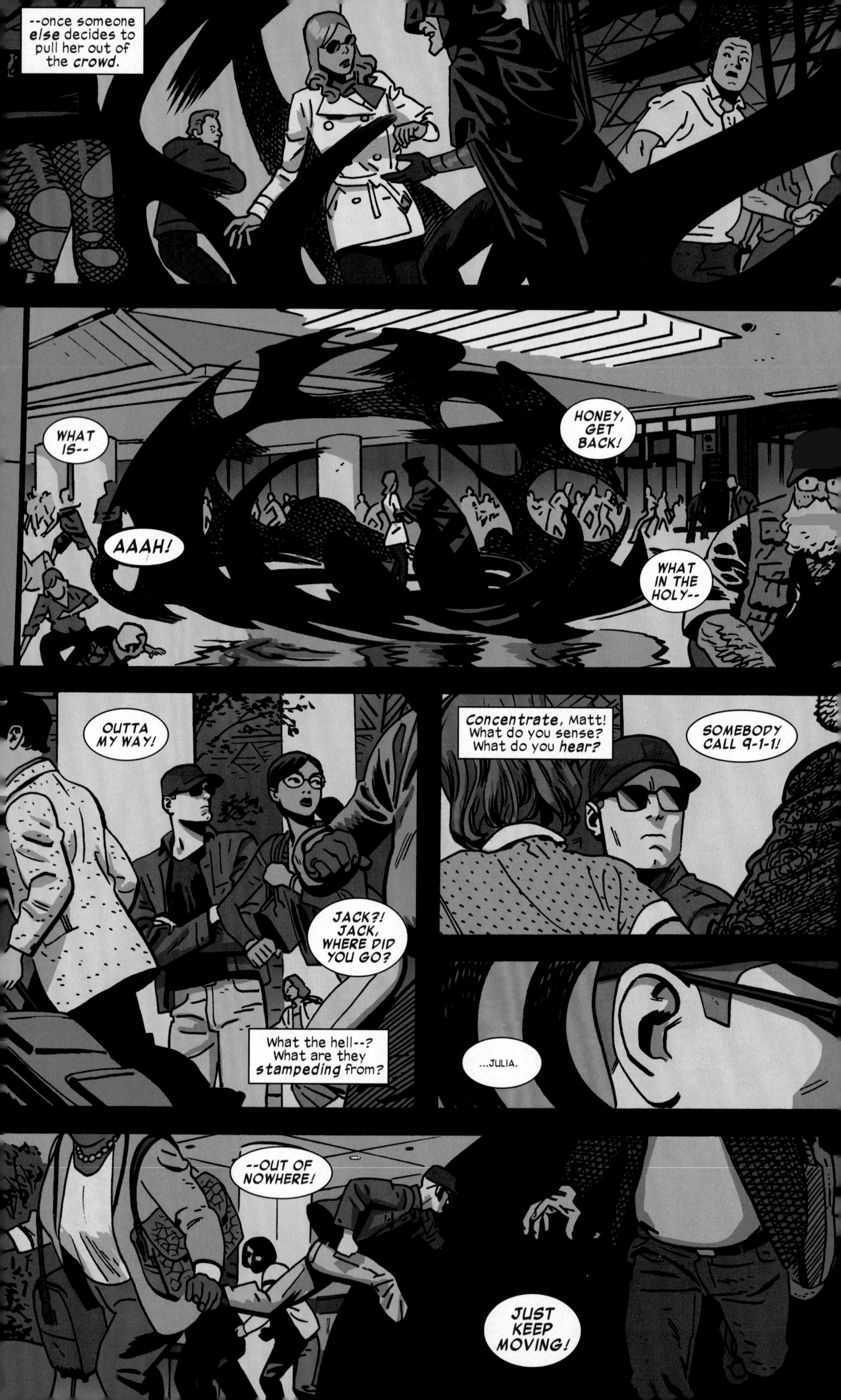
--once someone else decides to pull her out of the crowd.
WHAT IS--
HONEY, GET BACK!
AAAH!
WHAT IN THE HOLY--
OUTTA MY WAY!
JACK?! JACK, WHERE DID YOU GO?
What the hell--? What are they stampeding from?
Concentrate, Matt! What do you sense? What do you hear?
SOMEBODY CALL 9-1-1!
...JULIA.
--OUT OF NOWHERE!
JUST KEEP MOVING!

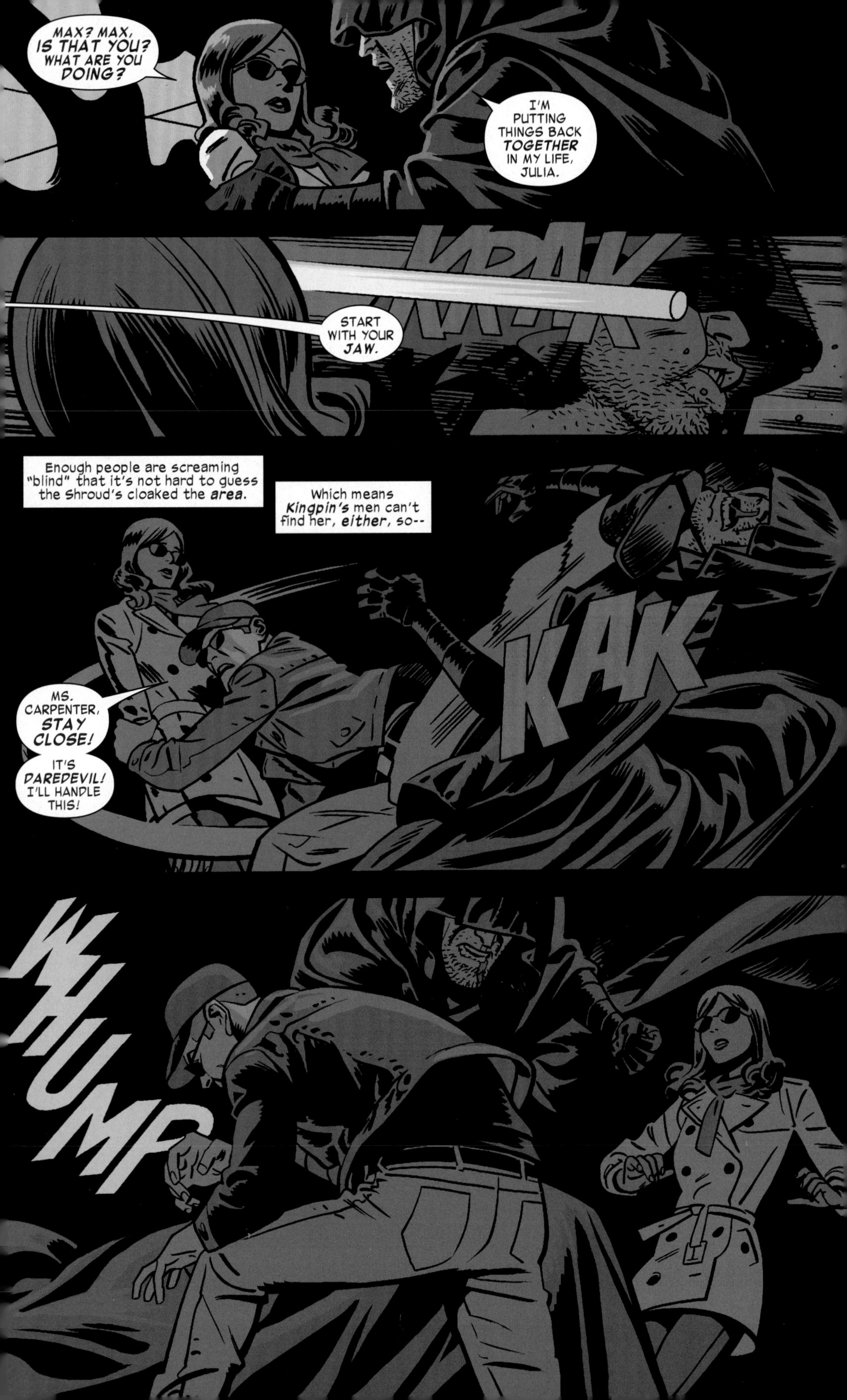
MAX? MAX, IS THAT YOU? WHAT ARE YOU DOING?
I'M PUTTING THINGS BACK TOGETHER IN MY LIFE, JULIA.
START WITH YOUR JAW.
Enough people are screaming "blind" that it's not hard to guess the Shroud's cloaked the area.
Which means Kingpin's men can't find her, either, so--
MS. CARPENTER, STAY CLOSE!
IT'S DAREDEVIL! I'LL HANDLE THIS!
KAK
WHUMP

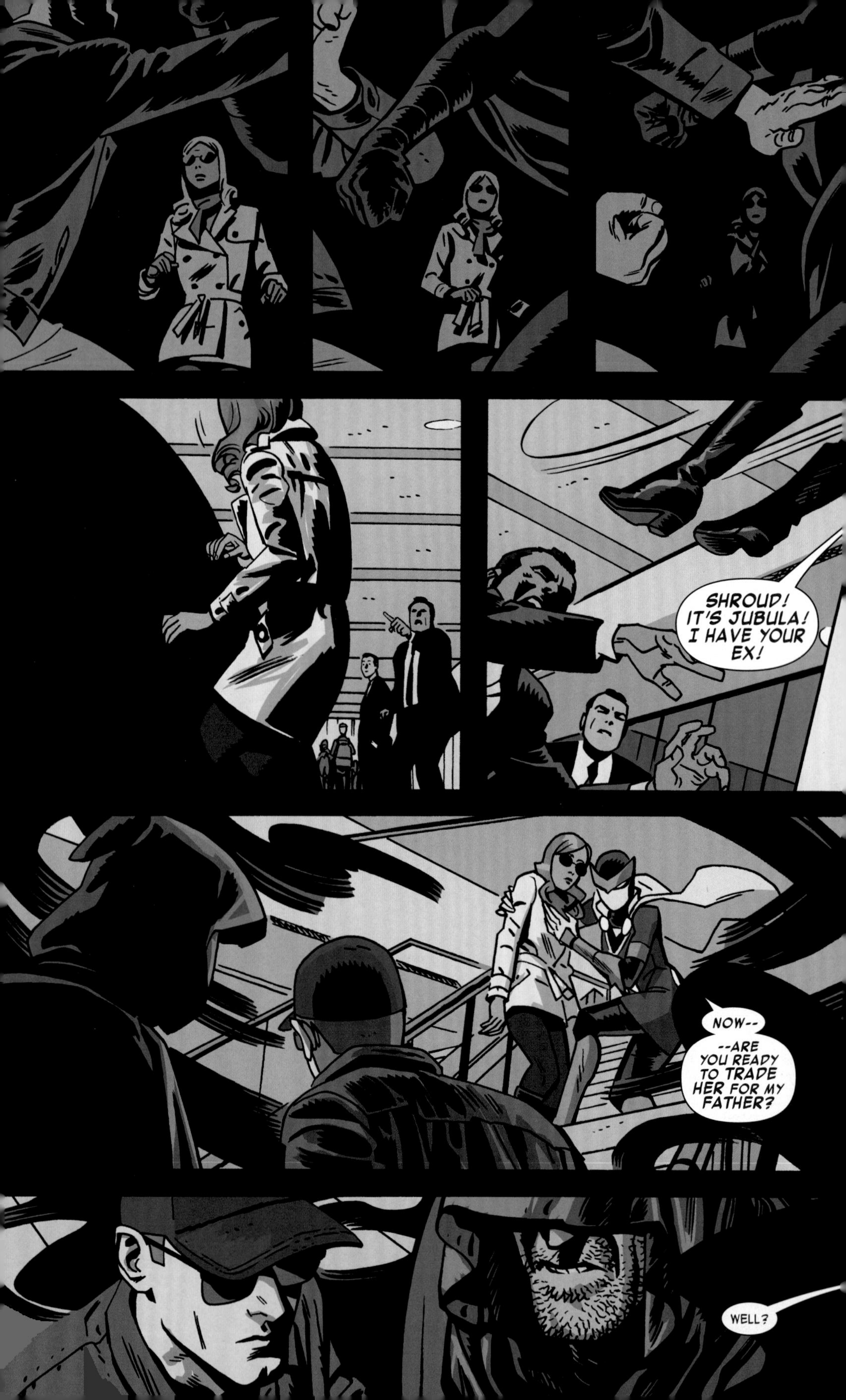
SHROUD! IT'S JUBULA! I HAVE YOUR EX!
NOW--
--ARE YOU READY TO TRADE HER FOR MY FATHER?
WELL?

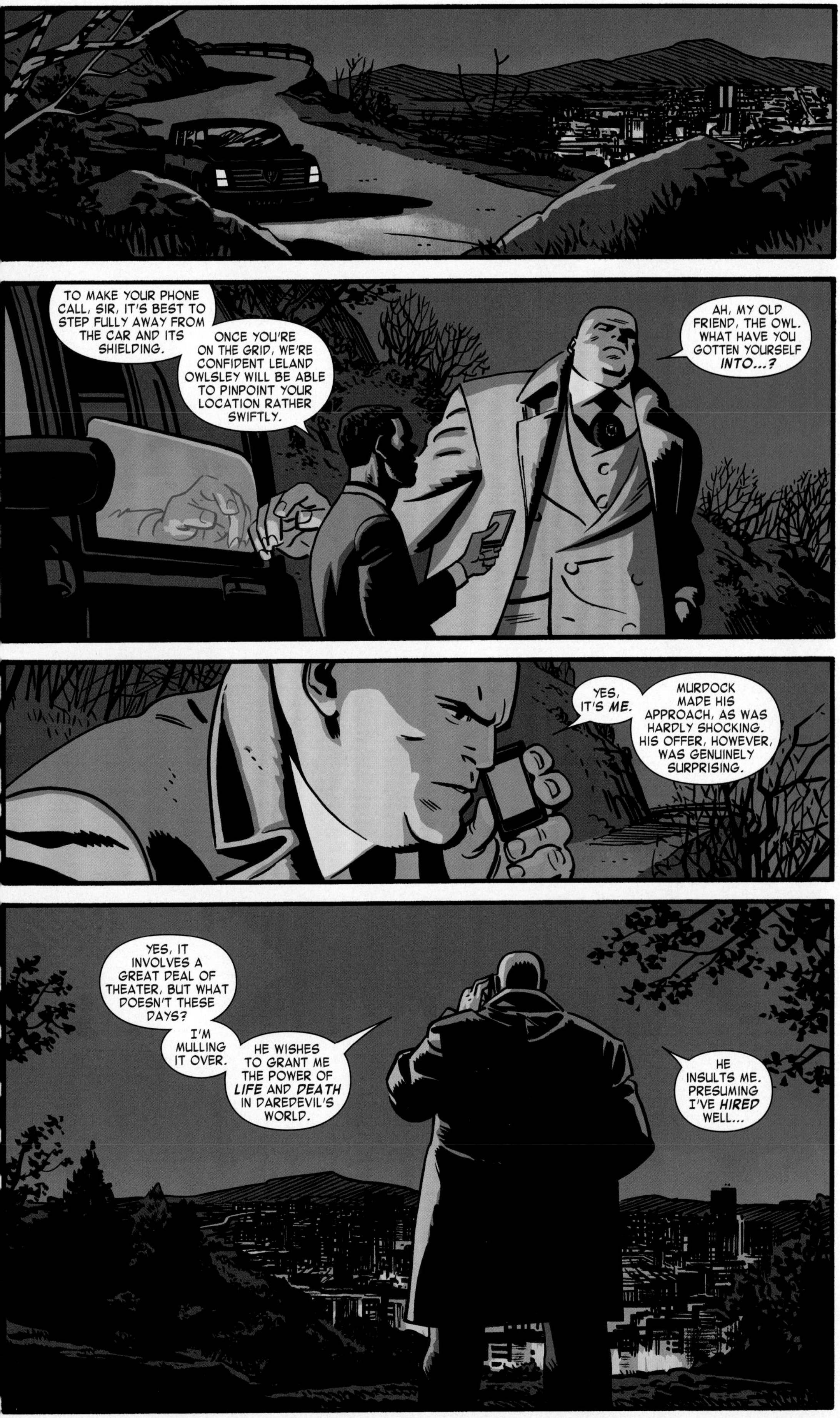
TO MAKE YOUR PHONE CALL, SIR, IT'S BEST TO STEP FULLY AWAY FROM THE CAR AND ITS SHIELDING.
ONCE YOU'RE ON THE GRID, WE'RE CONFIDENT LELAND OWLSLEY WILL BE ABLE TO PINPOINT YOUR LOCATION RATHER SWIFTLY.
AH, MY OLD FRIEND, THE OWL. WHAT HAVE YOU GOTTEN YOURSELF *INTO...?*
YES, IT'S *ME.*
MURDOCK MADE HIS APPROACH, AS WAS HARDLY SHOCKING. HIS OFFER, HOWEVER, WAS GENUINELY SURPRISING.
YES, IT INVOLVES A GREAT DEAL OF THEATER, BUT WHAT DOESN'T THESE DAYS?
I'M MULLING IT OVER.
HE WISHES TO GRANT ME THE POWER OF *LIFE* AND *DEATH* IN DAREDEVIL'S WORLD.
HE INSULTS ME. PRESUMING I'VE *HIRED* WELL...

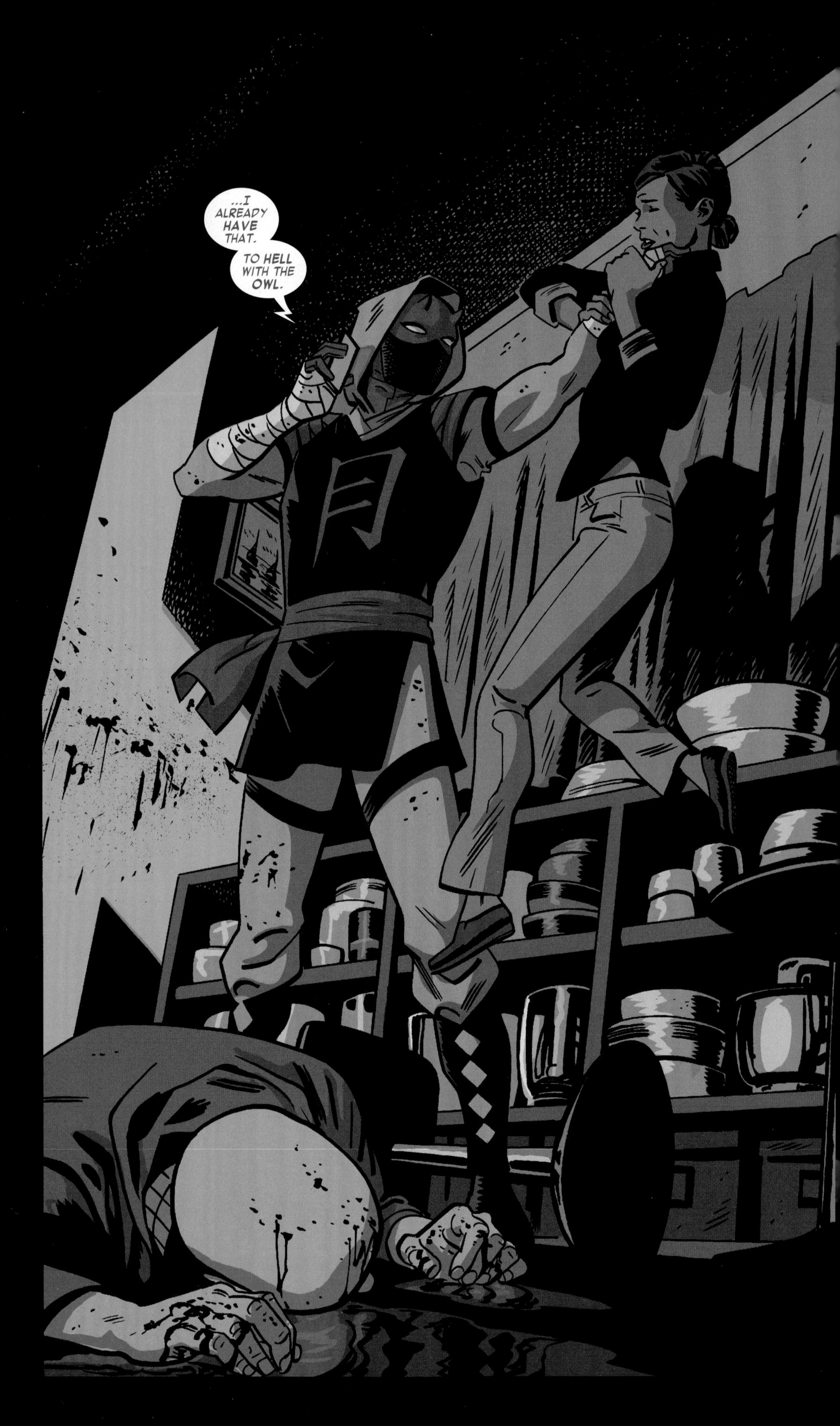
...I ALREADY HAVE THAT.
TO HELL WITH THE OWL.

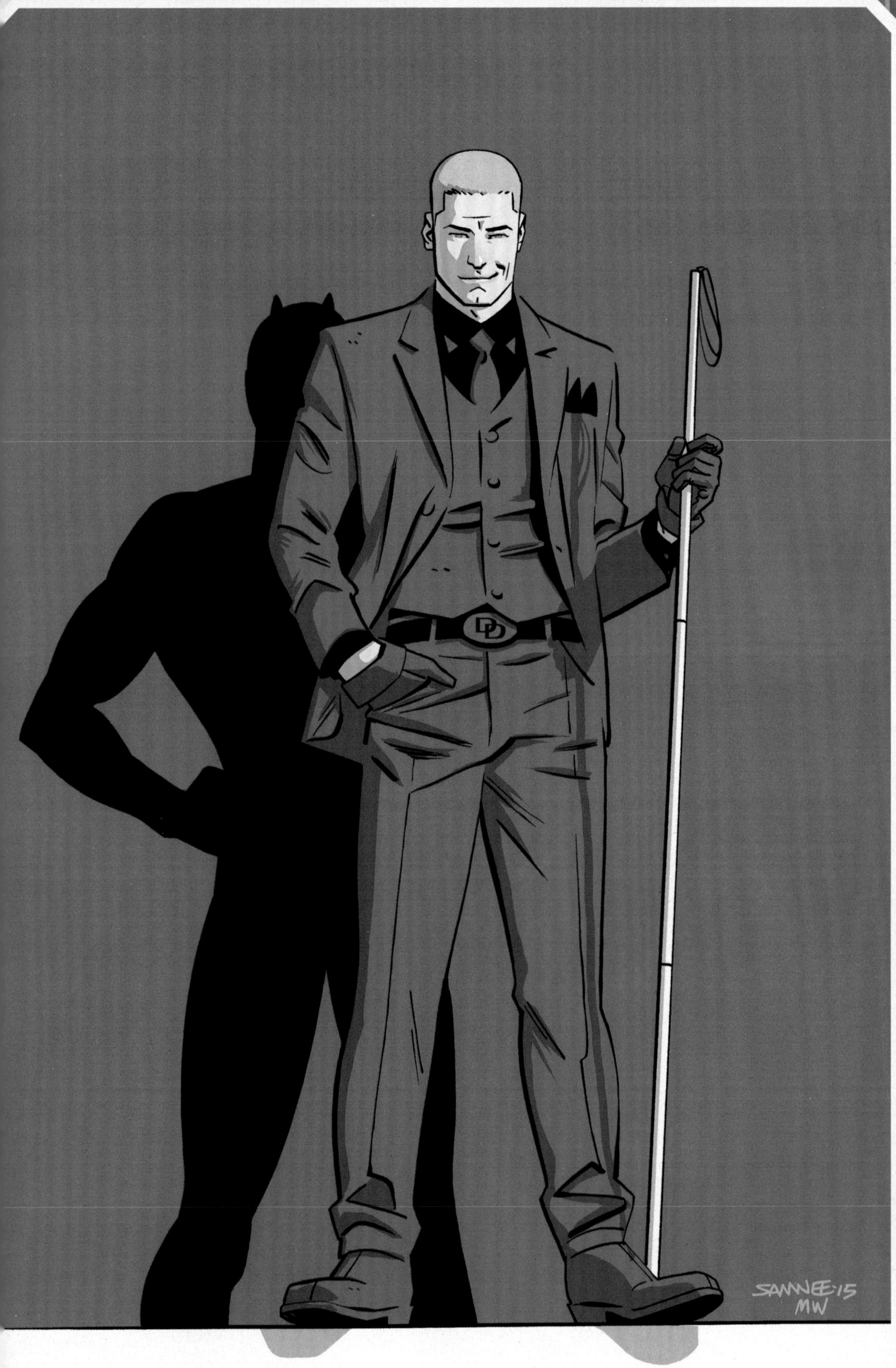
SAMNEE '15
MW

DAREDEVIL #17

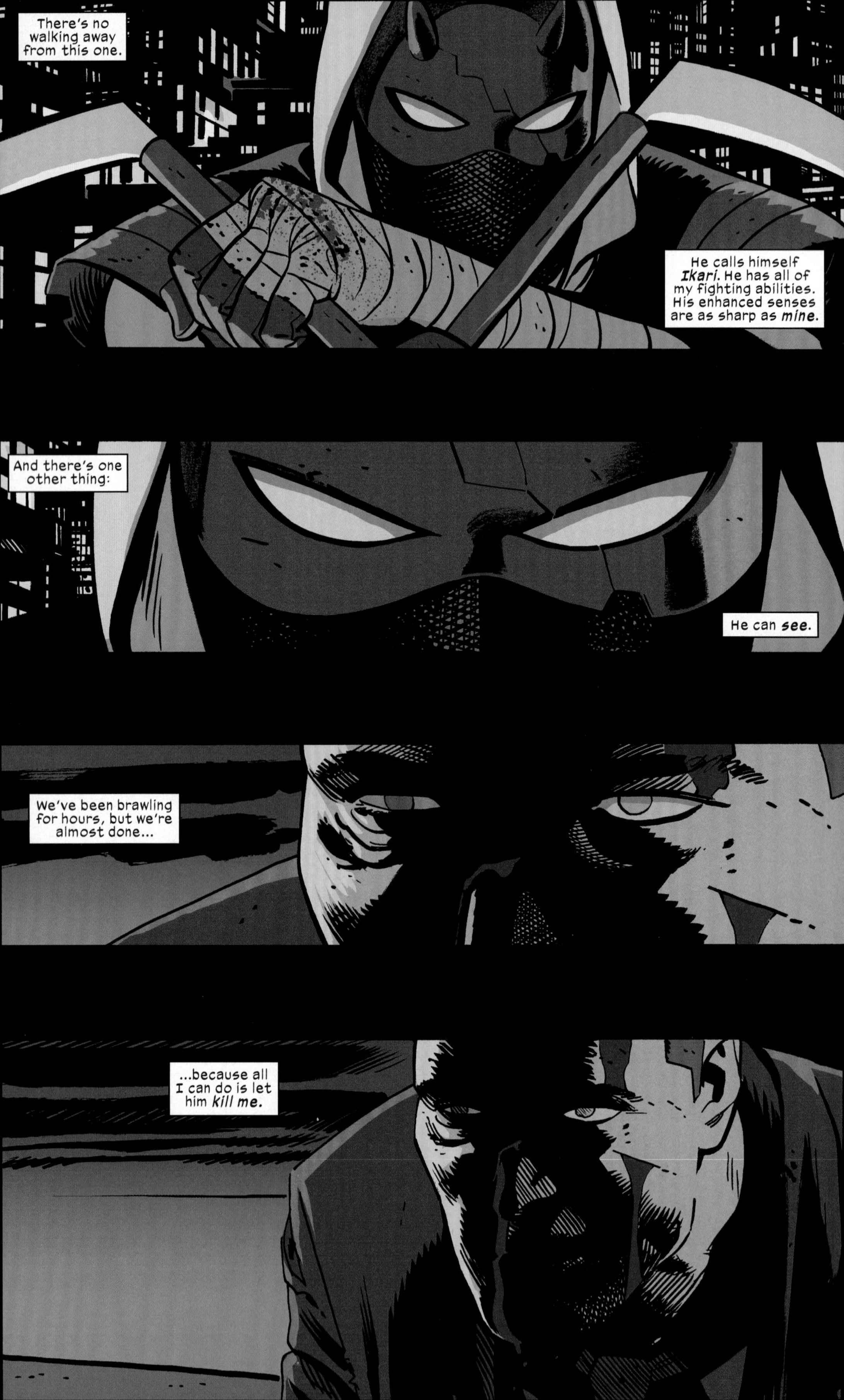

There's no walking away from this one.
He calls himself *Ikari*. He has all of my fighting abilities. His enhanced senses are as sharp as *mine*.
And there's one other thing:
He can *see*.
We've been brawling for hours, but we're almost done...
...because all I can do is let him *kill me*.

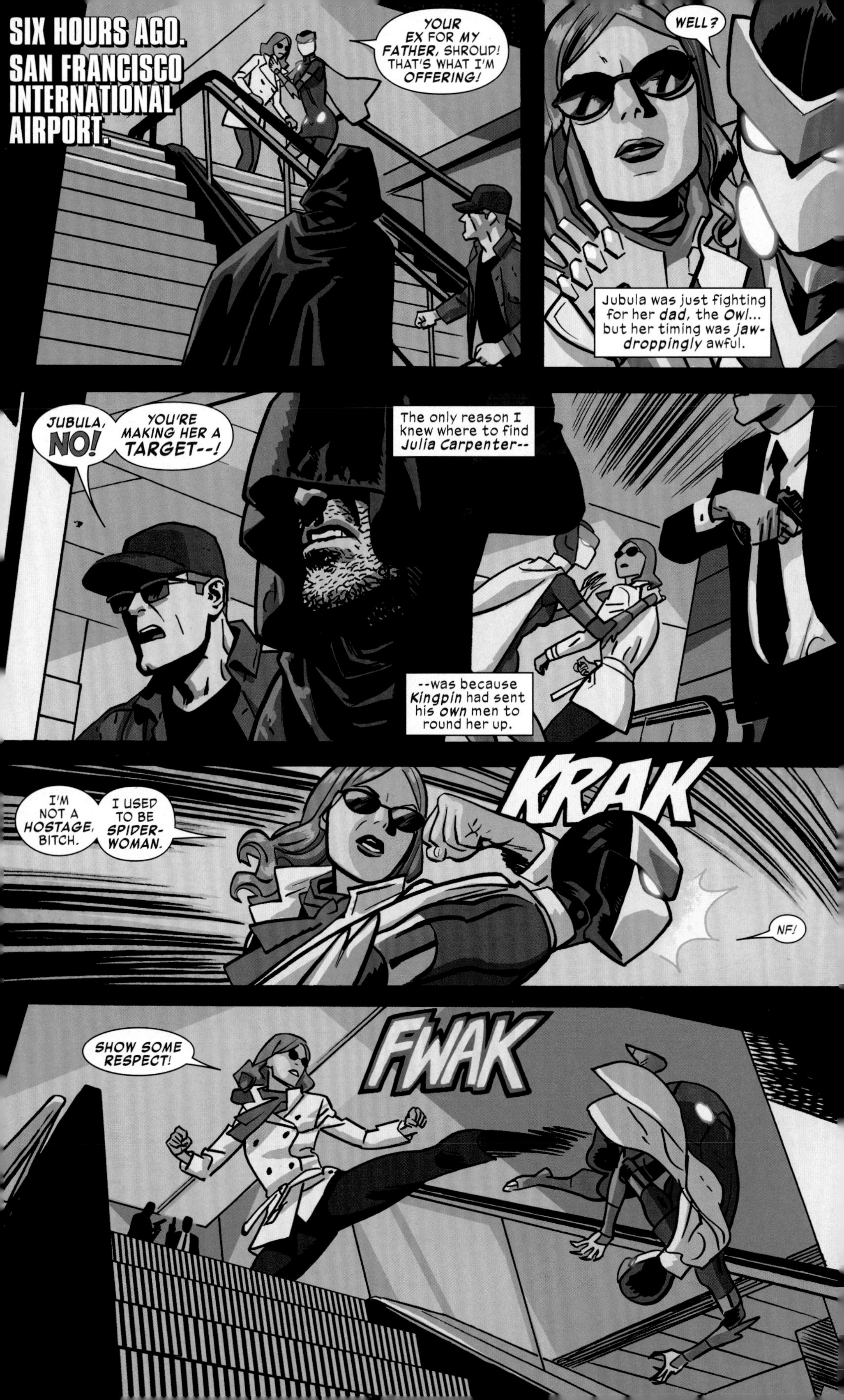
SIX HOURS AGO.
SAN FRANCISCO INTERNATIONAL AIRPORT.
YOUR EX FOR MY FATHER, SHROUD! THAT'S WHAT I'M OFFERING!
WELL?
Jubula was just fighting for her dad, the Owl... but her timing was jaw-droppingly awful.
JUBULA, NO!
YOU'RE MAKING HER A TARGET--!
The only reason I knew where to find Julia Carpenter--
--was because Kingpin had sent his own men to round her up.
I'M NOT A HOSTAGE, BITCH.
I USED TO BE SPIDER-WOMAN.
KRAK
NF!
SHOW SOME RESPECT!
FWAK

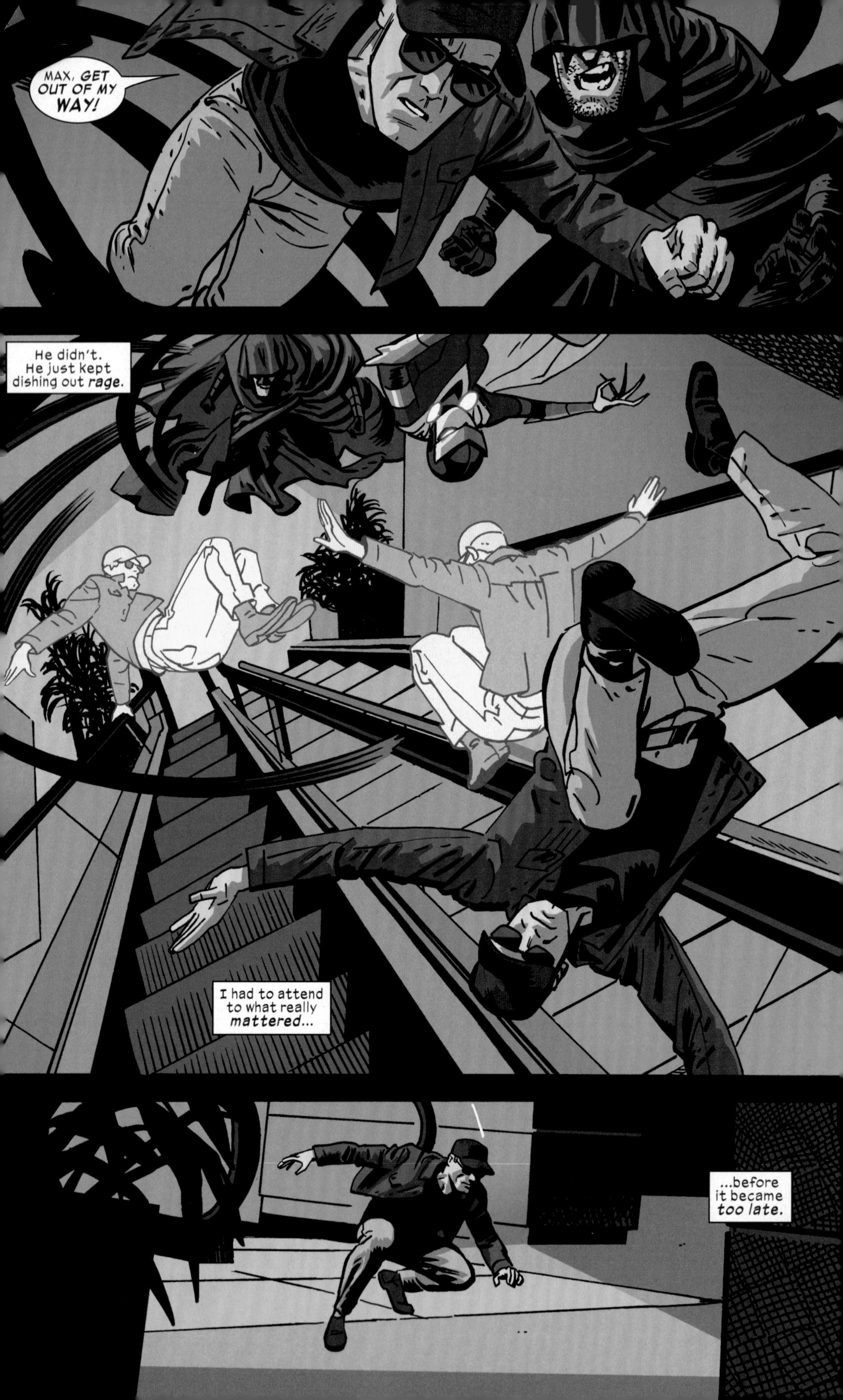
MAX, GET OUT OF MY WAY!
He didn't. He just kept dishing out rage.
I had to attend to what really mattered...
...before it became too late.

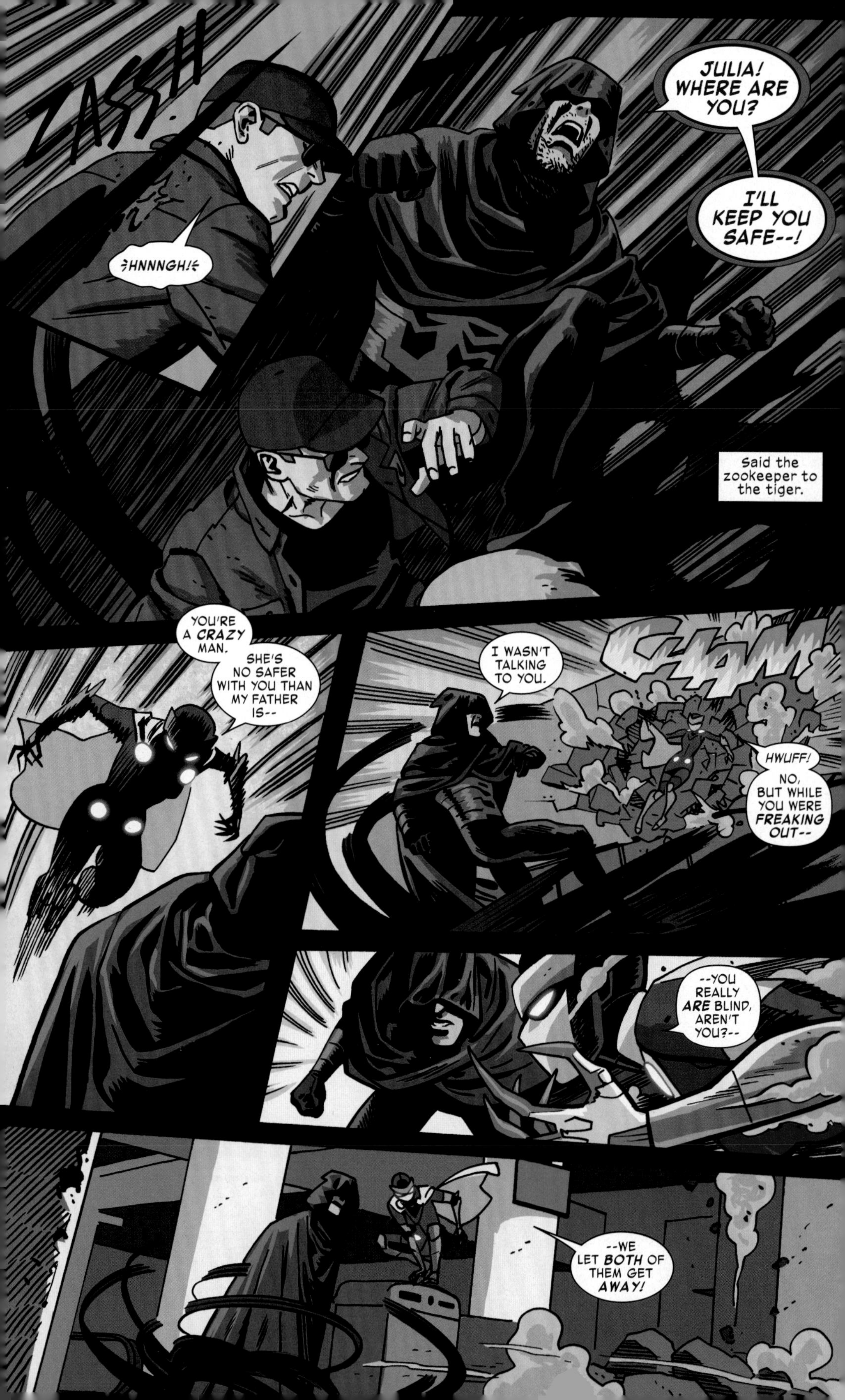
ZASSH
JULIA! WHERE ARE YOU?
I'LL KEEP YOU SAFE--!
HNNNGH!
Said the zookeeper to the tiger.
YOU'RE A CRAZY MAN.
SHE'S NO SAFER WITH YOU THAN MY FATHER IS--
I WASN'T TALKING TO YOU.
HWUFF!
NO, BUT WHILE YOU WERE FREAKING OUT--
--YOU REALLY ARE BLIND, AREN'T YOU?--
--WE LET BOTH OF THEM GET AWAY!

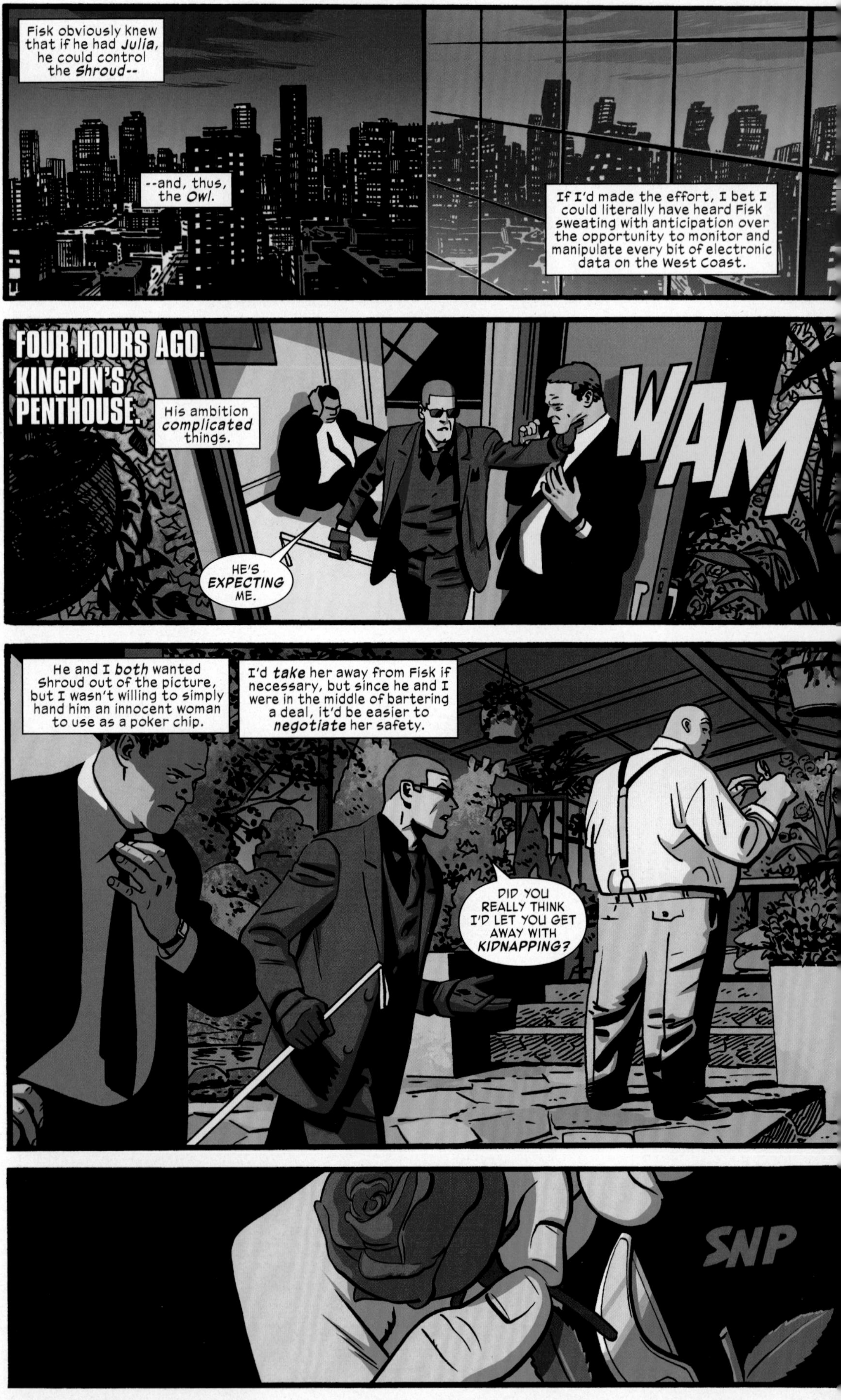

Fisk obviously knew that if he had *Julia*, he could control the *Shroud*--
--and, thus, the *Owl*.
If I'd made the effort, I bet I could literally have heard Fisk sweating with anticipation over the opportunity to monitor and manipulate every bit of electronic data on the West Coast.
FOUR HOURS AGO. KINGPIN'S PENTHOUSE.
His ambition *complicated* things.
WAM
HE'S *EXPECTING* ME.
He and I *both* wanted Shroud out of the picture, but I wasn't willing to simply hand him an innocent woman to use as a poker chip.
I'd *take* her away from Fisk if necessary, but since he and I were in the middle of bartering a deal, it'd be easier to *negotiate* her safety.
DID YOU REALLY THINK I'D LET YOU GET AWAY WITH *KIDNAPPING?*
SNP

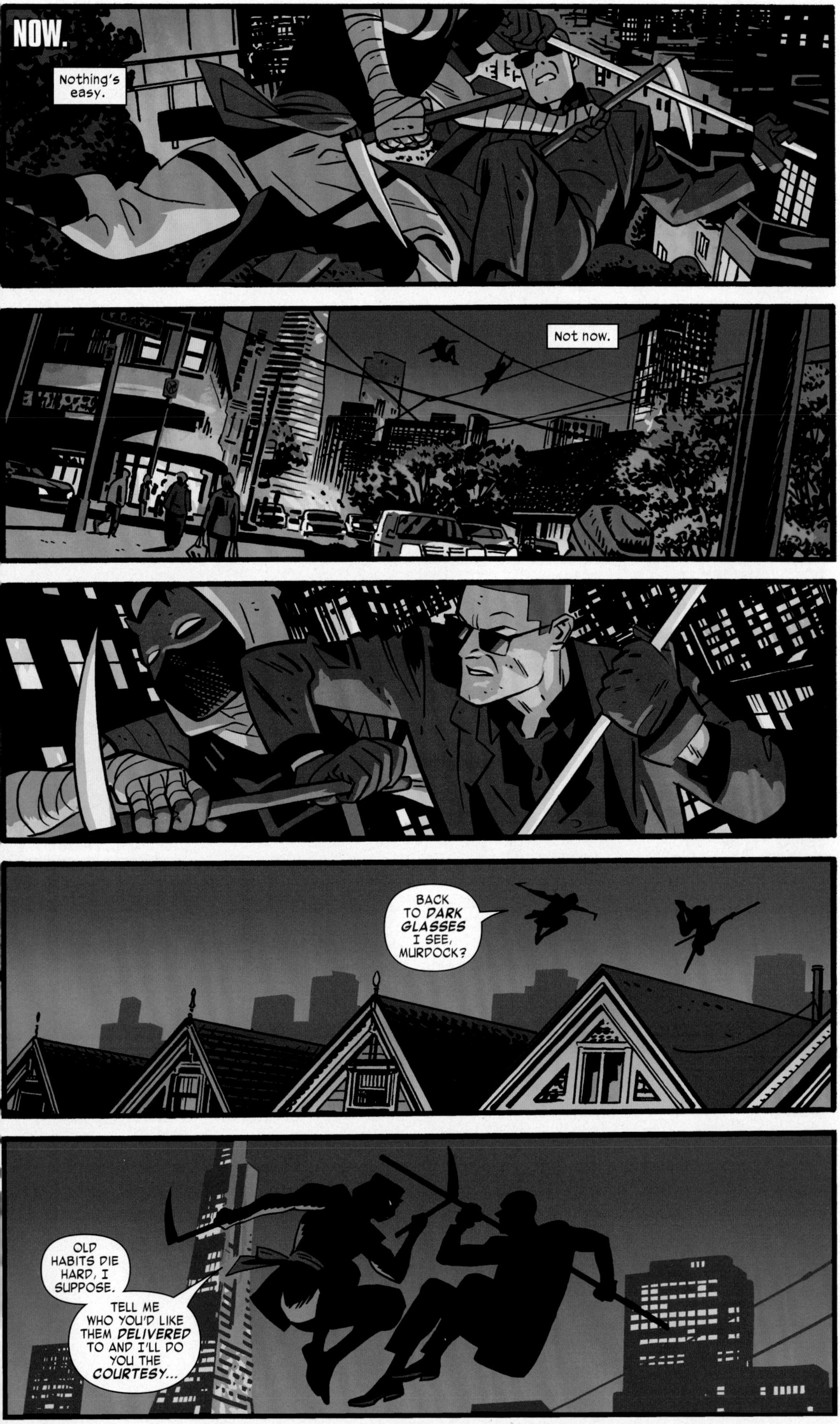
NOW.
Nothing's easy.
Not now.
BACK TO DARK GLASSES I SEE, MURDOCK?
OLD HABITS DIE HARD, I SUPPOSE.
TELL ME WHO YOU'D LIKE THEM DELIVERED TO AND I'LL DO YOU THE COURTESY...

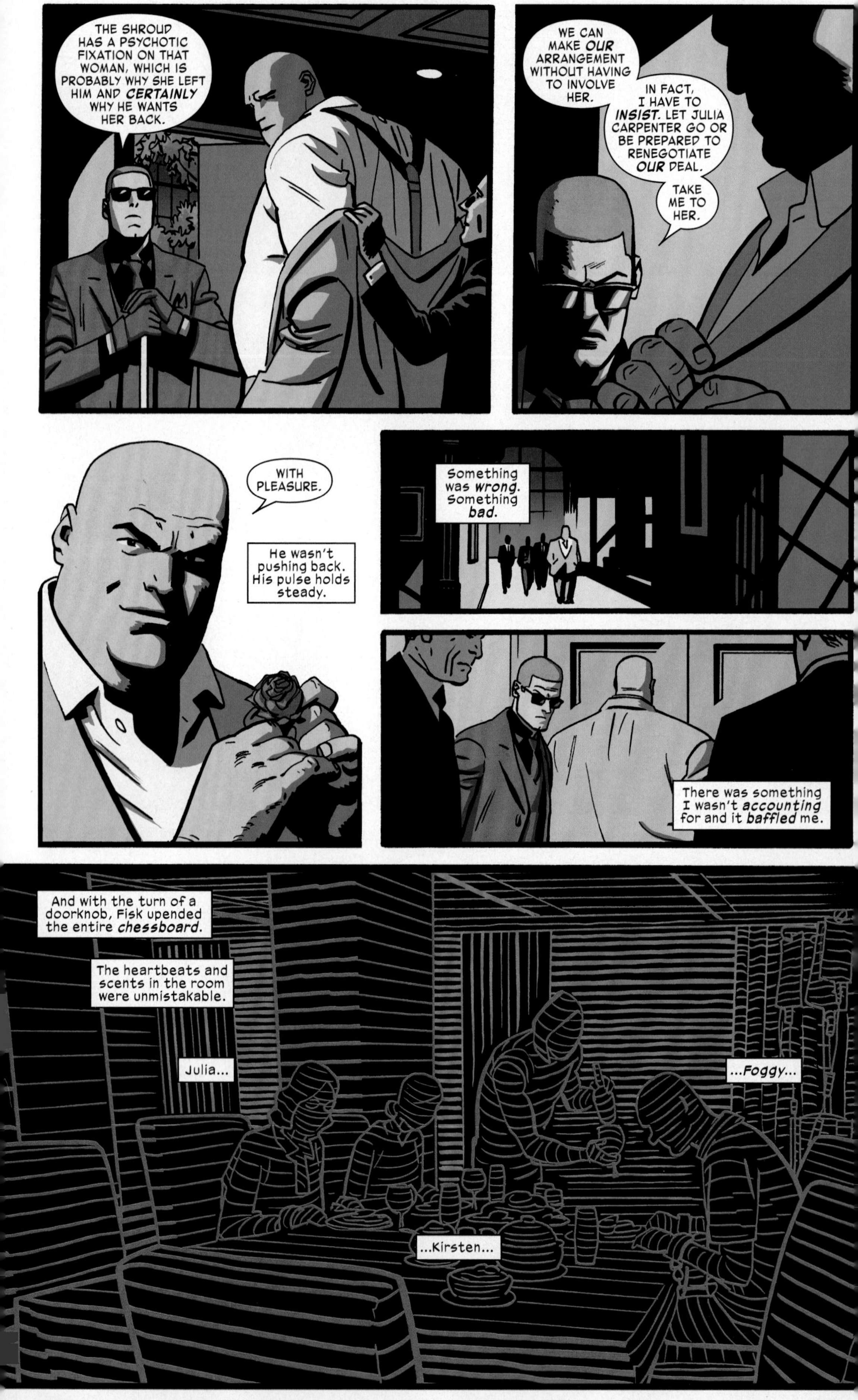
THE SHROUD HAS A PSYCHOTIC FIXATION ON THAT WOMAN, WHICH IS PROBABLY WHY SHE LEFT HIM AND CERTAINLY WHY HE WANTS HER BACK.
WE CAN MAKE OUR ARRANGEMENT WITHOUT HAVING TO INVOLVE HER.
IN FACT, I HAVE TO INSIST. LET JULIA CARPENTER GO OR BE PREPARED TO RENEGOTIATE OUR DEAL.
TAKE ME TO HER.
WITH PLEASURE.
He wasn't pushing back. His pulse holds steady.
Something was wrong. Something bad.
There was something I wasn't accounting for and it baffled me.
And with the turn of a doorknob, Fisk upended the entire chessboard.
The heartbeats and scents in the room were unmistakable.
Julia...
...Foggy...
...Kirsten...

...and *Ikari*.

MATT--!

ZZZK

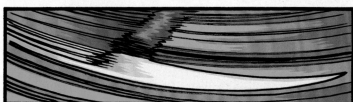

IF ANYONE HAS ANY *RENEGOTIATING* TO DO, COUNSELOR...

...IT'S *YOU.*

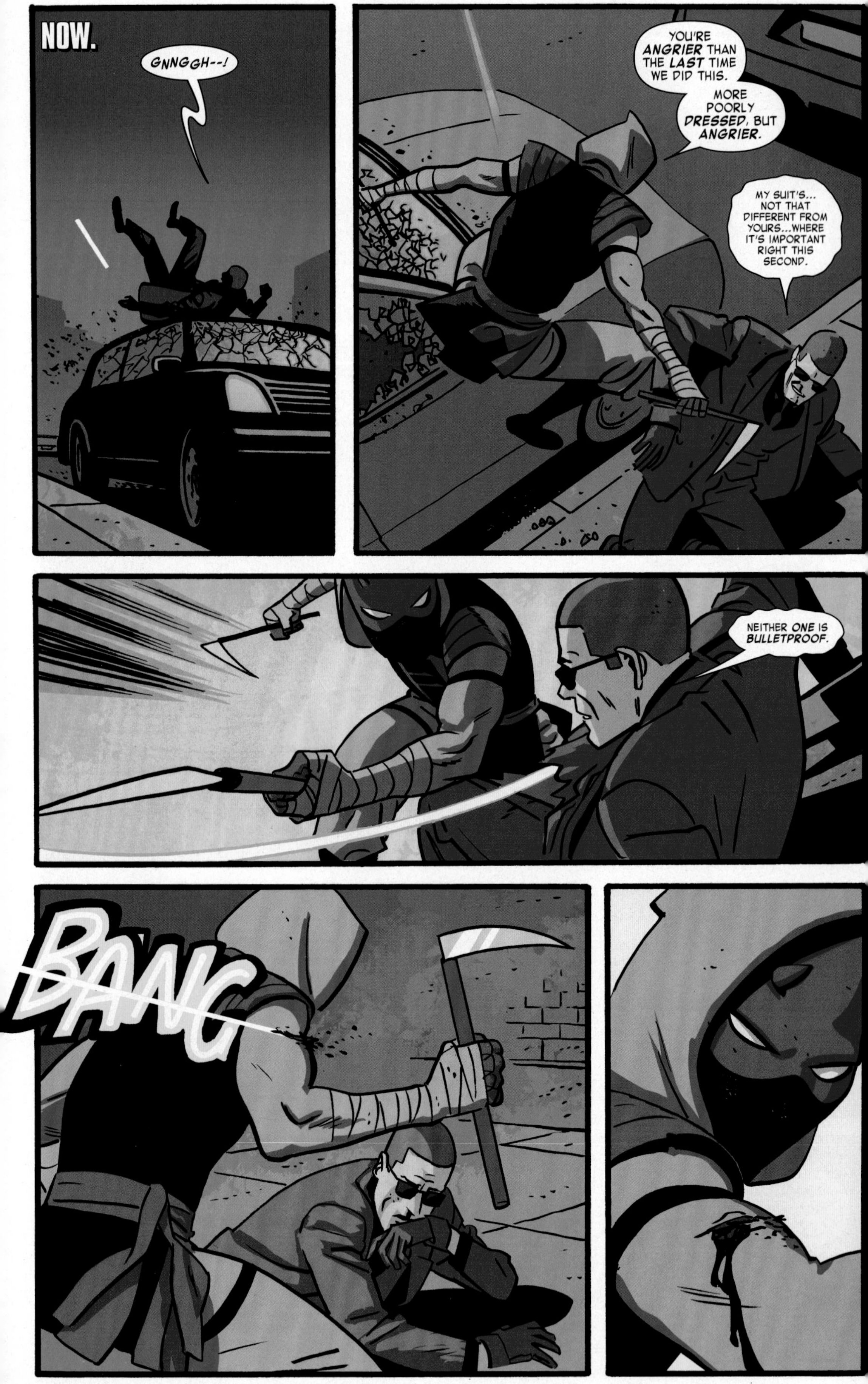
NOW.
GNNGGH--!
YOU'RE ANGRIER THAN THE LAST TIME WE DID THIS.
MORE POORLY DRESSED, BUT ANGRIER.
MY SUIT'S... NOT THAT DIFFERENT FROM YOURS...WHERE IT'S IMPORTANT RIGHT THIS SECOND.
NEITHER ONE IS BULLETPROOF.
BAANG

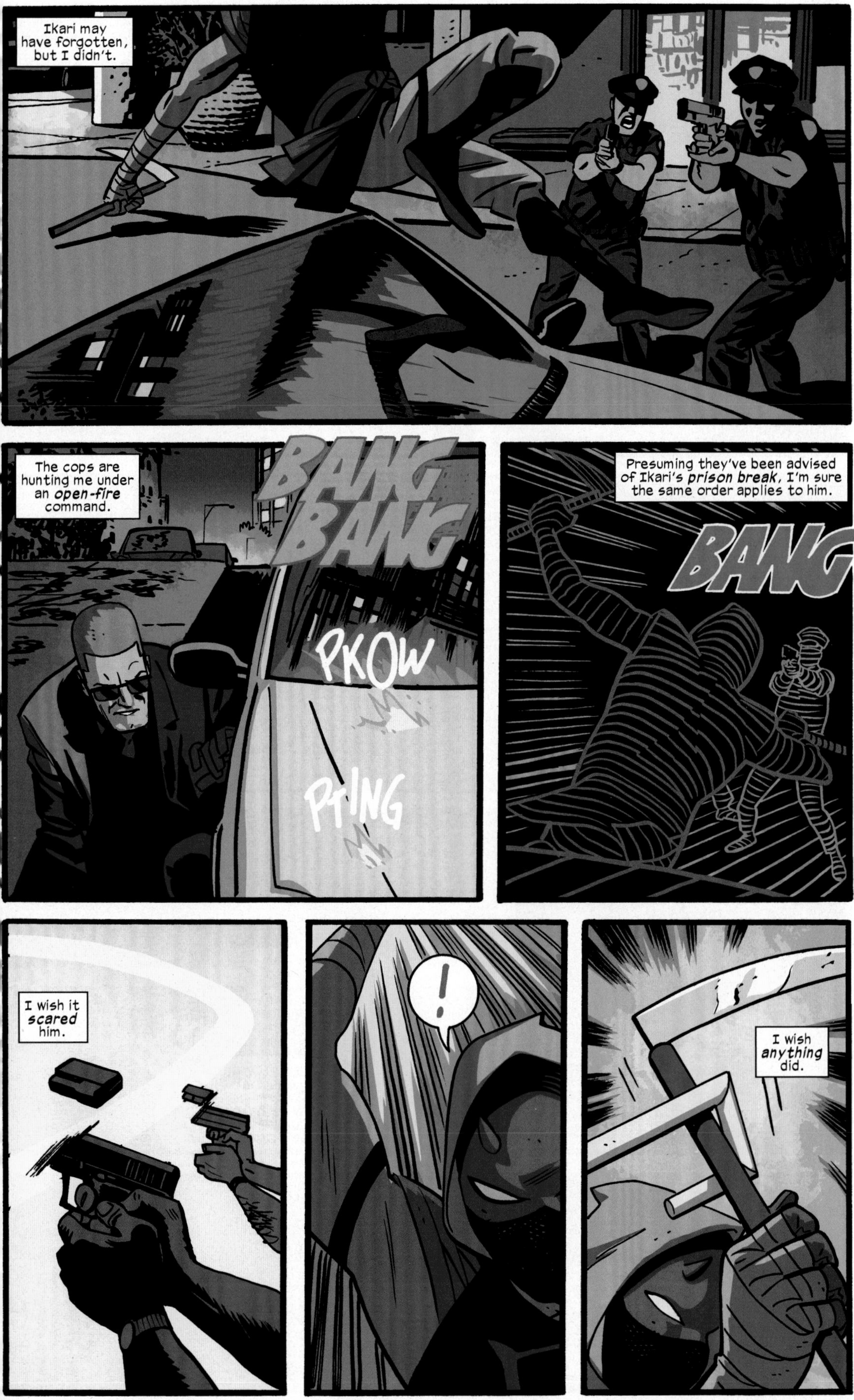
Ikari may have forgotten, but I didn't.
The cops are hunting me under an open-fire command.
BANG BANG
PKOW
PTING
Presuming they've been advised of Ikari's prison break, I'm sure the same order applies to him.
BANG
I wish it scared him.
!
I wish anything did.

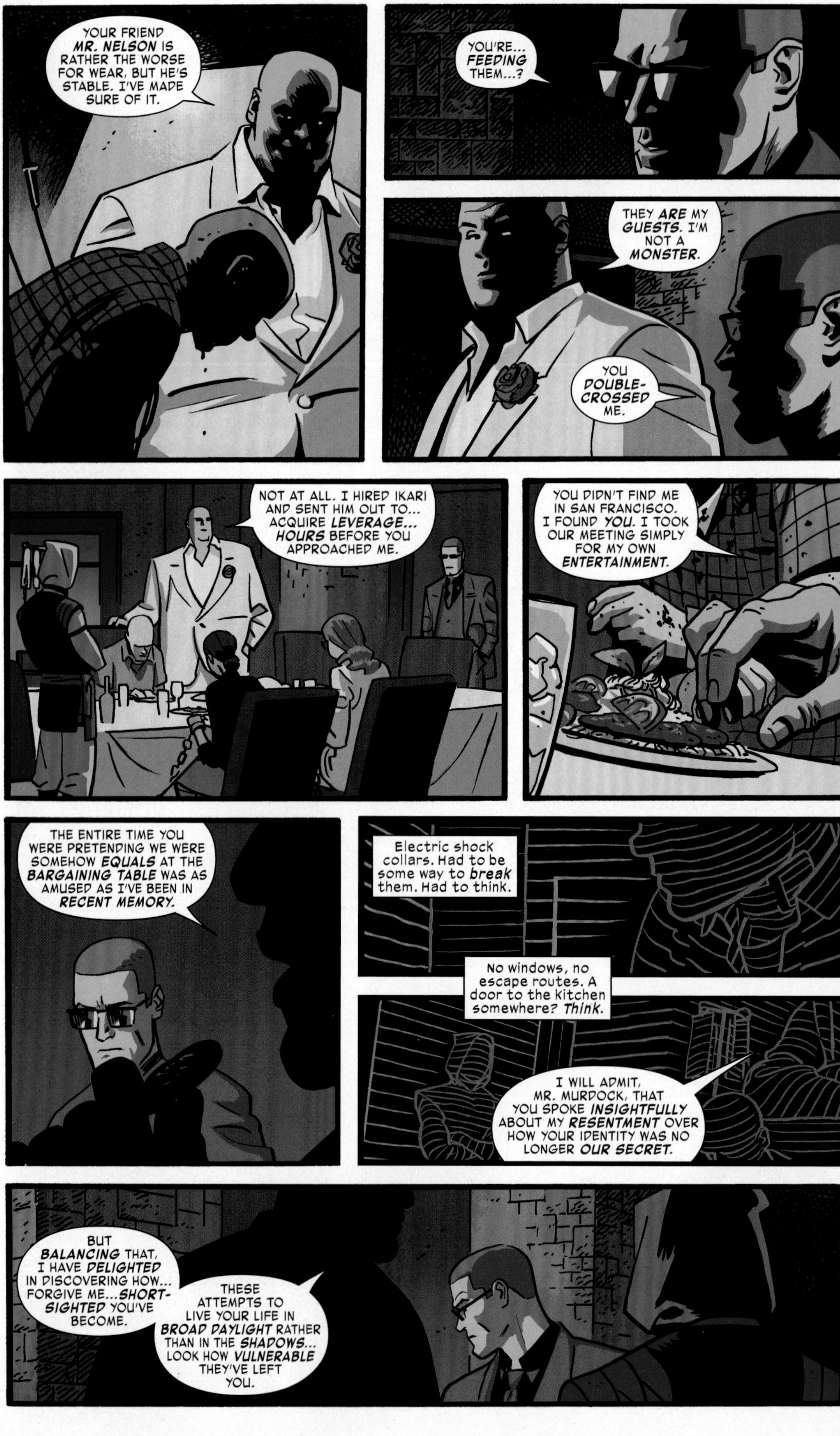
YOUR FRIEND MR. NELSON IS RATHER THE WORSE FOR WEAR, BUT HE'S STABLE. I'VE MADE SURE OF IT.
YOU'RE... FEEDING THEM...?
THEY ARE MY GUESTS. I'M NOT A MONSTER.
YOU DOUBLE-CROSSED ME.
NOT AT ALL. I HIRED IKARI AND SENT HIM OUT TO... ACQUIRE LEVERAGE... HOURS BEFORE YOU APPROACHED ME.
YOU DIDN'T FIND ME IN SAN FRANCISCO. I FOUND YOU. I TOOK OUR MEETING SIMPLY FOR MY OWN ENTERTAINMENT.
THE ENTIRE TIME YOU WERE PRETENDING WE WERE SOMEHOW EQUALS AT THE BARGAINING TABLE WAS AS AMUSED AS I'VE BEEN IN RECENT MEMORY.
Electric shock collars. Had to be some way to break them. Had to think.
No windows, no escape routes. A door to the kitchen somewhere? Think.
I WILL ADMIT, MR. MURDOCK, THAT YOU SPOKE INSIGHTFULLY ABOUT MY RESENTMENT OVER HOW YOUR IDENTITY WAS NO LONGER OUR SECRET.
BUT BALANCING THAT, I HAVE DELIGHTED IN DISCOVERING HOW... FORGIVE ME...SHORT-SIGHTED YOU'VE BECOME.
THESE ATTEMPTS TO LIVE YOUR LIFE IN BROAD DAYLIGHT RATHER THAN IN THE SHADOWS... LOOK HOW VULNERABLE THEY'VE LEFT YOU.

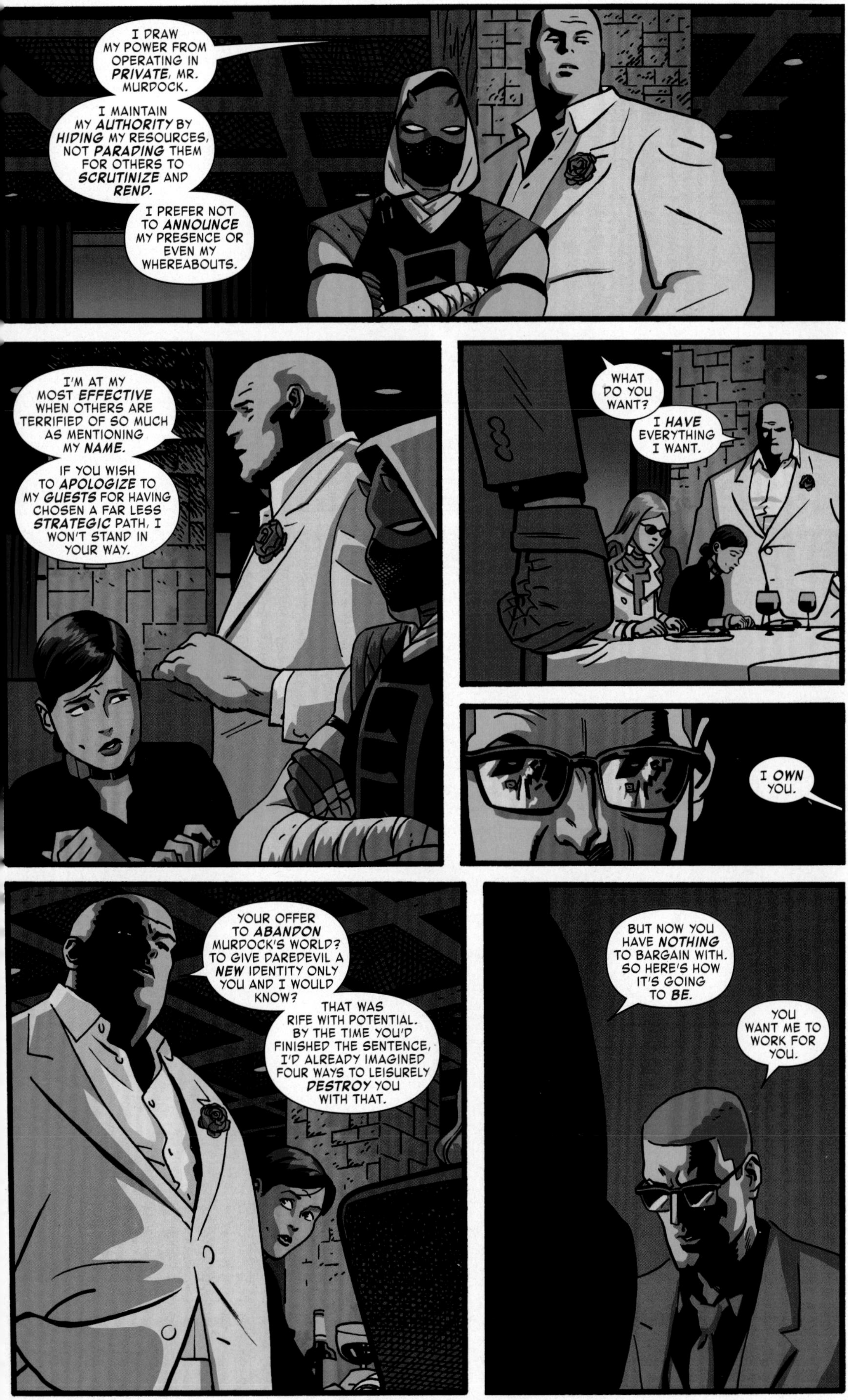
I DRAW MY POWER FROM OPERATING IN *PRIVATE*, MR. MURDOCK.
I MAINTAIN MY *AUTHORITY* BY *HIDING* MY RESOURCES, NOT *PARADING* THEM FOR OTHERS TO *SCRUTINIZE* AND *REND*.
I PREFER NOT TO *ANNOUNCE* MY PRESENCE OR EVEN MY WHEREABOUTS.
I'M AT MY MOST *EFFECTIVE* WHEN OTHERS ARE TERRIFIED OF SO MUCH AS MENTIONING MY *NAME*.
IF YOU WISH TO *APOLOGIZE* TO MY *GUESTS* FOR HAVING CHOSEN A FAR LESS *STRATEGIC* PATH, I WON'T STAND IN YOUR WAY.
WHAT DO YOU WANT?
I *HAVE* EVERYTHING I WANT.
I *OWN* YOU.
YOUR OFFER TO *ABANDON* MURDOCK'S WORLD? TO GIVE DAREDEVIL A *NEW* IDENTITY ONLY YOU AND I WOULD KNOW?
THAT WAS RIFE WITH POTENTIAL. BY THE TIME YOU'D FINISHED THE SENTENCE, I'D ALREADY IMAGINED FOUR WAYS TO LEISURELY *DESTROY* YOU WITH THAT.
BUT NOW YOU HAVE *NOTHING* TO BARGAIN WITH. SO HERE'S HOW IT'S GOING TO *BE*.
YOU WANT ME TO WORK FOR YOU.

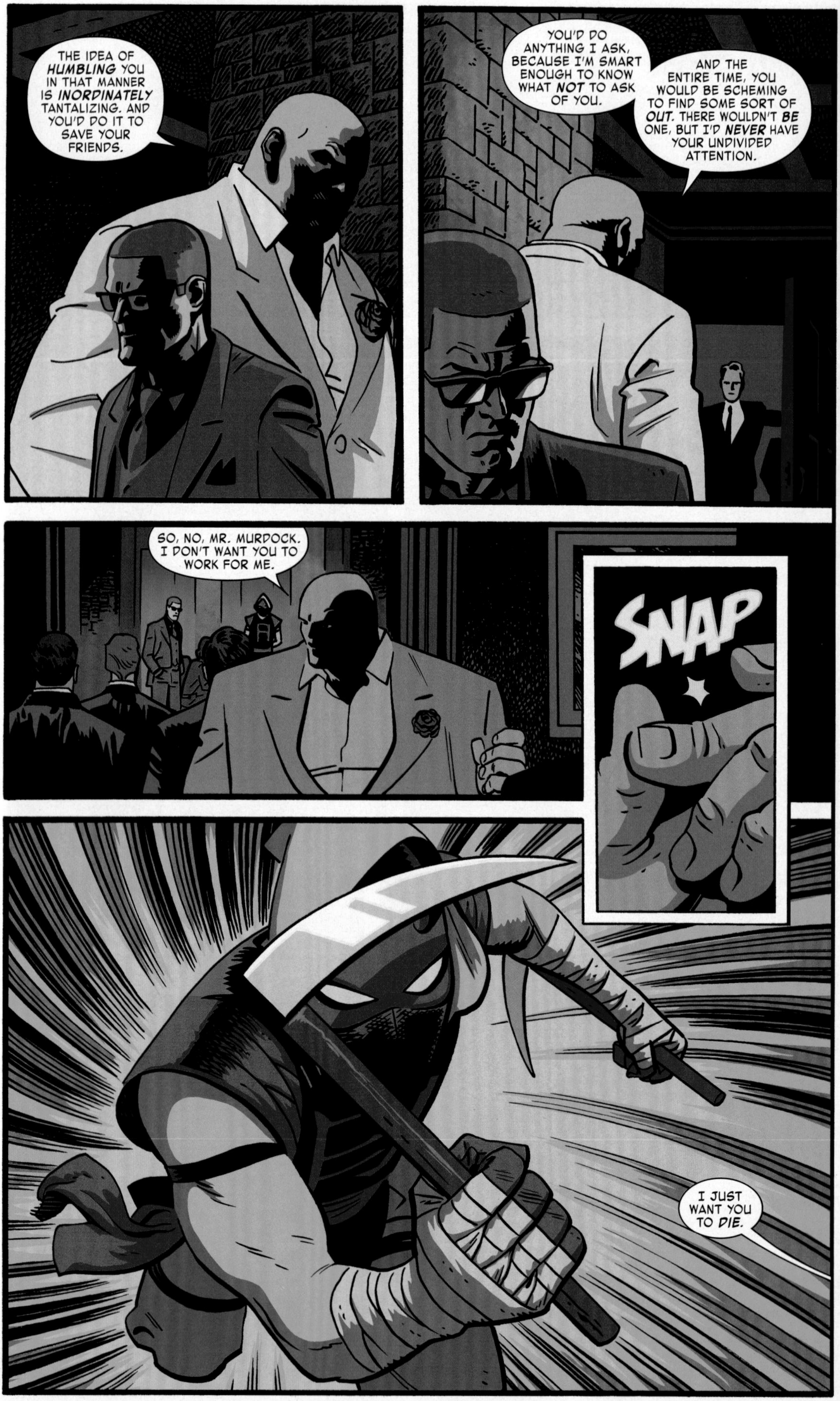

THE IDEA OF HUMBLING YOU IN THAT MANNER IS INORDINATELY TANTALIZING. AND YOU'D DO IT TO SAVE YOUR FRIENDS.
YOU'D DO ANYTHING I ASK, BECAUSE I'M SMART ENOUGH TO KNOW WHAT NOT TO ASK OF YOU.
AND THE ENTIRE TIME, YOU WOULD BE SCHEMING TO FIND SOME SORT OF OUT. THERE WOULDN'T BE ONE, BUT I'D NEVER HAVE YOUR UNDIVIDED ATTENTION.
SO, NO, MR. MURDOCK. I DON'T WANT YOU TO WORK FOR ME.
SNAP
I JUST WANT YOU TO DIE.

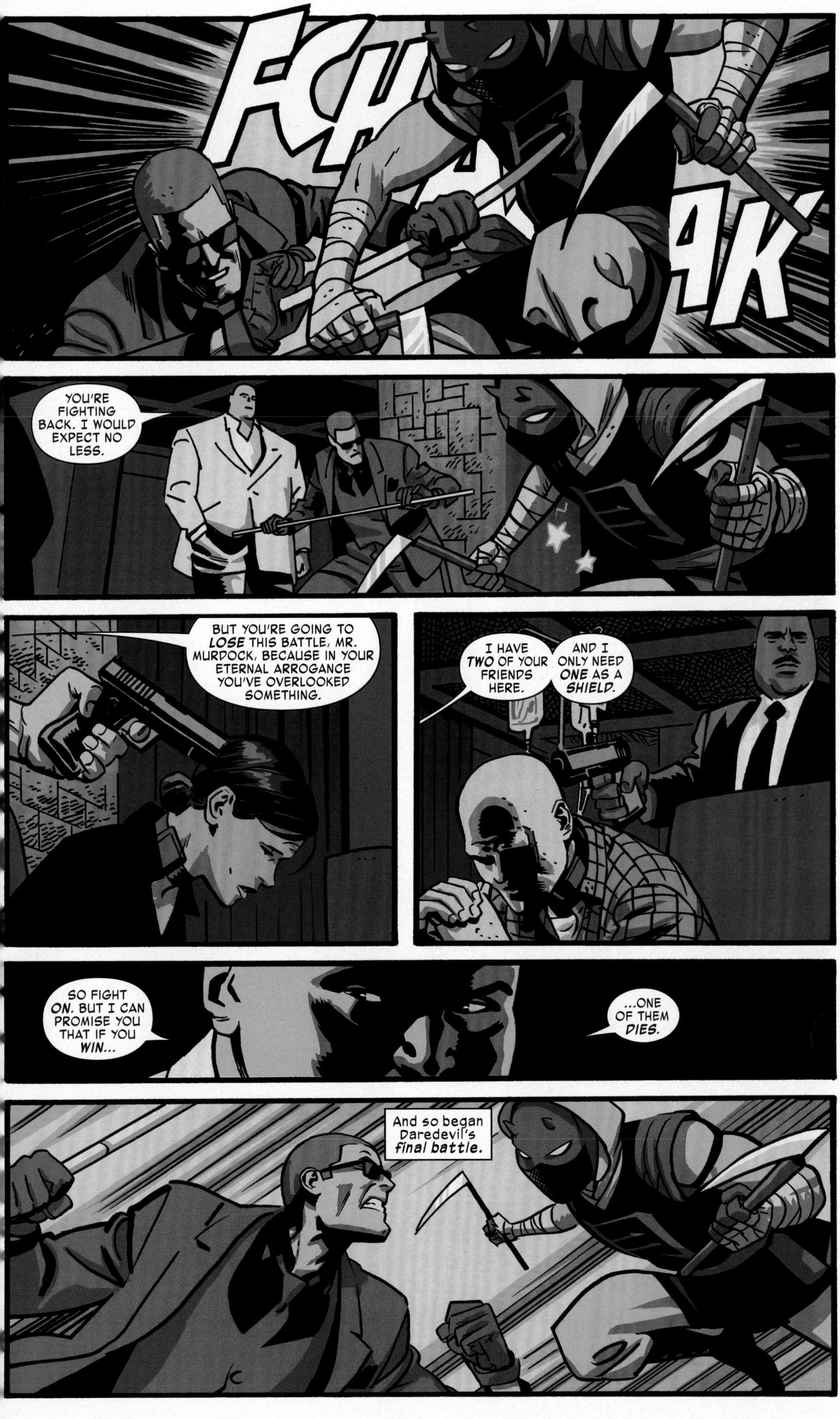
F-CHAK
YOU'RE FIGHTING BACK. I WOULD EXPECT NO LESS.
BUT YOU'RE GOING TO LOSE THIS BATTLE, MR. MURDOCK, BECAUSE IN YOUR ETERNAL ARROGANCE YOU'VE OVERLOOKED SOMETHING.
I HAVE TWO OF YOUR FRIENDS HERE.
AND I ONLY NEED ONE AS A SHIELD.
SO FIGHT ON. BUT I CAN PROMISE YOU THAT IF YOU WIN...
...ONE OF THEM DIES.
And so began Daredevil's final battle.

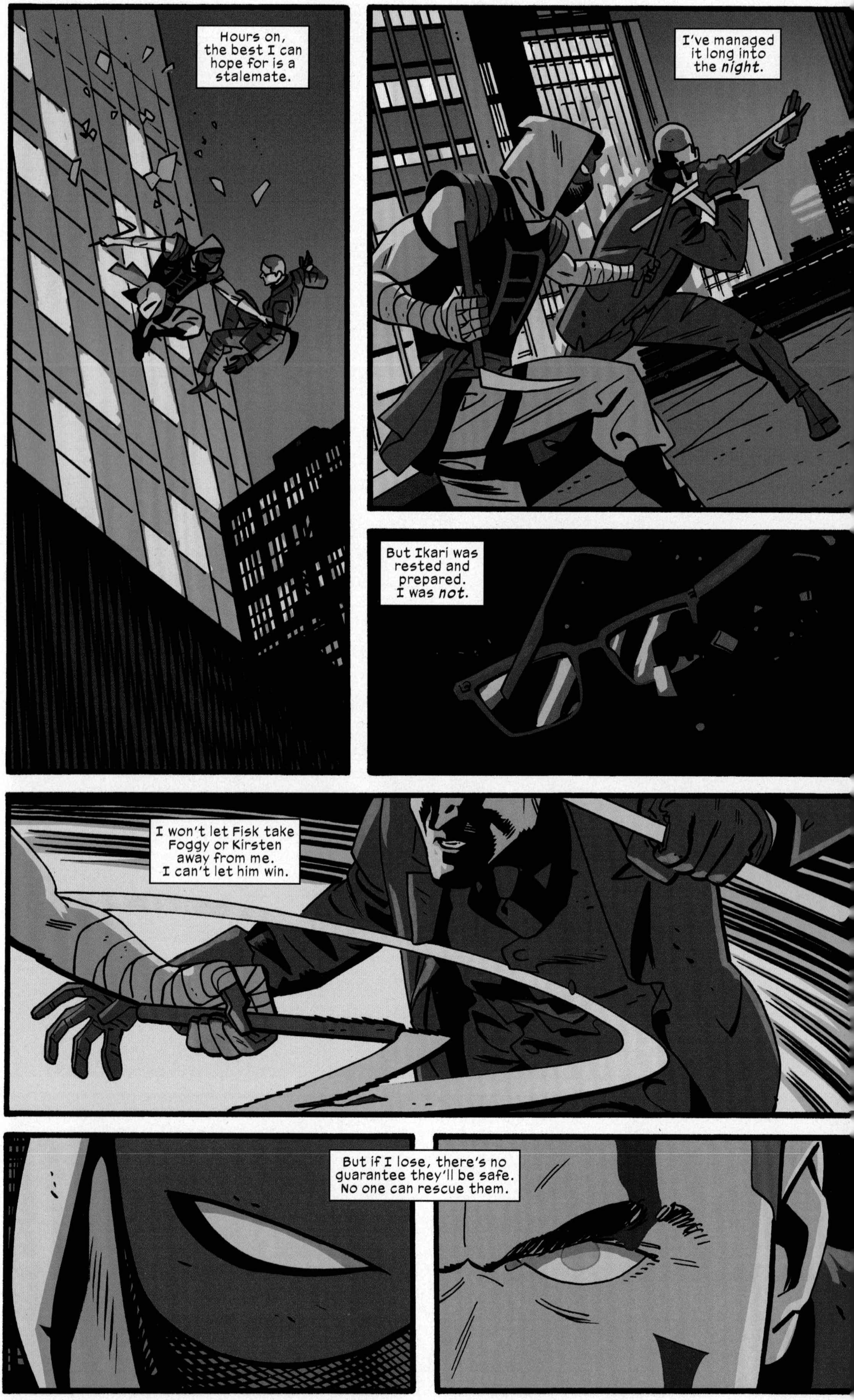
Hours on, the best I can hope for is a stalemate.
I've managed it long into the *night*.
But Ikari was rested and prepared. I was *not*.
I won't let Fisk take Foggy or Kirsten away from me. I can't let him win.
But if I lose, there's no guarantee they'll be safe. No one can rescue them.

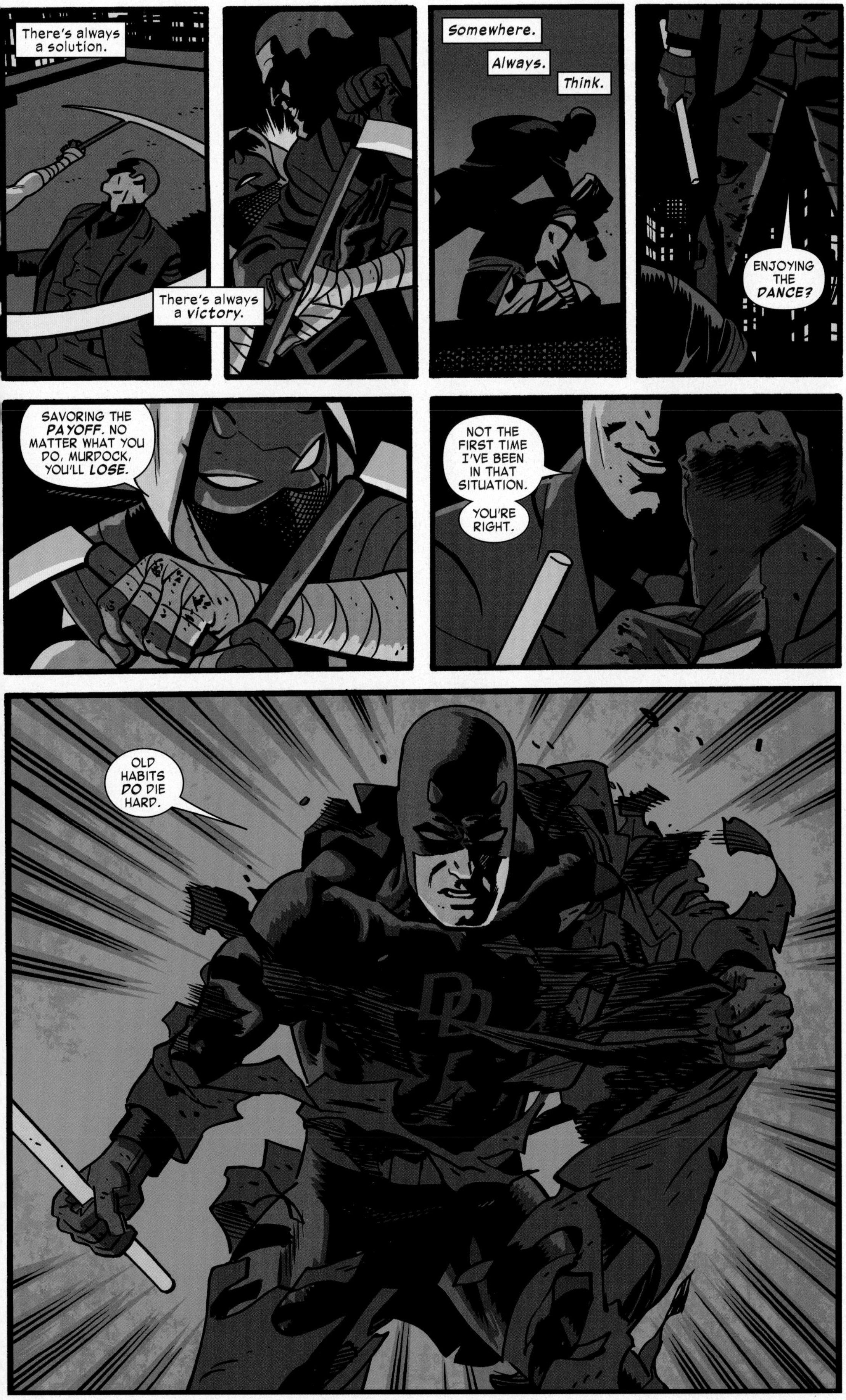
There's always a solution.
There's always a *victory*.
Somewhere.
Always.
Think.
ENJOYING THE *DANCE?*
SAVORING THE **PAYOFF**. NO MATTER WHAT YOU DO, MURDOCK, YOU'LL **LOSE**.
NOT THE FIRST TIME I'VE BEEN IN THAT SITUATION.
YOU'RE RIGHT.
OLD HABITS *DO* DIE HARD.

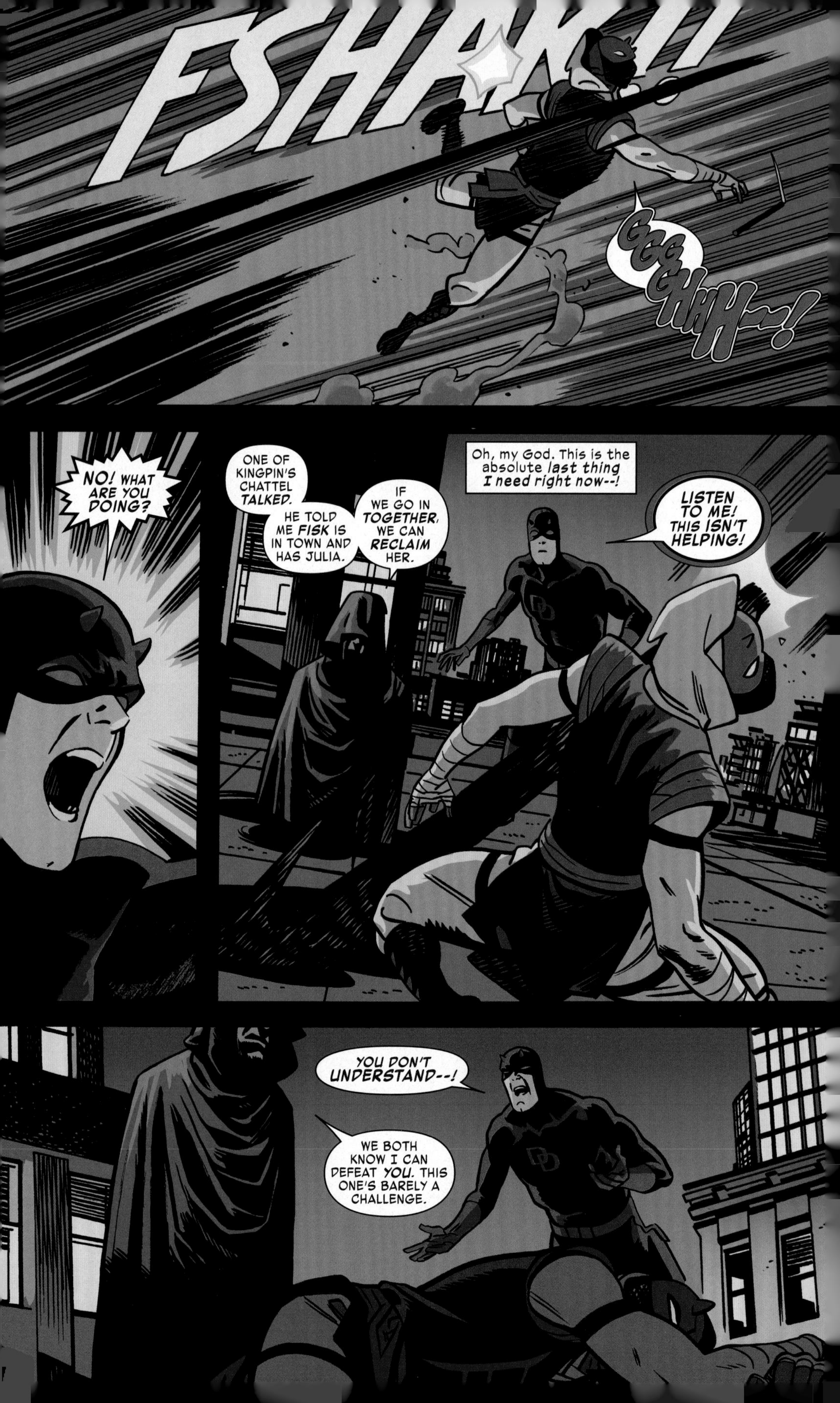
FSHAKK!!
GGGGHHH--!
NO! WHAT ARE YOU DOING?
ONE OF KINGPIN'S CHATTEL TALKED.
HE TOLD ME FISK IS IN TOWN AND HAS JULIA.
IF WE GO IN TOGETHER, WE CAN RECLAIM HER.
Oh, my God. This is the absolute last thing I need right now--!
LISTEN TO ME! THIS ISN'T HELPING!
YOU DON'T UNDERSTAND--!
WE BOTH KNOW I CAN DEFEAT YOU. THIS ONE'S BARELY A CHALLENGE.

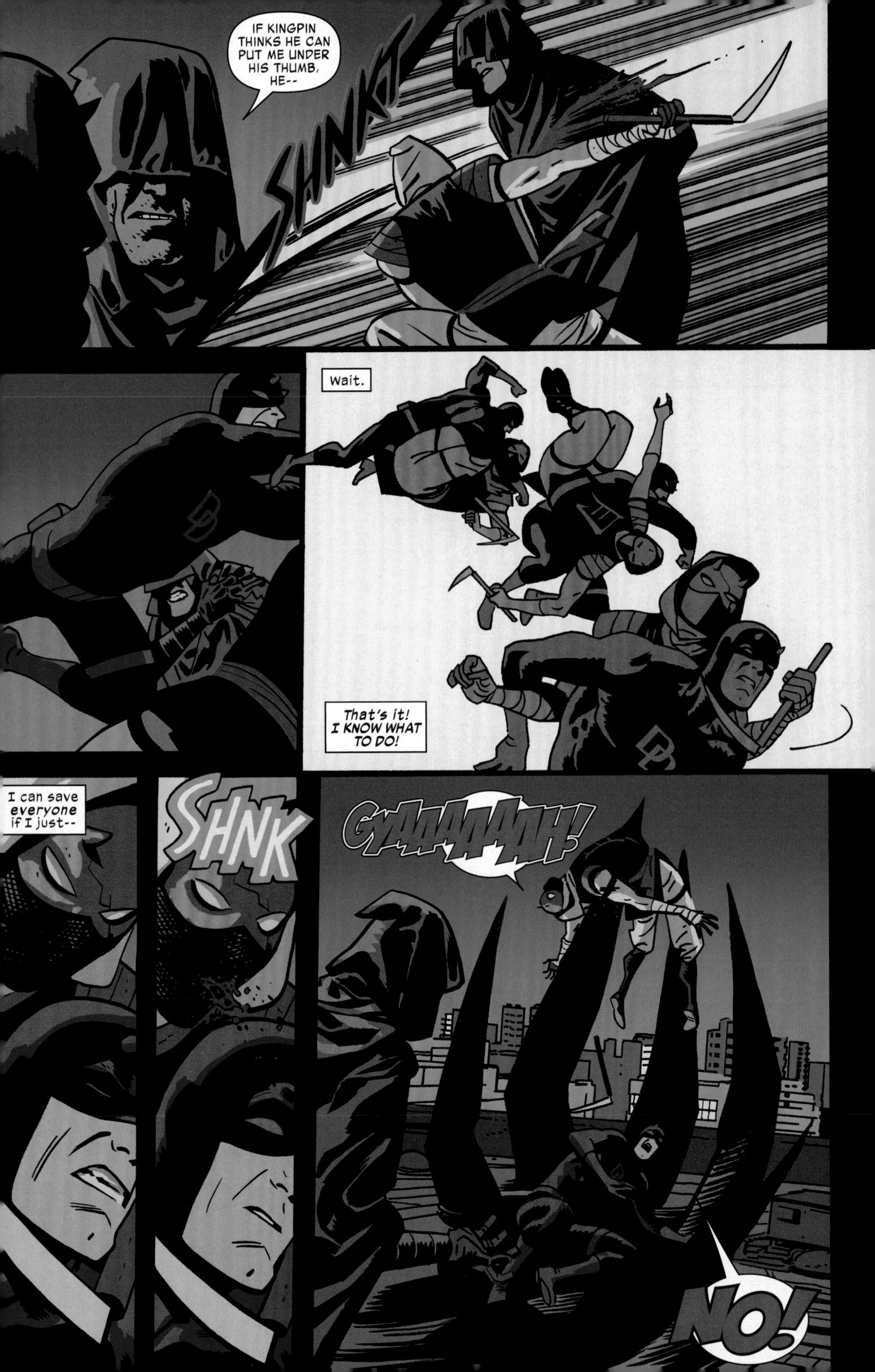

IF KINGPIN THINKS HE CAN PUT ME UNDER HIS THUMB, HE--
SHNKT
Wait.
That's it! I KNOW WHAT TO DO!
I can save *everyone* if I just--
SHNK
GYAAAAAAAH!
NO!

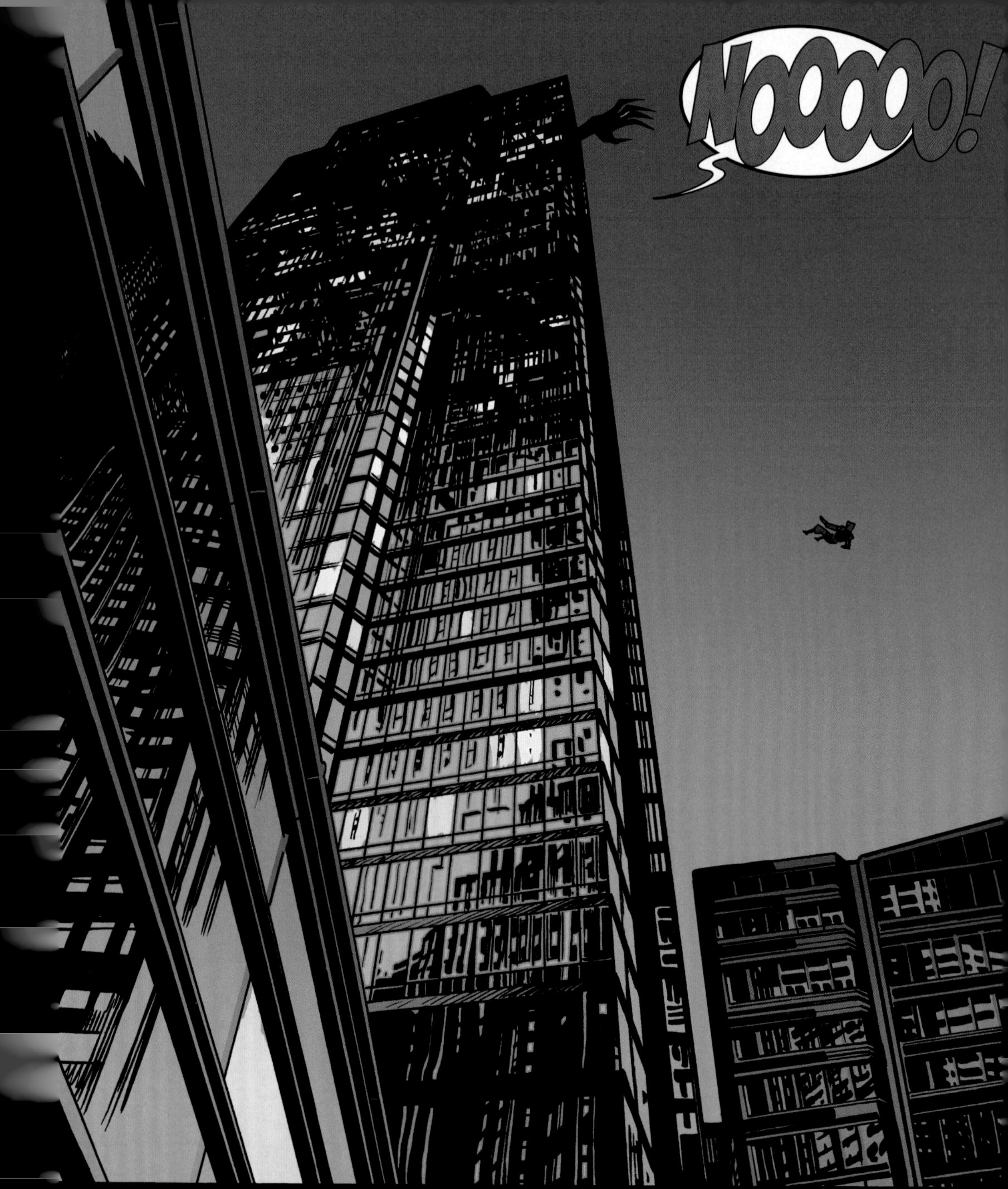
NOOOOO!

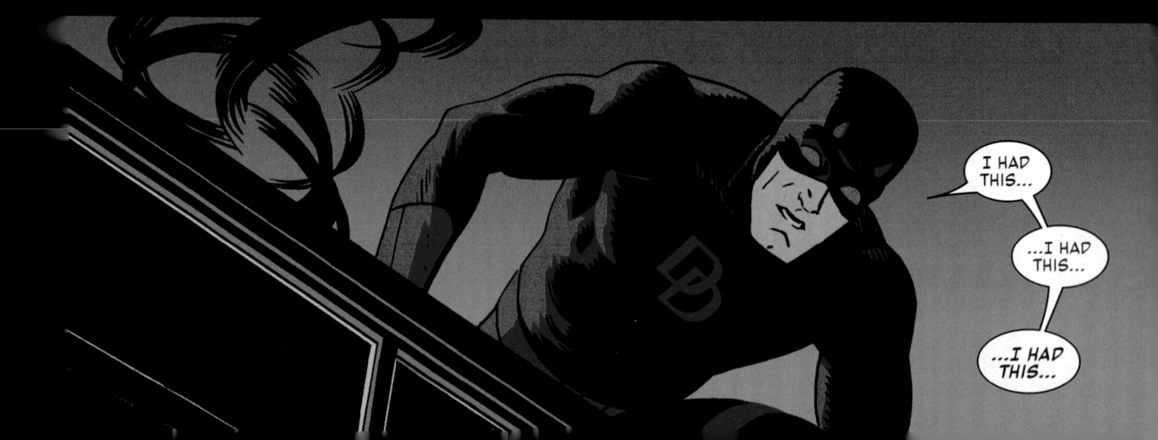
I HAD THIS...
...I HAD THIS...
...I HAD THIS...

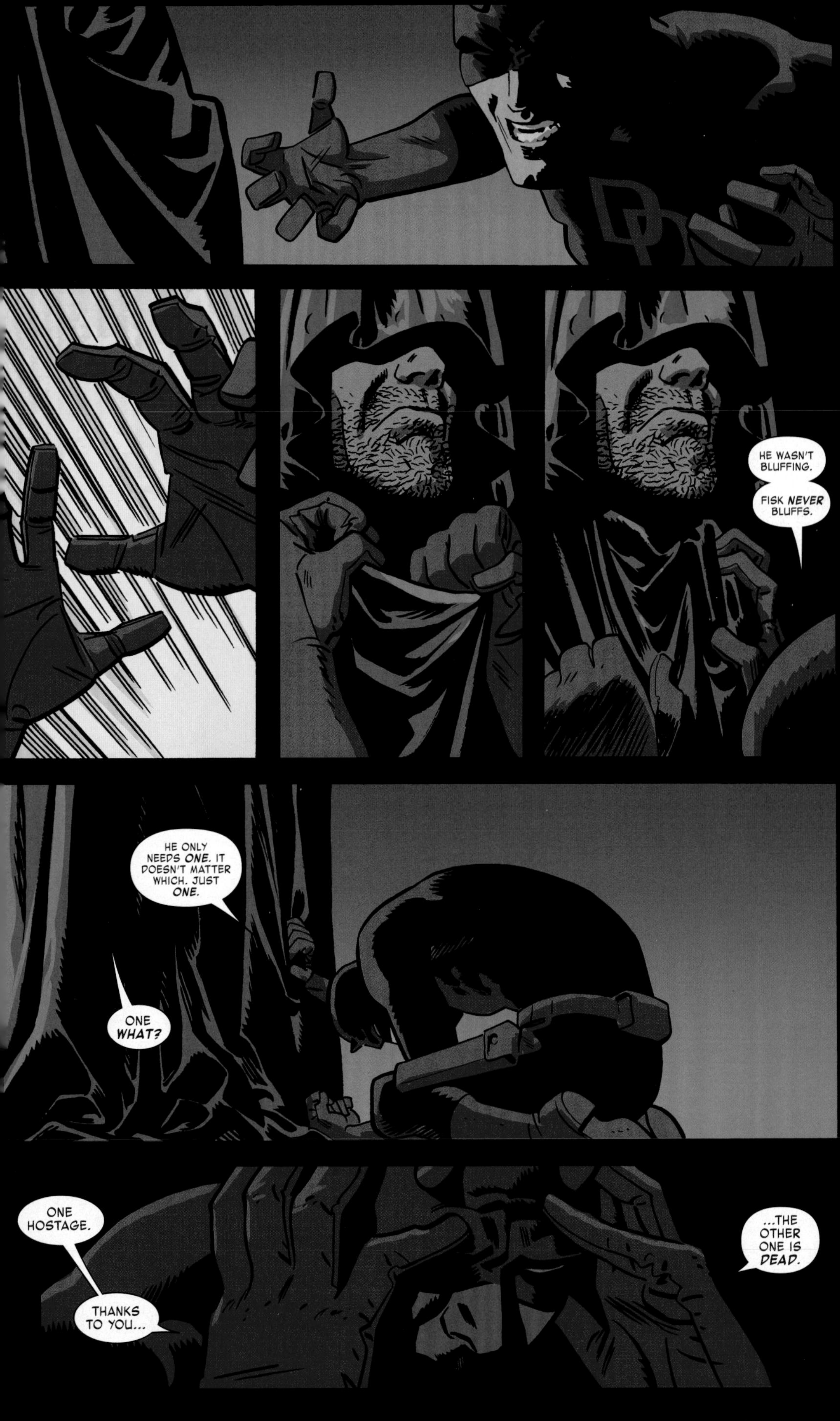
HE WASN'T BLUFFING.
FISK NEVER BLUFFS.
HE ONLY NEEDS ONE. IT DOESN'T MATTER WHICH. JUST ONE.
ONE WHAT?
ONE HOSTAGE.
THANKS TO YOU...
...THE OTHER ONE IS DEAD.

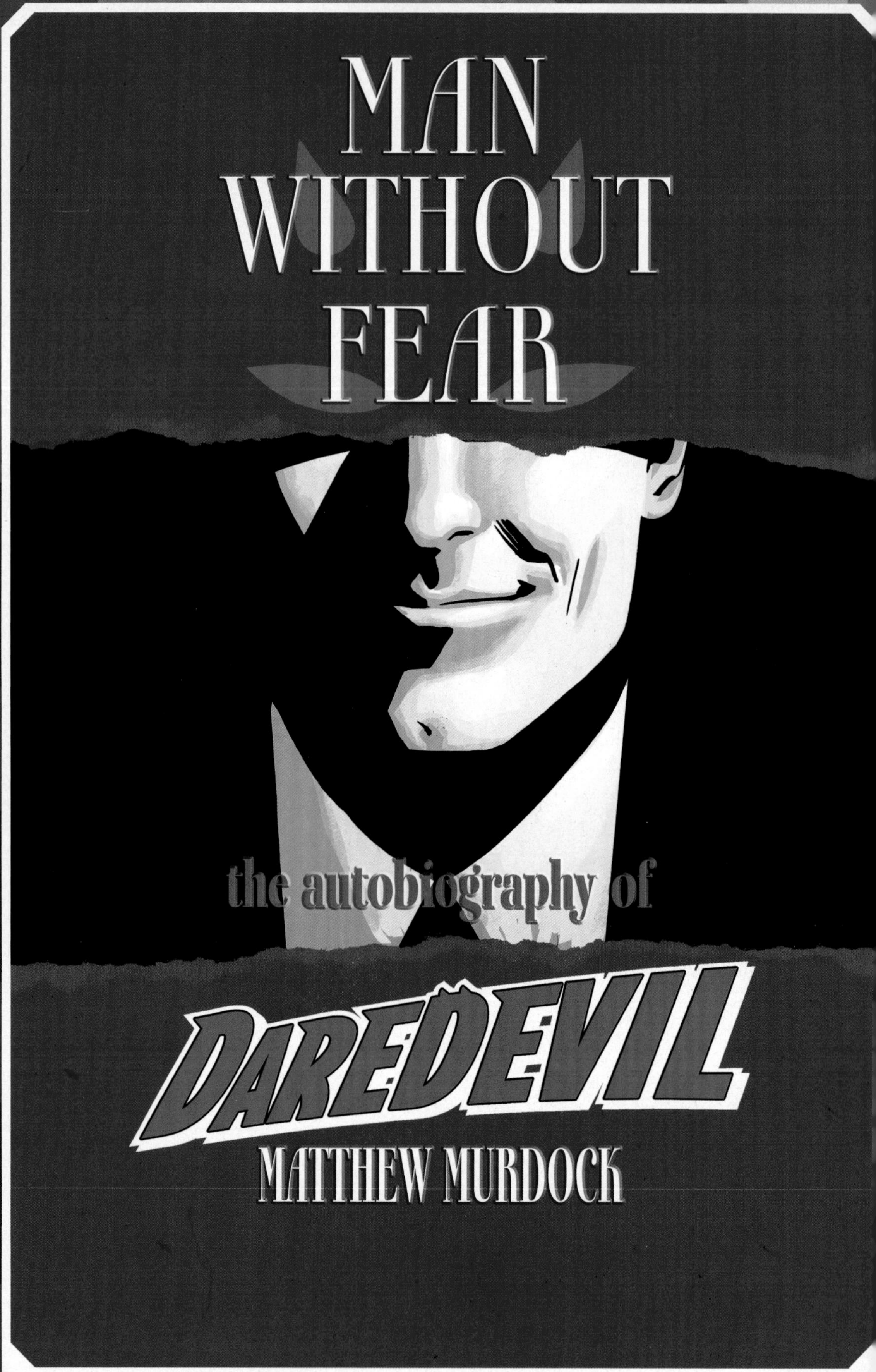

MAN WITHOUT FEAR

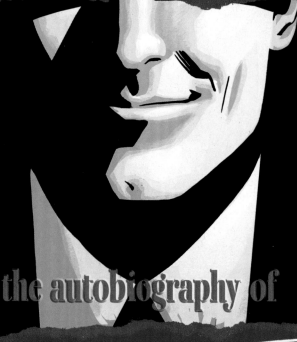

the autobiography of

DAREDEVIL

MATTHEW MURDOCK

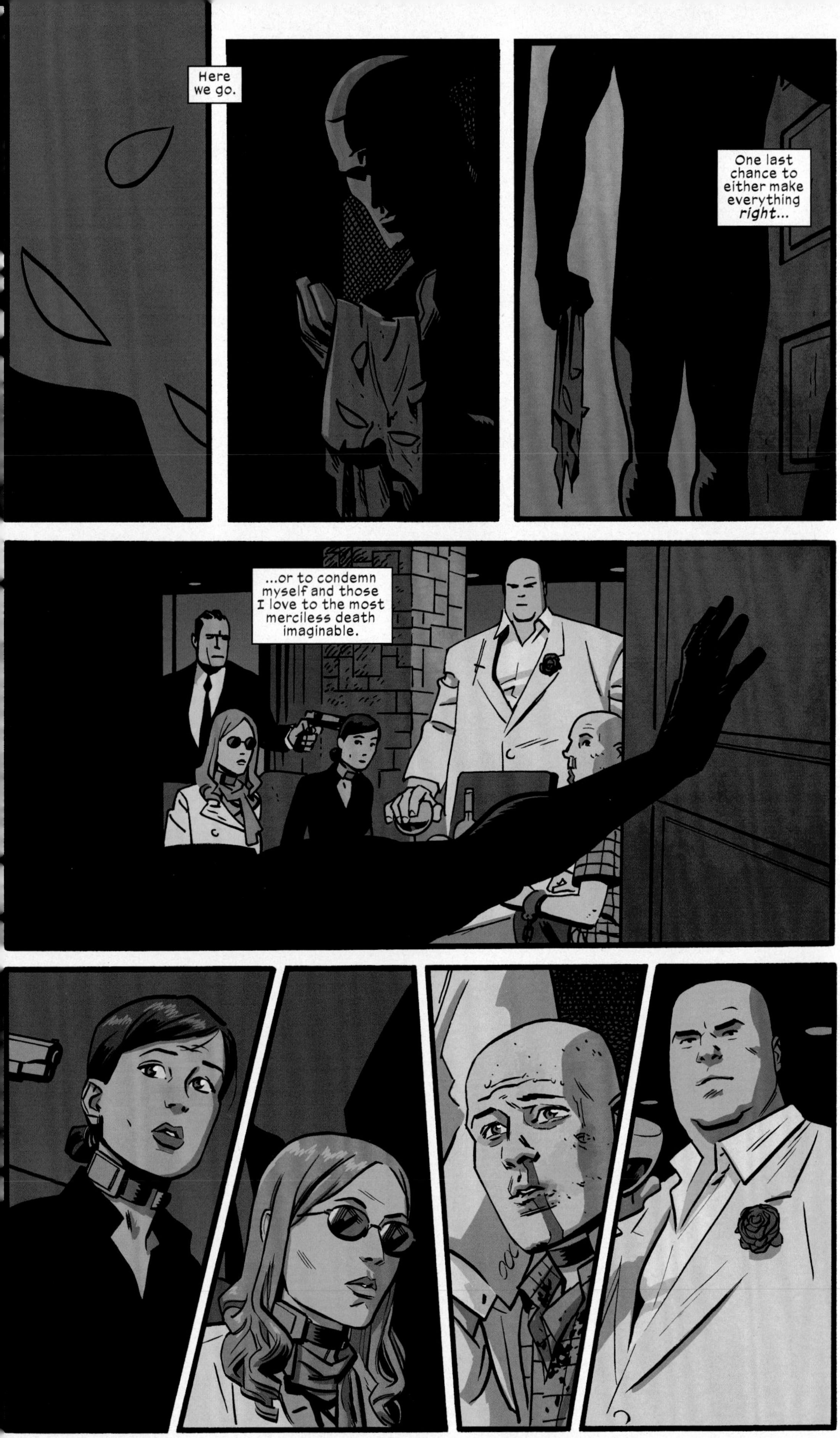
Here we go.
One last chance to either make everything *right*...
...or to condemn myself and those I love to the most merciless death imaginable.

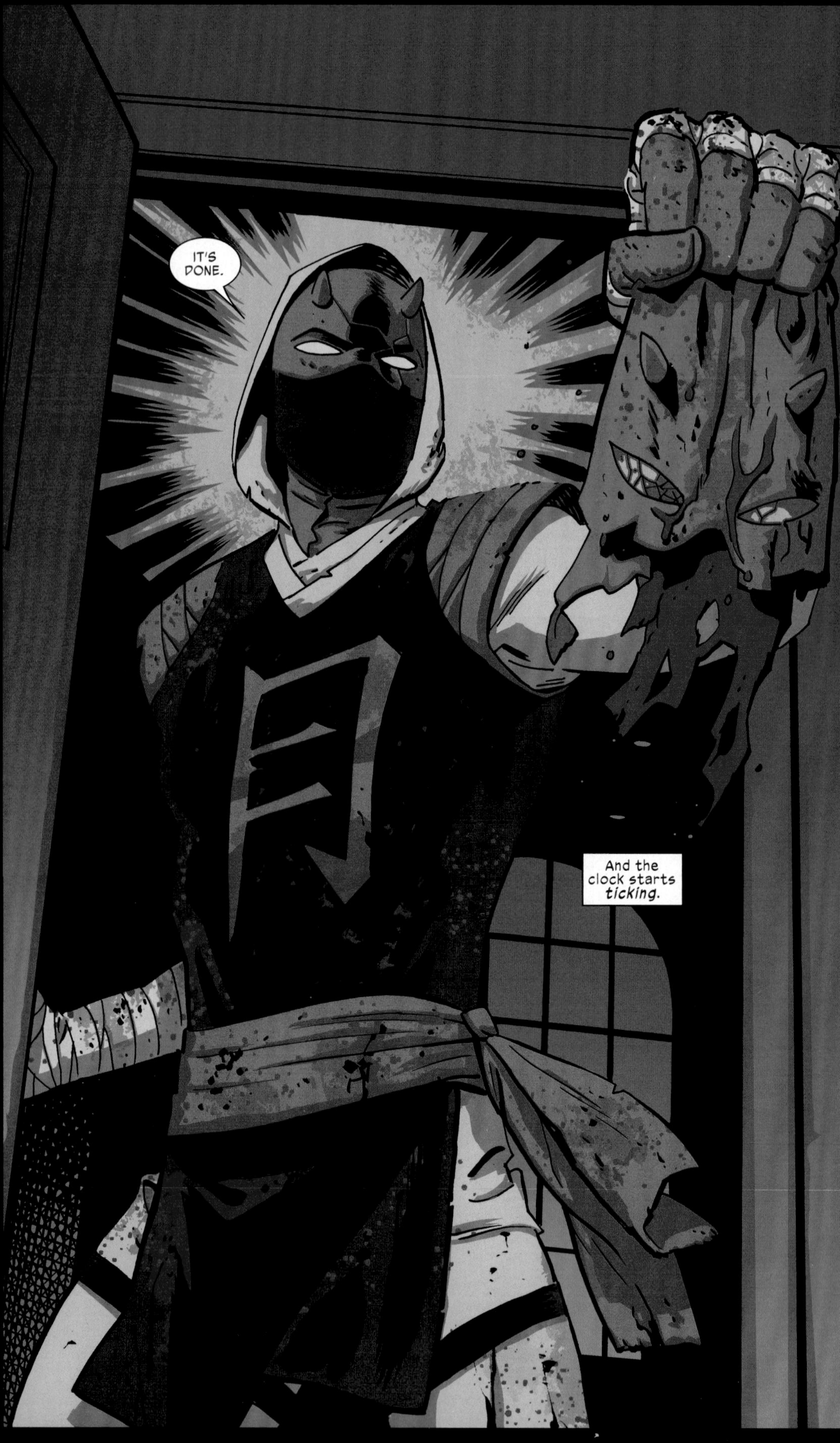
IT'S DONE.
And the clock starts *ticking*.

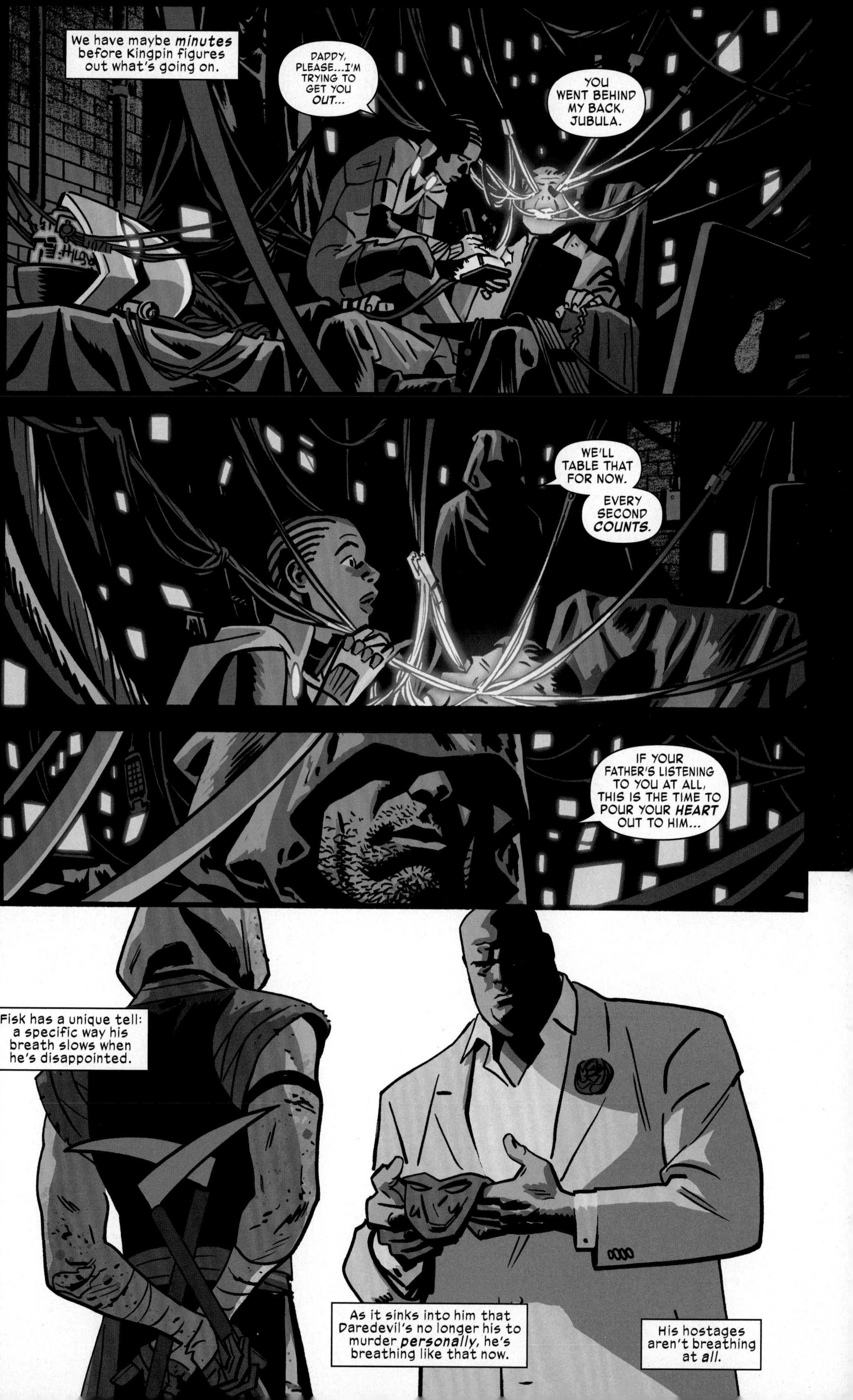
We have maybe *minutes* before Kingpin figures out what's going on.
DADDY, PLEASE...I'M TRYING TO GET YOU *OUT*...
YOU WENT BEHIND MY BACK, JUBULA.
WE'LL TABLE THAT FOR NOW.
EVERY SECOND *COUNTS.*
IF YOUR FATHER'S LISTENING TO YOU AT ALL, THIS IS THE TIME TO POUR YOUR *HEART* OUT TO HIM...
Fisk has a unique tell: a specific way his breath slows when he's disappointed.
As it sinks into him that Daredevil's no longer his to murder *personally*, he's breathing like that now.
His hostages aren't breathing at *all*.

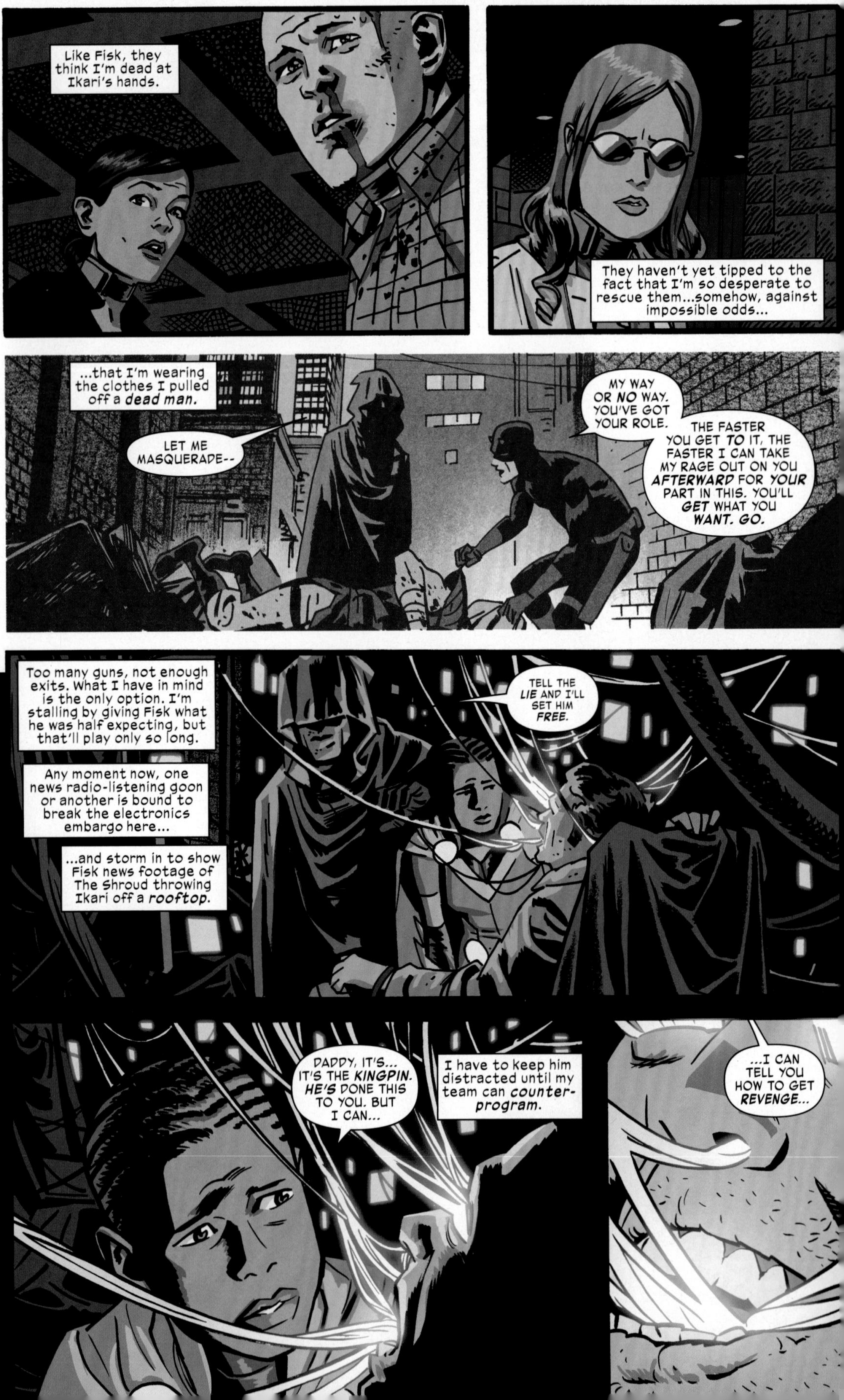
Like Fisk, they think I'm dead at Ikari's hands.
They haven't yet tipped to the fact that I'm so desperate to rescue them...somehow, against impossible odds...
...that I'm wearing the clothes I pulled off a *dead man.*
LET ME MASQUERADE--
MY WAY OR *NO* WAY. YOU'VE GOT YOUR ROLE.
THE FASTER YOU GET *TO* IT, THE FASTER I CAN TAKE MY RAGE OUT ON YOU *AFTERWARD* FOR *YOUR* PART IN THIS. YOU'LL *GET* WHAT YOU *WANT. GO.*
Too many guns, not enough exits. What I have in mind is the only option. I'm stalling by giving Fisk what he was half expecting, but that'll play only so long.
Any moment now, one news radio-listening goon or another is bound to break the electronics embargo here...
...and storm in to show Fisk news footage of The Shroud throwing Ikari off a *rooftop*.
TELL THE *LIE* AND I'LL SET HIM *FREE.*
DADDY, IT'S... IT'S THE *KINGPIN. HE'S* DONE THIS TO YOU. BUT I CAN...
I have to keep him distracted until my team can *counter-program*.
...I CAN TELL YOU HOW TO GET *REVENGE...*

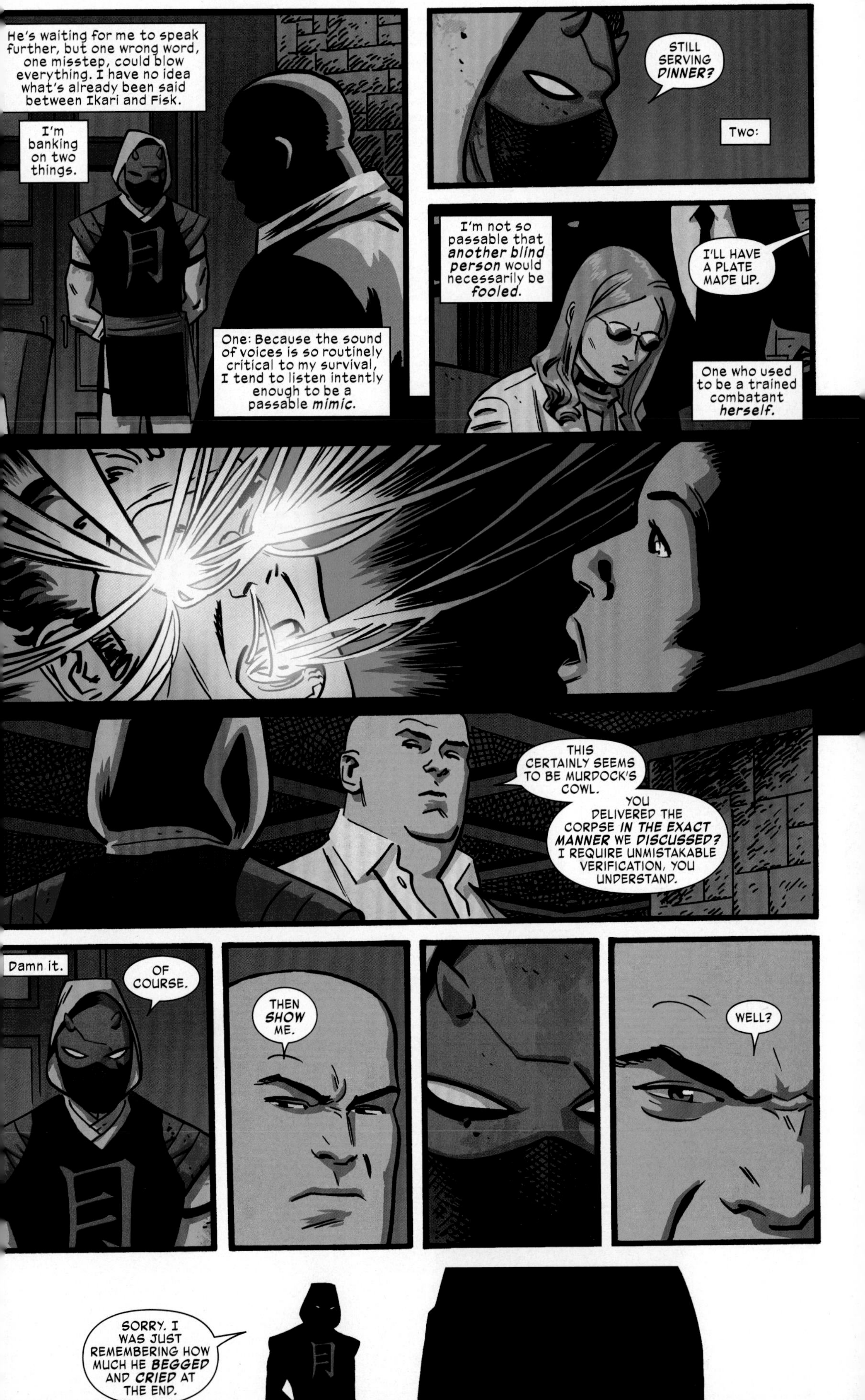
He's waiting for me to speak further, but one wrong word, one misstep, could blow everything. I have no idea what's already been said between Ikari and Fisk.
I'm banking on two things.
One: Because the sound of voices is so routinely critical to my survival, I tend to listen intently enough to be a passable *mimic*.
STILL SERVING *DINNER?*
Two:
I'm not so passable that *another blind person* would necessarily be *fooled*.
I'LL HAVE A PLATE MADE UP.
One who used to be a trained combatant *herself*.
THIS CERTAINLY SEEMS TO BE MURDOCK'S COWL.
YOU DELIVERED THE CORPSE *IN THE EXACT MANNER* WE *DISCUSSED?* I REQUIRE UNMISTAKABLE VERIFICATION, YOU UNDERSTAND.
Damn it.
OF COURSE.
THEN *SHOW* ME.
WELL?
SORRY. I WAS JUST REMEMBERING HOW MUCH HE *BEGGED* AND *CRIED* AT THE END.

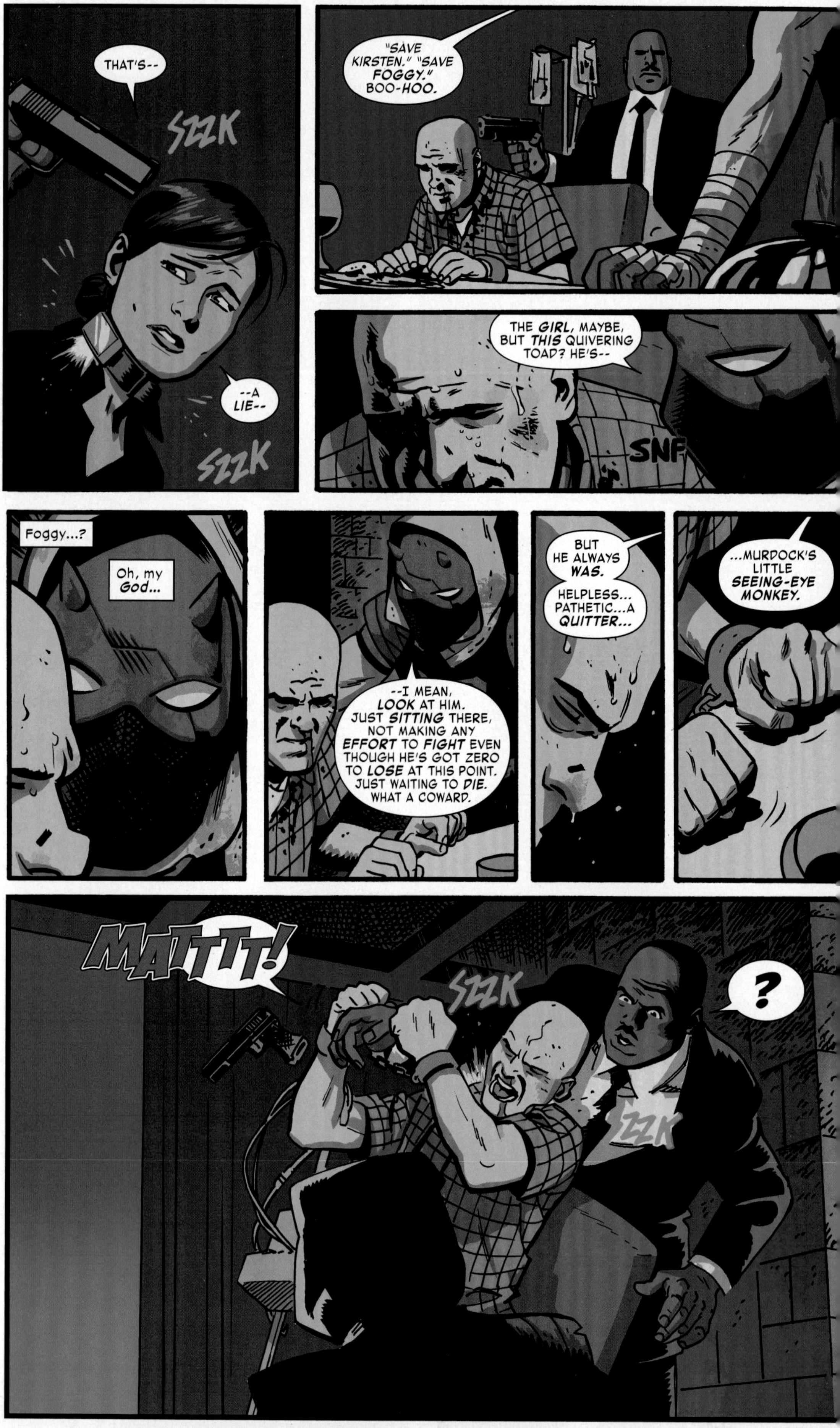

THAT'S--
SZZK
--A LIE--
SZZK
"SAVE KIRSTEN." "SAVE FOGGY." BOO-HOO.
THE GIRL, MAYBE, BUT THIS QUIVERING TOAD? HE'S--
SNF
Foggy...?
Oh, my God...
--I MEAN, LOOK AT HIM. JUST SITTING THERE, NOT MAKING ANY EFFORT TO FIGHT EVEN THOUGH HE'S GOT ZERO TO LOSE AT THIS POINT. JUST WAITING TO DIE. WHAT A COWARD.
BUT HE ALWAYS WAS.
HELPLESS... PATHETIC...A QUITTER...
...MURDOCK'S LITTLE SEEING-EYE MONKEY.
MATTTT!
SZZK
?
SZZK

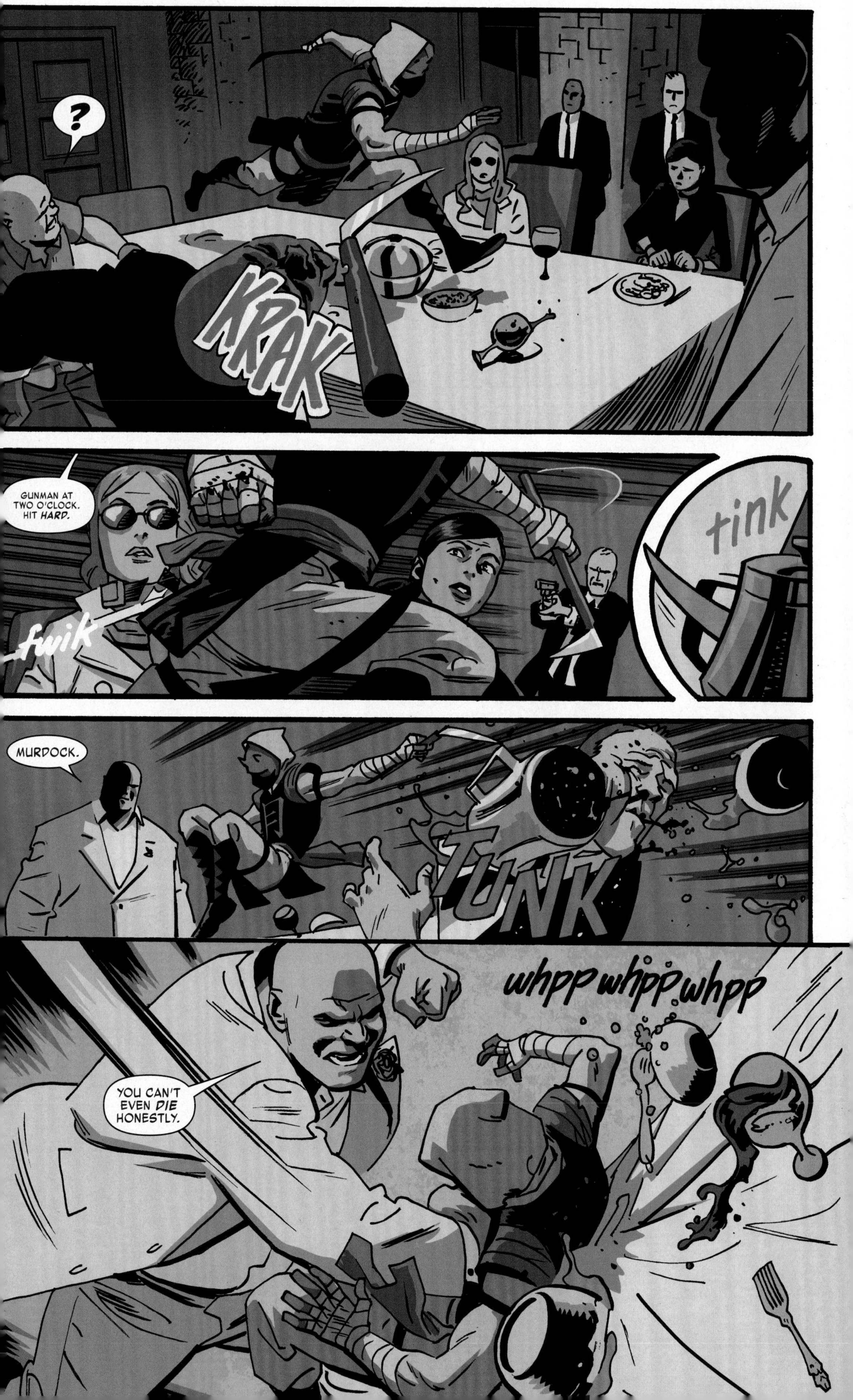
?
KRAK
GUNMAN AT TWO O'CLOCK. HIT HARD.
fwik
tink
MURDOCK.
TUNK
whpp whpp whpp
YOU CAN'T EVEN DIE HONESTLY.

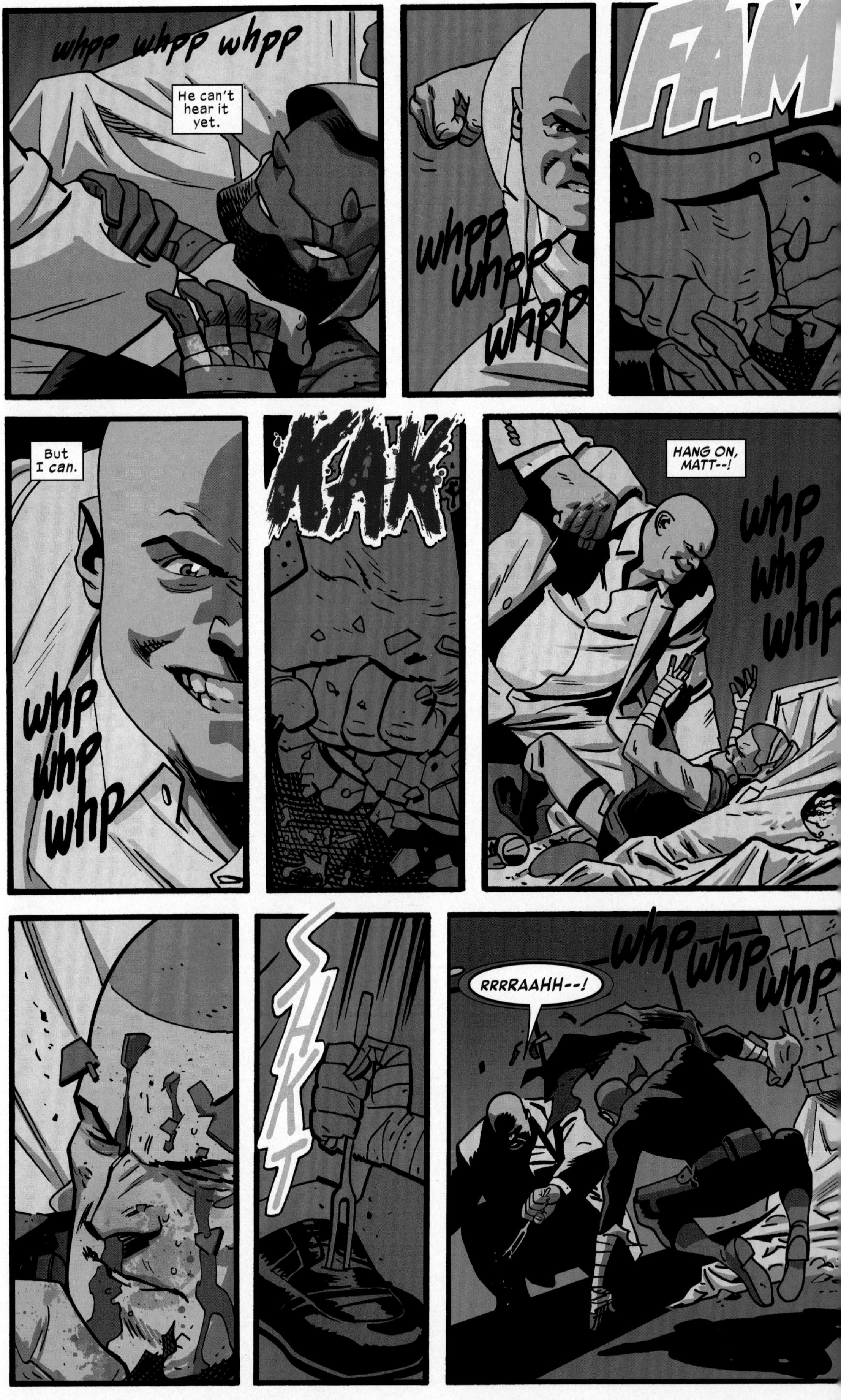
whpp whpp whpp
He can't hear it yet.
whpp whpp whpp
FAM
But I can.
whp whp whp
KAK
HANG ON, MATT--!
whp whp whp
SHKT
whp whp whp
RRRRAAHH--!

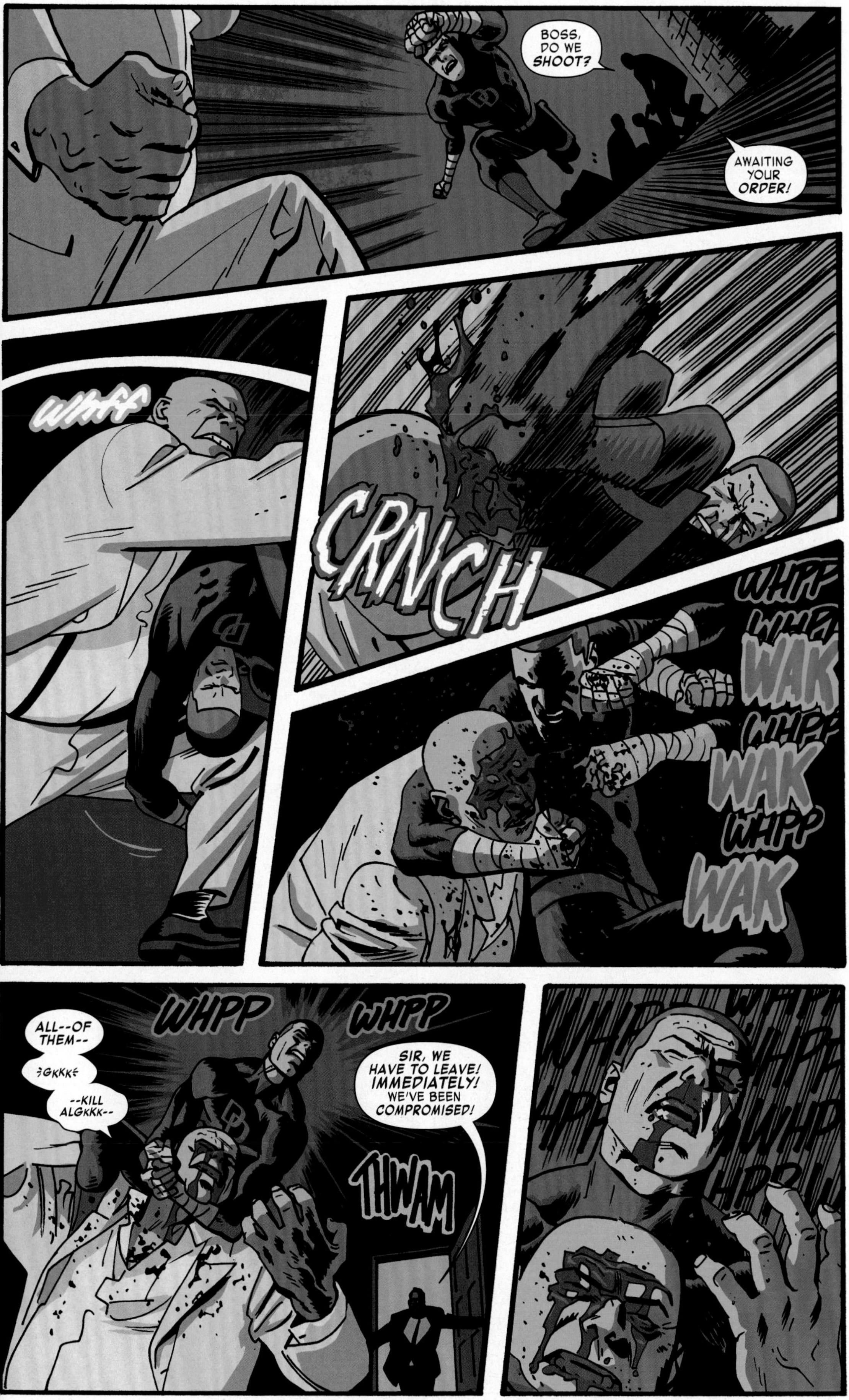
BOSS, DO WE SHOOT?
AWAITING YOUR ORDER!
WHFF
CRNCH
WHPP
WHPP
WAK
WHPP
WAK
WHPP
WAK
WHPP
ALL--OF THEM--
GKKK
--KILL ALGKKK--
WHPP
SIR, WE HAVE TO LEAVE! IMMEDIATELY! WE'VE BEEN COMPROMISED!
THWAM

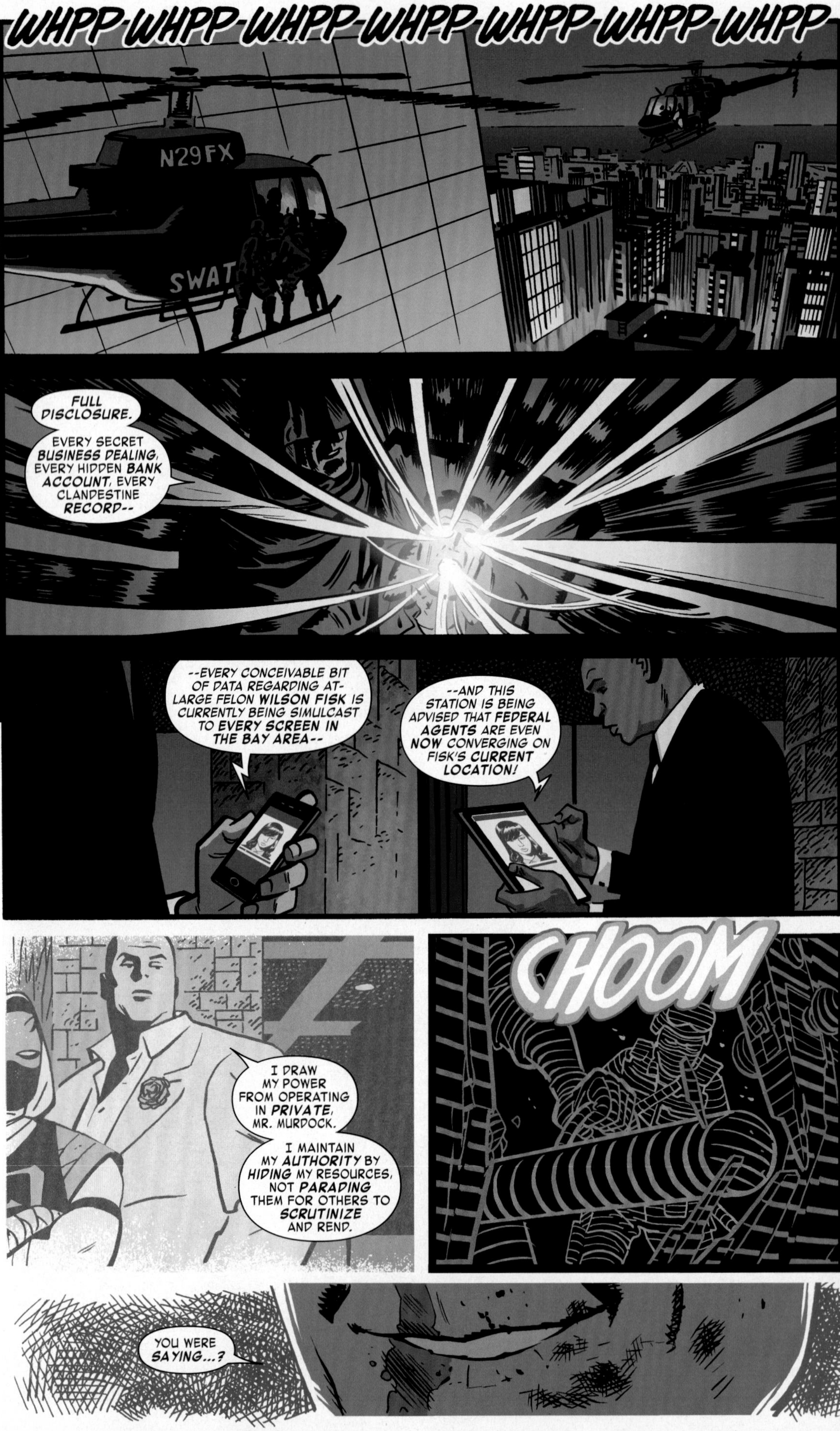
WHPP-WHPP-WHPP-WHPP-WHPP-WHPP-WHPP
N29FX
SWAT
FULL DISCLOSURE.
EVERY SECRET BUSINESS DEALING, EVERY HIDDEN BANK ACCOUNT, EVERY CLANDESTINE RECORD--
--EVERY CONCEIVABLE BIT OF DATA REGARDING AT-LARGE FELON WILSON FISK IS CURRENTLY BEING SIMULCAST TO EVERY SCREEN IN THE BAY AREA--
--AND THIS STATION IS BEING ADVISED THAT FEDERAL AGENTS ARE EVEN NOW CONVERGING ON FISK'S CURRENT LOCATION!
I DRAW MY POWER FROM OPERATING IN PRIVATE, MR. MURDOCK.
I MAINTAIN MY AUTHORITY BY HIDING MY RESOURCES, NOT PARADING THEM FOR OTHERS TO SCRUTINIZE AND REND.
CHOOM
YOU WERE SAYING...?

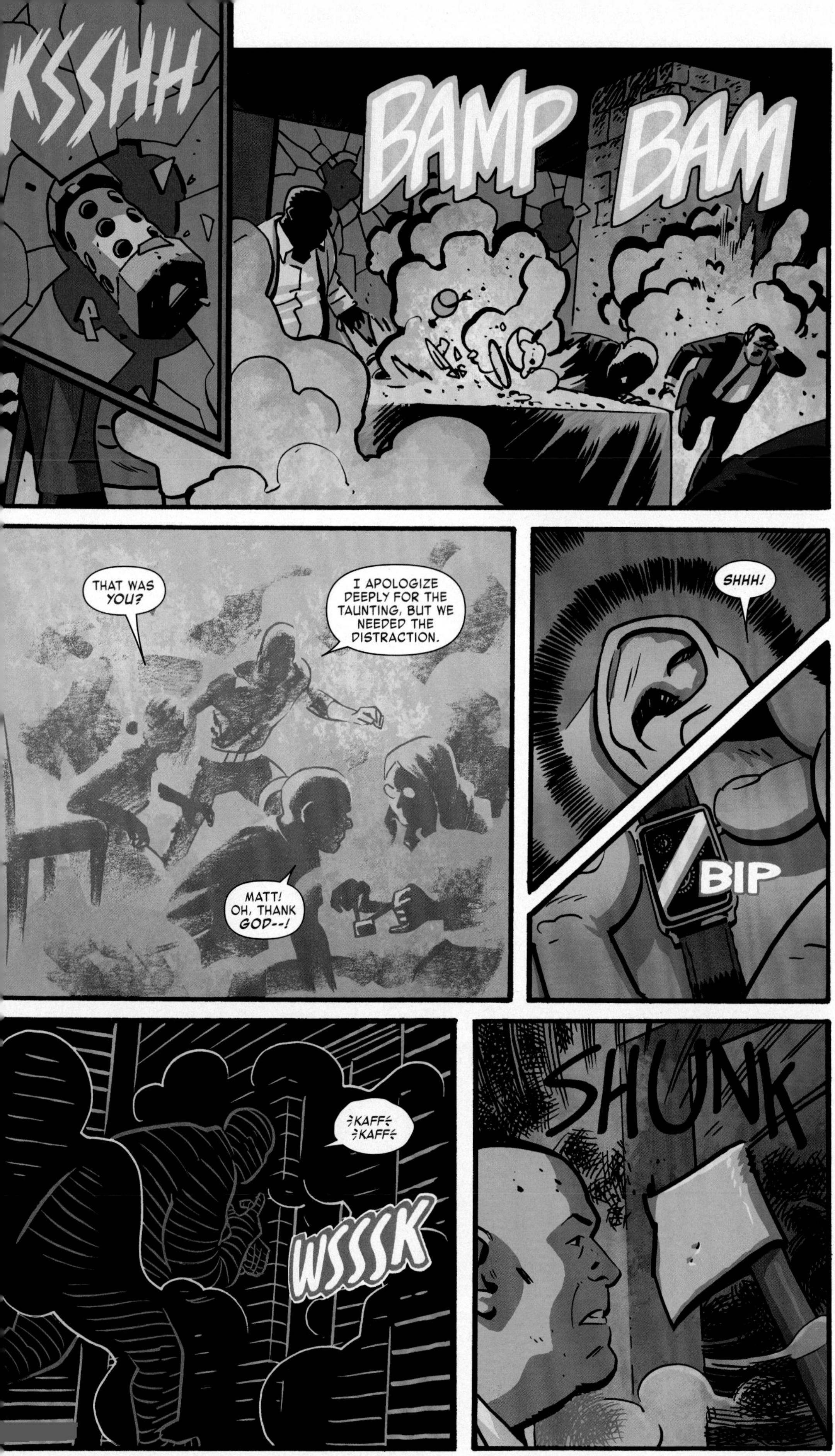
KSSHH
BAMP BAM
THAT WAS YOU?
I APOLOGIZE DEEPLY FOR THE TAUNTING, BUT WE NEEDED THE DISTRACTION.
MATT! OH, THANK GOD--!
SHHH!
BIP
KAFF KAFF
WSSSK
SHUNK

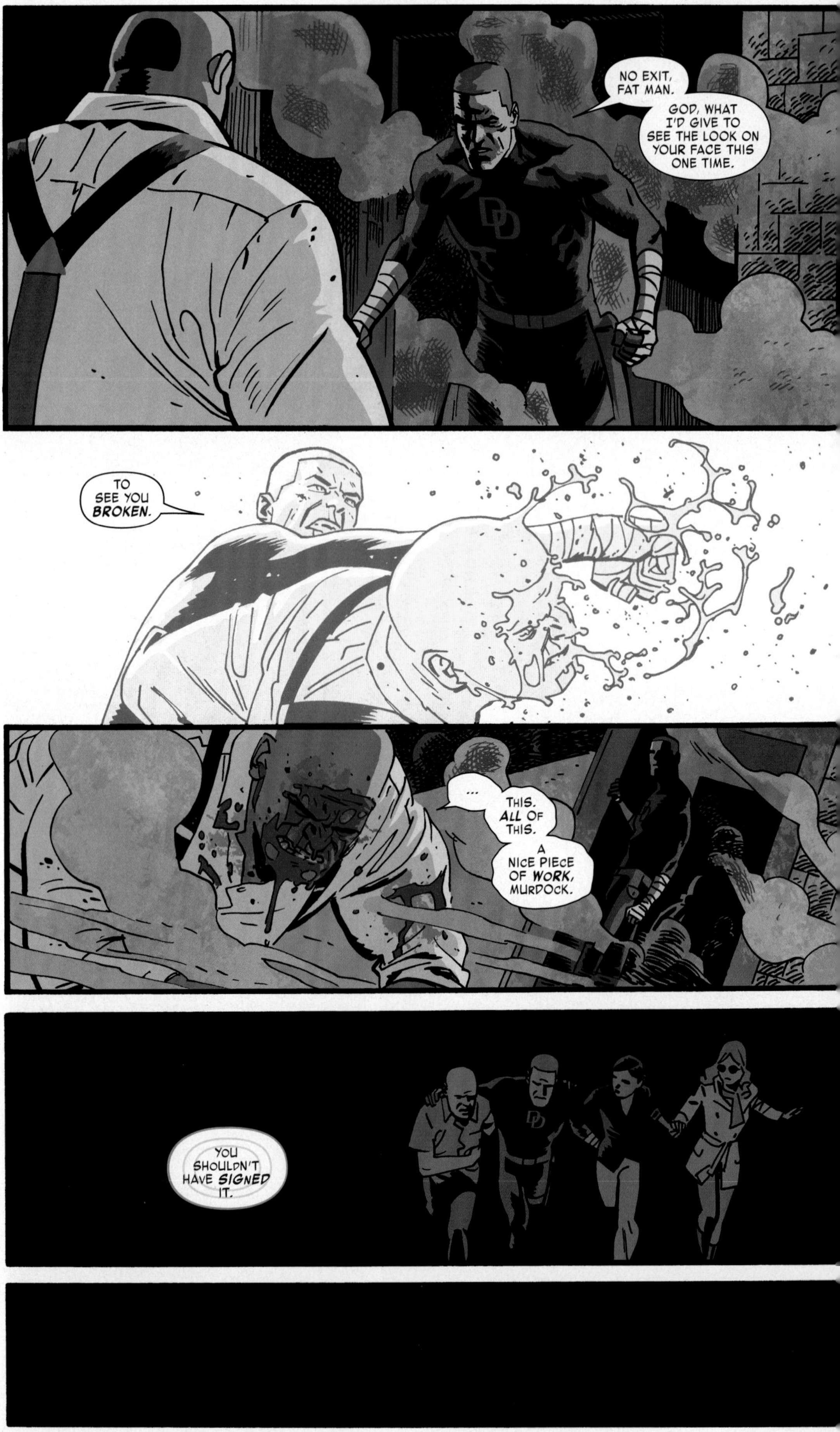
NO EXIT, FAT MAN.
GOD, WHAT I'D GIVE TO SEE THE LOOK ON YOUR FACE THIS ONE TIME.
TO SEE YOU **BROKEN.**
...
THIS. **ALL** OF THIS.
A NICE PIECE OF **WORK,** MURDOCK.
YOU SHOULDN'T HAVE **SIGNED** IT.

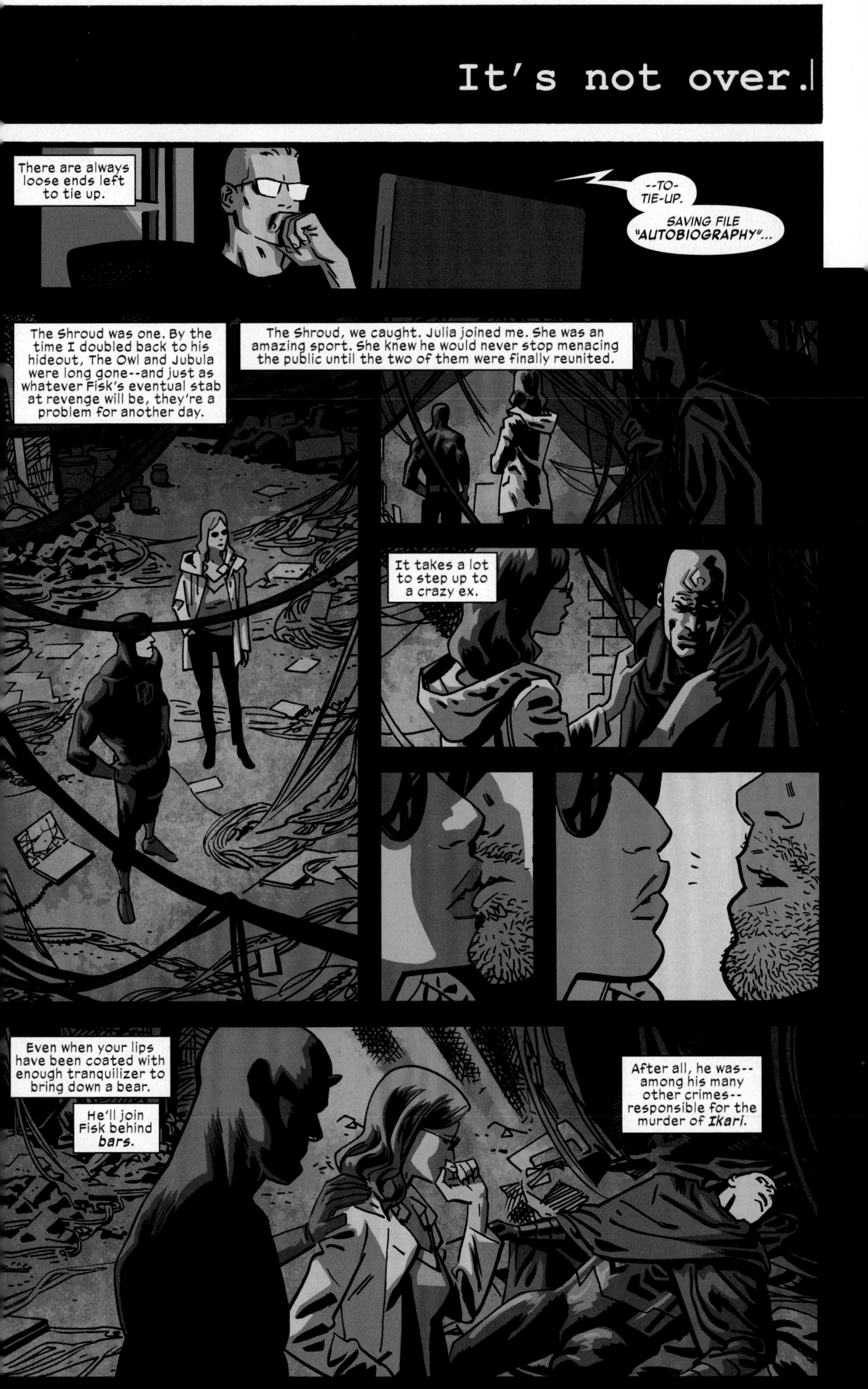
It's not over.
There are always loose ends left to tie up.
--TO-TIE-UP.
SAVING FILE "AUTOBIOGRAPHY"...
The Shroud was one. By the time I doubled back to his hideout, The Owl and Jubula were long gone--and just as whatever Fisk's eventual stab at revenge will be, they're a problem for another day.
The Shroud, we caught. Julia joined me. She was an amazing sport. She knew he would never stop menacing the public until the two of them were finally reunited.
It takes a lot to step up to a crazy ex.
Even when your lips have been coated with enough tranquilizer to bring down a bear.
He'll join Fisk behind *bars*.
After all, he was--among his many other crimes--responsible for the murder of *Ikari*.

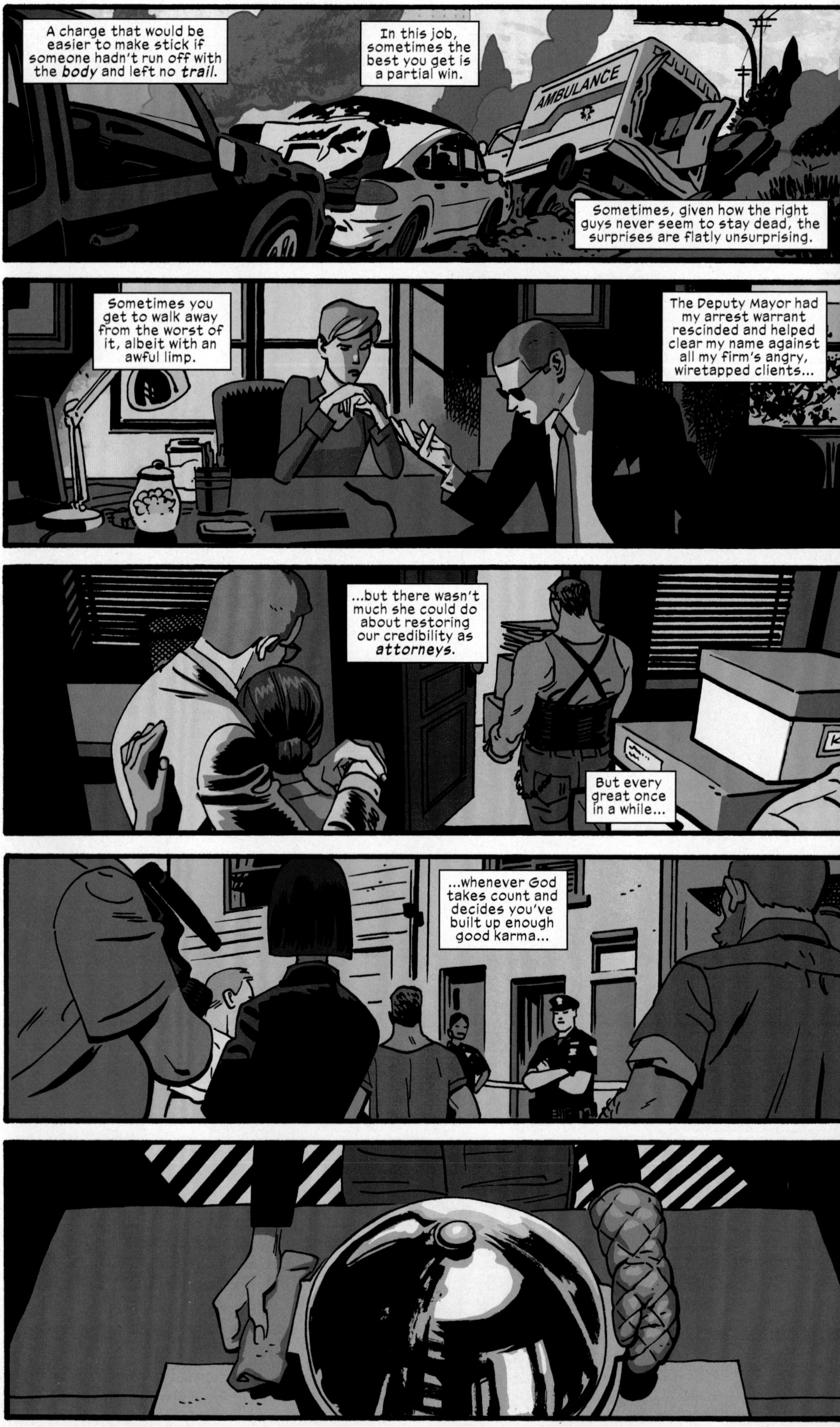
A charge that would be easier to make stick if someone hadn't run off with the *body* and left no *trail.*
In this job, sometimes the best you get is a partial win.
AMBULANCE
Sometimes, given how the right guys never seem to stay dead, the surprises are flatly unsurprising.
Sometimes you get to walk away from the worst of it, albeit with an awful limp.
The Deputy Mayor had my arrest warrant rescinded and helped clear my name against all my firm's angry, wiretapped clients...
...but there wasn't much she could do about restoring our credibility as *attorneys.*
But every great once in a while...
...whenever God takes count and decides you've built up enough good karma...
...

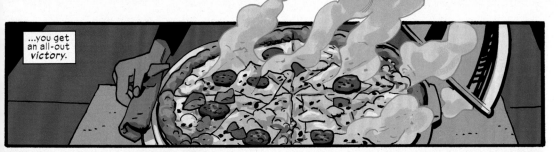

...you get an all-out *victory.*

OH, *GOD,* FOGGY--!

...*MMMM!* yyysdd I clld ≥MMPPH≤ hvve MMM-ything...

BECAUSE I DIDN'T KNOW THERE WAS SUCH A THING AS WEAPONS-GRADE *HEAD CHEESE!*

Iffff ≥SMACK≤ my pzzza.

THAT'S NOT *PIZZA.* PIZZA DOESN'T MAKE ANGELS *CRY.* WHY IS THERE KETCHUP ON IT?

BE GLAD YOU'RE NOT THE ONE WHO VOLUNTEERED TO MAKE IT FOR HIM. HE'S RUINED ENTIRE *FOOD GROUPS* FOR ME.

I'VE MISSED THESE LITTLE LECTURES.

YOU'RE THE TWO WHO SUGGESTED WE *CELEBRATE.*

WHEN I CAUGHT A WHIFF OF YOUR *BODY CHEMISTRY* BACK IN FISK'S DINING ROOM, I NEARLY BROKE CHARACTER. IT GAVE ME *HOPE.*

HOPE *REWARDED.* MY DOCTOR SAYS MY CANCER'S IN *FULL REMISSION.*

CONGRATULATIONS, SIR. WELL DESERVED.

TOMORROW, BACK TO A SENSIBLE DIET?

I PROMISE. TODAY, I DINE LIKE A SEVEN-YEAR-OLD WITH A PRIVATE CHEF.

GARCÓN! MY PORK RINDS AU JUS, PLEASE!

DESSERT IS FOR *CLOSERS.* ARE YOU TWO READY TO GO JOIN MY DAD AGAINST A SEA OF *REPORTERS* SO WE CAN GET ON WITH OUR *LIVES?*

THAT WAS THE DEAL.

THAT KEPT HIM FROM CANCELLING MY AUTOBIOGRAPHY AND *SUING* ME.

SMALL PRICE. C'MON. THIS IS A *WALK* OF THE *CAKE* VARIETY. THEY JUST WANT TO KNOW DEETS LIKE WHY YOU FAKED FOGGY'S DEATH, WHY OUR CLIENTS GOT RECORDED, ETCETERA.

ALL OF WHICH YOU HAVE PERFECTLY GOOD ANSWERS FOR.

PUT ON YOUR *CHARM,* DO THAT WHOLE *GRATINGLY TRANSPARENT* THING, AND WE CAN FINALLY MOVE ON TO WHATEVER'S *NEXT* IN THIS WACKO LIFE.

READY?

AFTER YOU.

CAN WE GET THIS SHOW ON THE ROAD, PLEASE?

SORRY. GANG'S ALL HERE, DAD.

OH?

MATTY, WHAT THE *HELL*--?

COUNSELOR, WHAT'S *WRONG?* DON'T TELL ME YOU'VE GOT *COLD FEET* ALL OF A SUDDEN!

HEY, MATT MURDOCK IS THE *MAN WITHOUT FEA*--

THAT'S *CRAP!* STOP *SAYING* THAT!

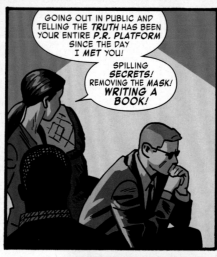

GOING OUT IN PUBLIC AND TELLING THE *TRUTH* HAS BEEN YOUR ENTIRE *P.R. PLATFORM* SINCE THE DAY I *MET* YOU!

SPILLING *SECRETS!* REMOVING THE *MASK!* WRITING A *BOOK!*

NOW, ALL OF A *SUDDEN*, BEING *HONEST* HAS YOU *SCARED?* NOW?

I WAS NEVER BEING *HONEST* EXCEPT ON *MY* TERMS! I WAS BEING *DEFIANT!*

THIS IS THE SECRET TO BEING "*FEARLESS*," OKAY? YOU ATTACK A PROBLEM BEFORE IT CAN ATTACK *YOU.*

OUTING MYSELF *THAT HARD* AND *THAT THOROUGHLY* WASN'T AN ACT OF INTEGRITY. IT WAS *RECKLESSNESS.*

IT WAS AN ATTEMPT TO *OUT-CLEVER* EVERYONE. TO TAKE MY SECRETS *OUT* OF THE MIX BEFORE THEY COULD BE USED *AGAINST* ME. THAT'S ALL. AND IT *BACKFIRED.* THAT WAS MY *AMMO.* THAT WAS OUR *PROTECTION.*

NOW WHAT DO WE HAVE TO *SHIELD* US?

EVERY DAY STANDING *NEXT* TO ME IS A *GAMBLE!*

WHO AM I TO BE SO *ARROGANT* AS TO BELIEVE I CAN ALWAYS *SAVE* YOU?

PERMISSION TO CROSS-EXAMINE.

NO OBJECTION.

IT'S THE 21st CENTURY. NO ONE GETS TO HIDE *SAFELY* BEHIND A *MASK* ANYMORE.

LISTEN TO ME.

THE *HORSE.*

IS *OUT.*

OF THE *BARN.*

YOU *TRIED* TO WHEN YOU WERE FIRST EXPOSED. YOU *"SAVED"* US, YOUR FRIENDS, BY *DOUBLING DOWN* AND LYING *POINT-BLANK* TO A GROUP OF REPORTERS *JUST LIKE THE ONE OUTSIDE,* SWEARING YOU *WEREN'T* WHO THEY *KNEW* YOU WERE--

--AND I HAVE *NEVER* FELT *LESS SAFE* IN MY *LIFE* BECAUSE YOU ARE MY *BEST FRIEND* AND I *DID NOT LIKE YOU* WHEN I SAW THE TRUTH!

MOTION TO STRIKE.

SHUT UP.

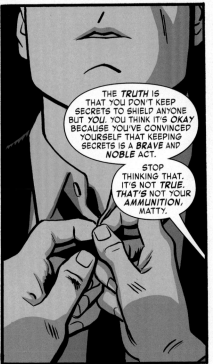

THE *TRUTH* IS THAT YOU DON'T KEEP SECRETS TO SHIELD ANYONE BUT *YOU.* YOU THINK IT'S *OKAY* BECAUSE YOU'VE CONVINCED YOURSELF THAT KEEPING SECRETS IS A *BRAVE* AND *NOBLE* ACT.

STOP THINKING THAT. IT'S NOT *TRUE. THAT'S* NOT YOUR *AMMUNITION,* MATTY.

WHEN YOU WERE A KID, YOU GOT BLINDED JUST TRYING TO HELP AN OLD MAN ACROSS THE STREET. THAT WASN'T FAIR.

EVER SINCE THEN, YOU'VE DEVOTED YOUR *LIFE* TO BALANCING THOSE SCALES. TO MAKING THE WORLD A *FAIRER PLACE* FOR EVERYONE *ELSE* DESPITE THE FACT THAT IT IS A *VAST, RANDOM ENTITY* OF *INCOMPREHENSIBLE POWER.*

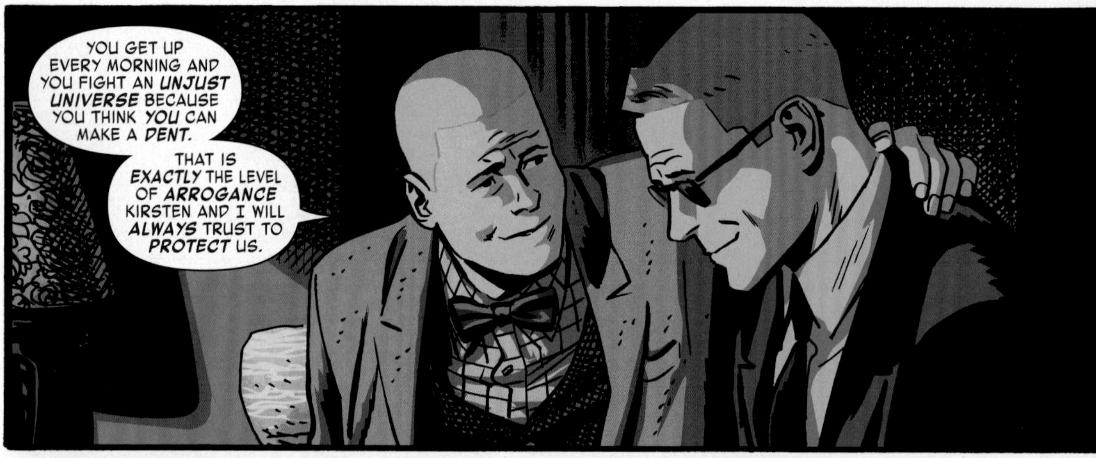
YOU GET UP EVERY MORNING AND YOU FIGHT AN UNJUST UNIVERSE BECAUSE YOU THINK YOU CAN MAKE A DENT.
THAT IS EXACTLY THE LEVEL OF ARROGANCE KIRSTEN AND I WILL ALWAYS TRUST TO PROTECT US.

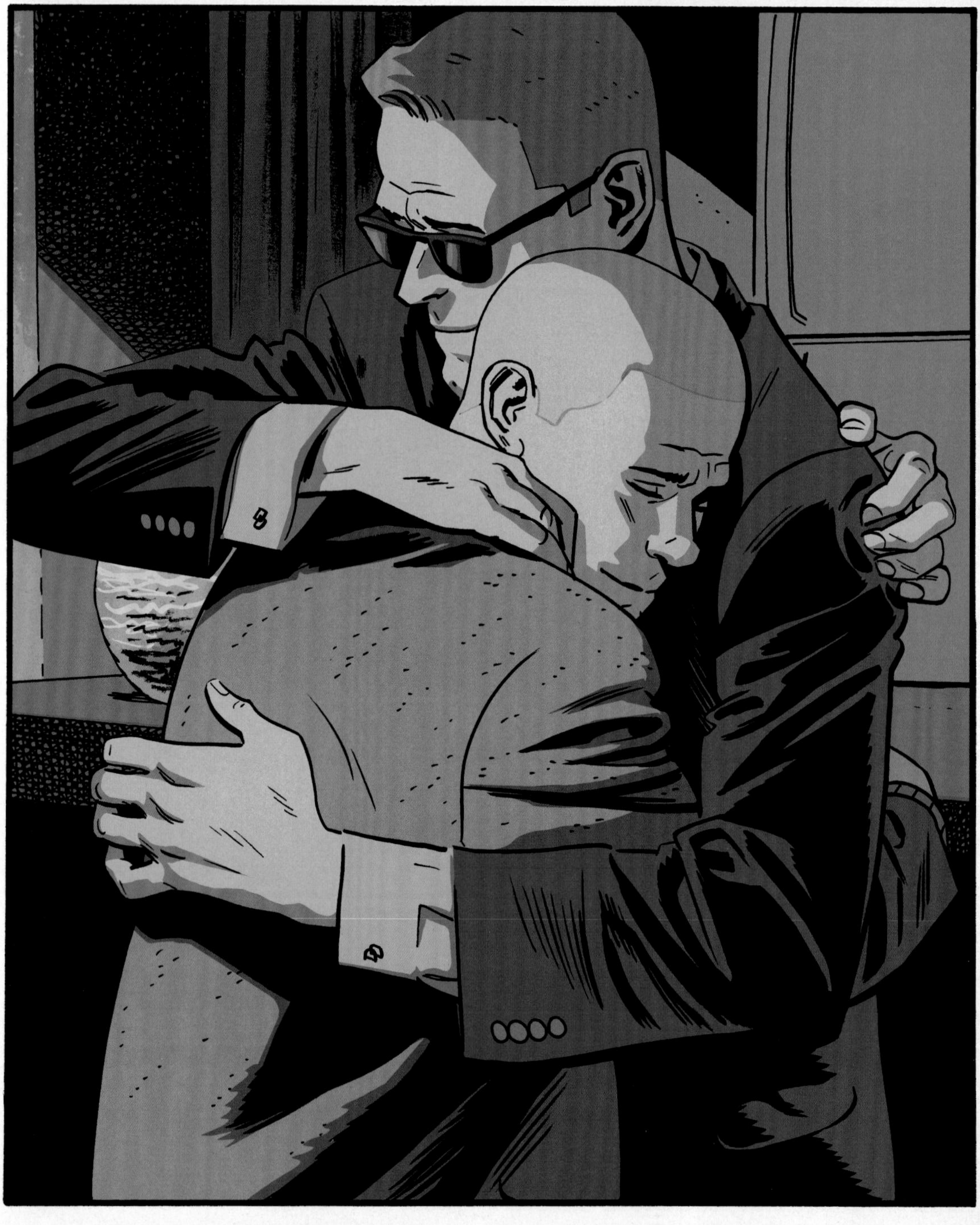

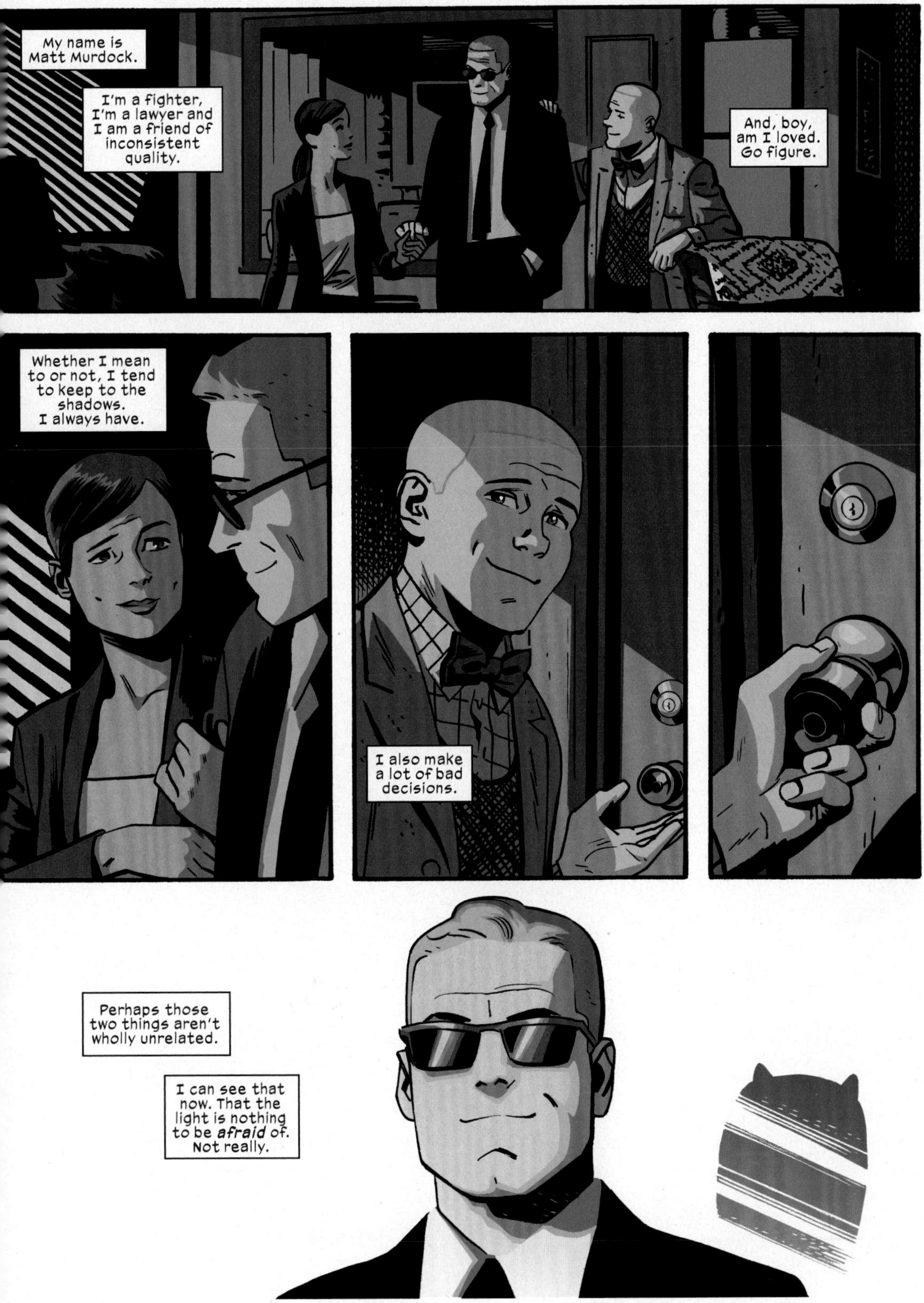
My name is Matt Murdock.
I'm a fighter, I'm a lawyer and I am a friend of inconsistent quality.
And, boy, am I loved. Go figure.
Whether I mean to or not, I tend to keep to the shadows. I always have.
I also make a lot of bad decisions.
Perhaps those two things aren't wholly unrelated.
I can see that now. That the light is nothing to be *afraid* of. Not really.

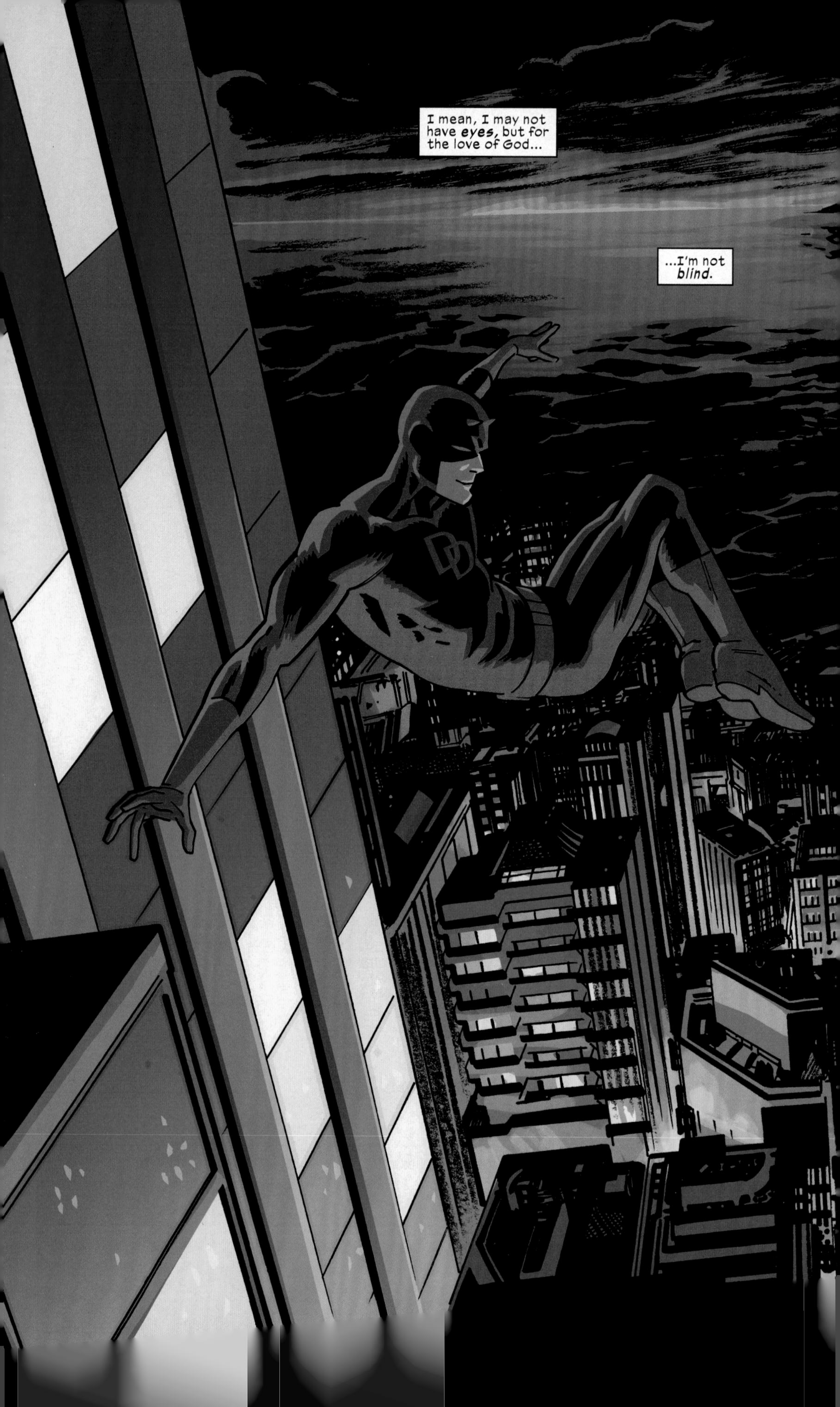
I mean, I may not have *eyes*, but for the love of God...
...I'm not *blind*.

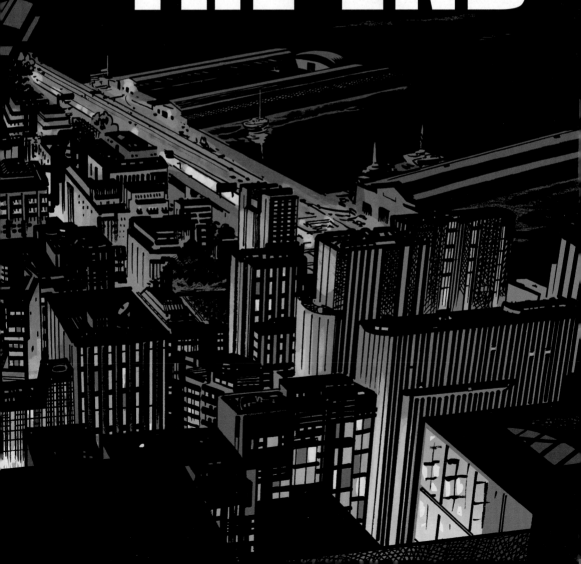

THE END

HERE COMES...

DAREDEVIL

THE MAN WITHOUT FEAR!

I have never had a better creative experience in comics than with Daredevil, and I hope it showed. I never dreamed I'd ever get this far into Matt Murdock's head, and now it's going to be a hell of a task to get back out of it. Every day still, as I have for the last four years, whenever I see or hear new things I immediately wonder how Matt would interpret them with his senses. It's been a weird but insightful habit.

I've been lucky enough to enjoy the longest unbroken run anyone's ever had on Daredevil, and that's only because I've been blessed with brilliant editors and collaborators. Steve Wacker, Ellie Pyle, and Sana Amanat have always had my back. Paolo Rivera, Marcos Martin, Javier Rodriguez, Matt Wilson and the inestimable Joe Caramagna elevated every issue. And when it comes to the staggeringly talented Chris Samnee, it's been pretty cool working with a guy who we all know is destined to be regarded as a giant in the field.

Thank you all for supporting us every issue. We've always tried hard to entertain and to be respectful to the characters, and your support would seem to indicate that we've succeeded. We're not going to give you a chance to miss us, though; the whole creative team--Chris, Matt, Joe and I--will be moving on to another Marvel series that you'll be hearing about soon. Best of luck to Charles Soule and Ron Garney as they take the baton (or billy club, if you will)--they won't let you down.

Mark Waid

• • • • • • • • • • • • • • • • •

Before the door closes behind us let me just say a huge thanks to my amazing collaborators Mark, Javier, Matt & Joe (who have made me look better than I have any right to), our wonderful editors (who have had our backs at every turn) and all the readers out there for all of your support.

This has been a wild few years-- and I can't thank you all enough for making my time on Daredevil such an enjoyable one.

Chris Samnee

• • • • • • • • • • • • • • • • •

I couldn't be happier to be a part of this terrific run. I've enjoyed my year on the book, and I'm grateful to the editors and creative team for having me on.

I've also greatly appreciated all the support that the Daredevil fans have shown for the book. You all have been a great crowd to make comics for, and I'll miss making this comic for all of you every month.

Every time I use red in my colors from now on I'll think of good ol' DD!

Matt Wilson

• • • • • • • • • • • • • • • • •

This run of Daredevil has been the single greatest experience of my professional career. Mark Waid, Chris Samnee, Matt Wilson, Paolo and Joe Rivera, Marcos Martin, and Javier Rodriguez are not only masters of their craft, they're unselfish collaborators and genuinely good people.

What has made DD so great for so long is the respect and admiration that each member of the team has for the others. Mark and Chris have insisted that the entire creative team be involved in every step of the process from the beginning, and in spite of my best efforts to stay out of their way, they not only welcome the input of the rest of us, they demand and value it.

Best wishes to the next #TeamDD led by Charles Soule and Ron Garney! I can't wait to see where they take ol' hornhead next!

Joe Caramagna

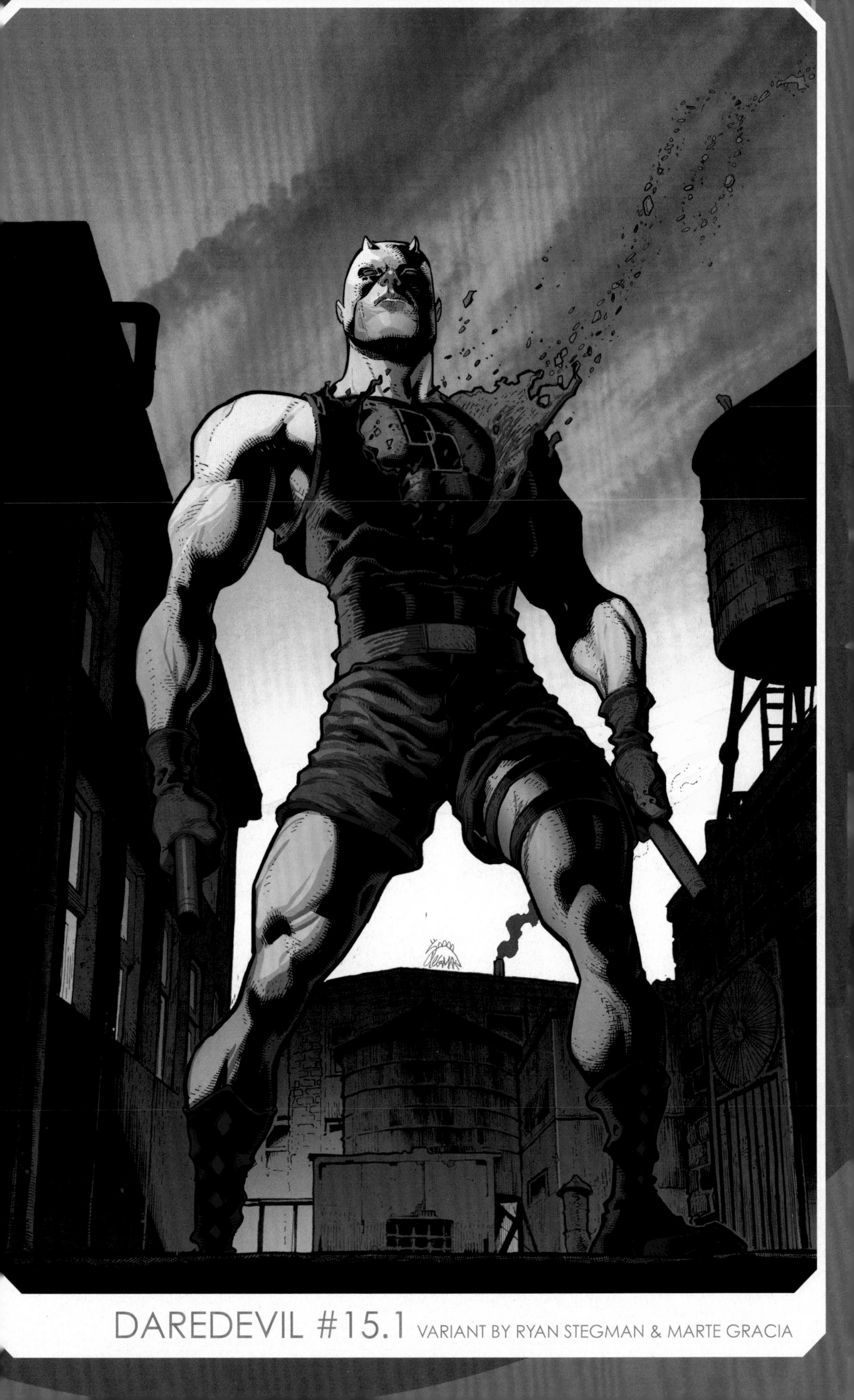

DAREDEVIL #15.1 VARIANT BY RYAN STEGMAN & MARTE GRACIA

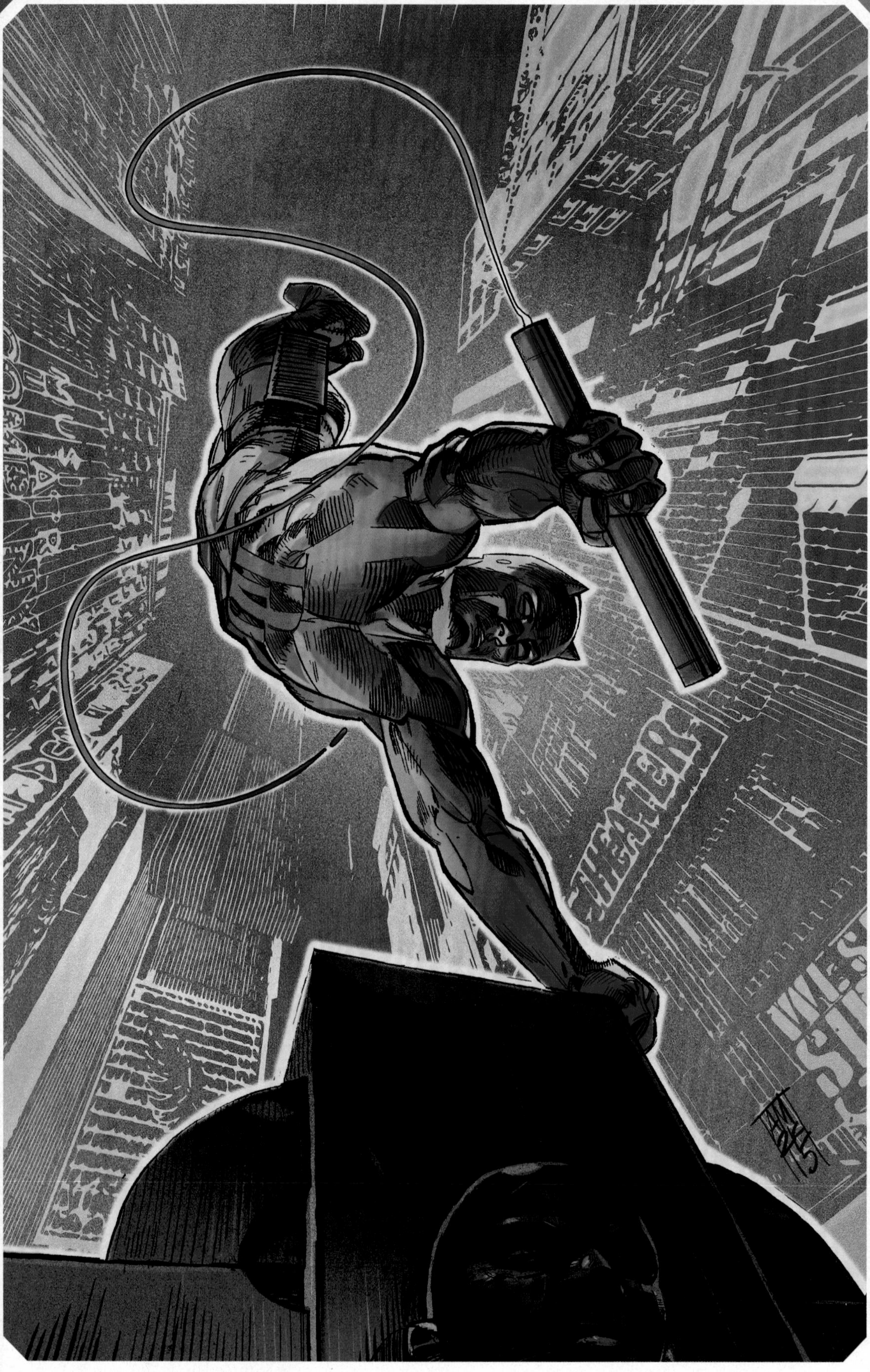

DAREDEVIL #16 VARIANT BY ALEX MALEEV

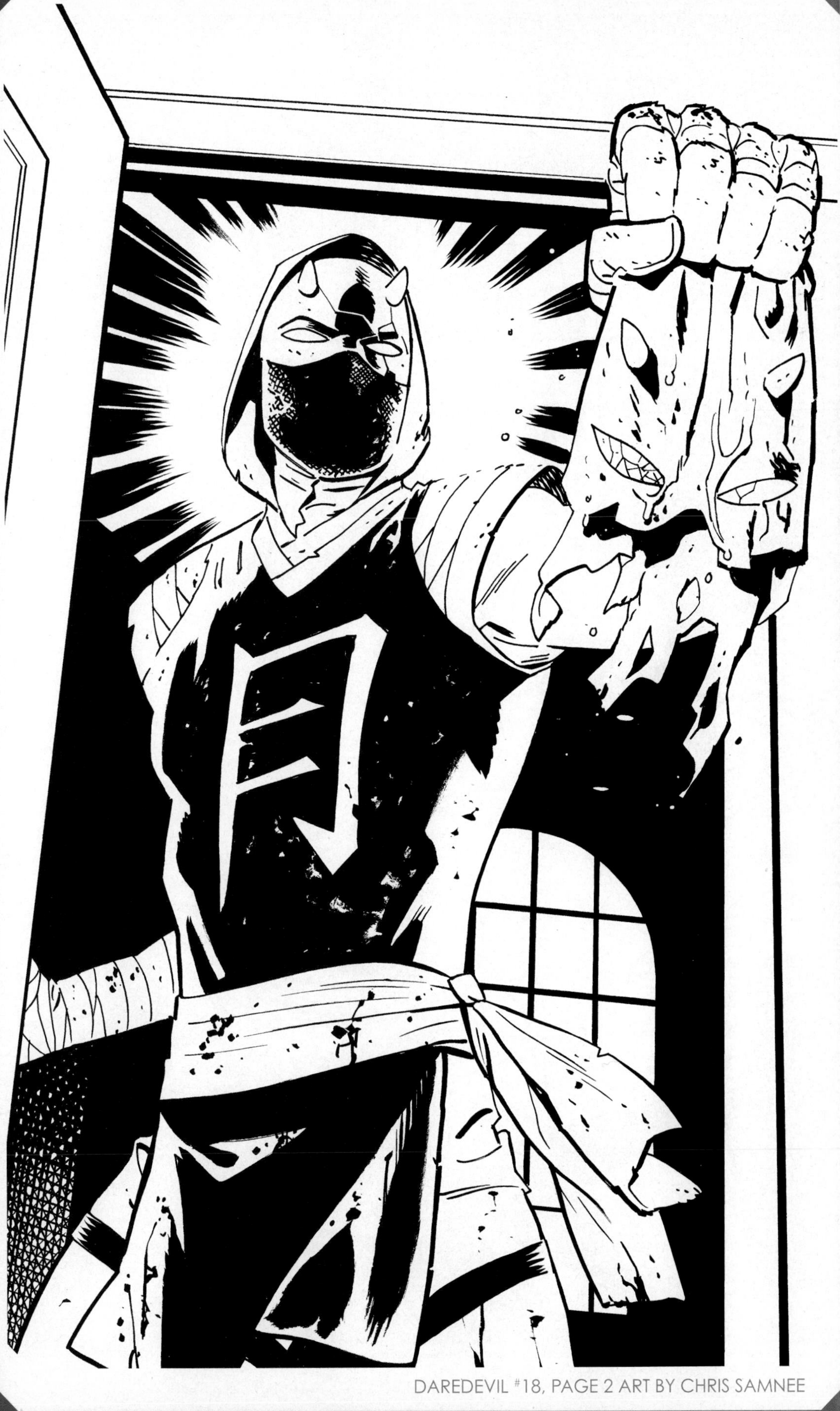

DAREDEVIL #18, PAGE 2 ART BY CHRIS SAMNEE

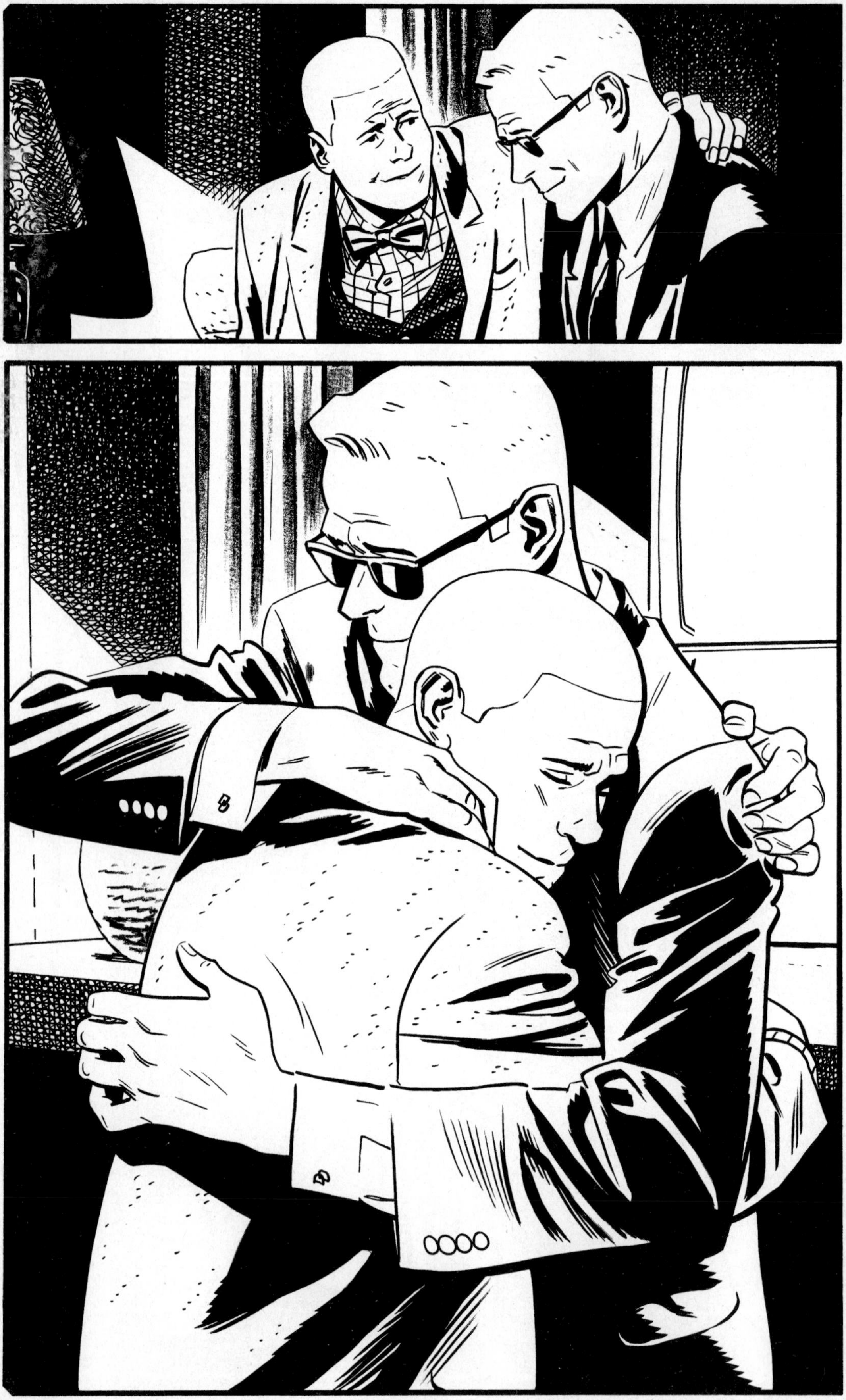

DAREDEVIL #18, PAGE 18 ART BY CHRIS SAMNEE